Why Demography Matters

Why Demography Matters

Danny Dorling

Stuart Gietel-Basten

polity

Copyright © Danny Dorling and Stuart Gietel-Basten 2018

The right of Danny Dorling and Stuart Gietel-Basten to be identified as Author of this Work has been asserted in accordance with the UK Copyright, Designs and Patents Act 1988.

First published in 2018 by Polity Press

Polity Press
65 Bridge Street
Cambridge CB2 1UR, UK

Polity Press
101 Station Landing
Suite 300,
Medford, MA 02155
USA

ISBN-13: 978-0-7456-9840-3
ISBN-13: 978-0-7456-9841-0(pb)

A catalogue record for this book is available from the British Library.

Library of Congress Cataloging-in-Publication Data

Names: Dorling, Daniel, author. | Gietel-Basten, Stuart, author.
Title: Why demography matters / Danny Dorling, Stuart Gietel-Basten.
Description: Cambridge, UK ; Malden, MA : Polity Press, 2017. | Includes
  bibliographical references and index.
Identifiers: LCCN 2017019477 (print) | LCCN 2017035266 (ebook) | ISBN
  9780745698434 (Mobi) | ISBN 9780745698441 (Epub) | ISBN 9780745698403
  (hardback) | ISBN 9780745698410 (pbk.)
Subjects: LCSH: Demography.
Classification: LCC HB871 (ebook) | LCC HB871 .D67 2017 (print) | DDC
  304.6--dc23
LC record available at https://lccn.loc.gov/2017019477

Typeset in 10.5 on 12 pt Plantin by
Servis Filmsetting Ltd, Stockport, Cheshire
Printed and bound in the UK by CPI Group (UK) Ltd, Croydon, CR0 4YY

The publisher has used its best endeavours to ensure that the URLs for external websites referred to in this book are correct and active at the time of going to press. However, the publisher has no responsibility for the websites and can make no guarantee that a site will remain live or that the content is or will remain appropriate.

Every effort has been made to trace all copyright holders, but if any have been inadvertently overlooked the publisher will be pleased to include any necessary credits in any subsequent reprint or edition.

For further information on Polity, visit our website: politybooks.com

To Celia, Nerice and Paul

Because births, marriages and deaths are not just
'demographic occurrences' or bases for statistical calculations.
They are life-changing human events.

Contents

Contents

List of Figures and Tables

Chapter 5: Why No Children?

Chapter 6: Population Ageing

Acknowledgements

We are grateful to Jonathan Skerrett at Polity for all his encouragement to produce, revise and finish this book on time, and to two anonymous reviewers for many very useful comments on an earlier draft. Mark Fransham and David Dorling very kindly commented on the entire later manuscript, and Adam Keefe redrew all our diagrams to a common standard. Many thanks are also due to Clare Ansell and Rachel Moore at Polity, who worked on the production of this book so efficiently, and to Tim Clark, who proofread the book extremely diligently. All errors remain our responsibility. Demographers know that there are always errors.

1

Introduction

There is no such thing as destiny. We ourselves shape our own lives.

The ticking time bomb of ageing.
The population explosion (and implosion).
The migration bomb.

Demography appears to promise more bombs and explosions than a Hollywood blockbuster. To continue the movie metaphor: the demographic future is presented like *Die Hard* (and its four sequels), as an endless fight against explosion after explosion; the best we can hope for is to emulate the cast of *The Hurt Locker*, trying (sometimes in vain) to defuse all these ticking time bombs. This, so the traditional alarmist narrative goes, is *why demography matters*. It matters because China's ageing population means its future economic growth might soon be checked, with disastrous consequences worldwide. It matters, some say, because migration into the UK will inevitably lead to its public services being overwhelmed. It matters because the tremendous population growth in much of sub-Saharan Africa, coupled with climate change, could lead to conflict, drought, mass relocation and disaster. This *could* happen, and some might claim that it already partly has. But this is not to say that it *will*. Indeed, what will happen in terms of numbers of people is far from certain; and what will happen as a result of whatever level our population eventually reaches is even less predictable.

I think we're fucked.

There are not many lines in books on demography that our undergraduate students can directly quote, but this one from Stephen

Emmott's recent study of the environmental consequences of population growth is certainly a contender. In *Ten Billion*, Emmott sets out the challenges that have accompanied rapid population growth in the twentieth century, and offers a vision of how they will progress in the current century. His conclusion is profoundly pessimistic. The passage at the end of the book that precedes the line above is as follows: 'We urgently need to do – and I mean actually do – something radical to avert a global catastrophe. But I don't think we will' (Emmott 2013: 202).

Ten Billion is just one of a huge number of books, articles and press headlines describing the potentially negative consequences of population change. We began writing this book during the build-up to the UK's referendum on EU membership. The 'Brexit' campaign presented horror stories of an 'out-of-control' immigration system, a 'break down of public services', projected overwhelming population growth soon to be hitting our 'crowded island' leading to the building over of the English greenbelt, and much more besides. In the aftermath, one key aspect of demography – immigration – was presented as the single most important reason to explain why the UK voted to leave. There was also a rise in fear, hatred and racist attacks. It became apparent that control over immigration was the main factor shaping debate over the process of how to withdraw from the EU. When the vote was analysed demographically the results showed that it was the old who voted for Brexit in the largest numbers, the old who 'feared' the migrants most, or who thought that limiting immigration would somehow help younger generations (see Dorling, 2016a).

If fertility in the UK had been higher in the past then there would have been more young voters. Had UK society not become so individualistic over the last four decades more of the young might have turned out to vote, and economic inequalities might not have risen so high. We would have been a very different population and had a very different political and demographic make-up had we had a few more children in the 1930s or a few more emigrants in the 1990s. Demography shapes our politics. Politics shapes our demography.

A number of recently published books, mainly emanating from the United States, have sought to paint a bleak future for Europe based upon a convergence of problems associated with its low fertility rates, rapidly ageing population and, in some cases, the fear of some imagined vigorous growth of Islamic culture in Europe (Coleman and Basten, 2015). In China and India, population ageing leading to eventual economic decline is projected to be a core factor in shaping their relative futures, with India perceived to have an 'in-built' economic advantage as it already has far more children.

In Europe, demographic change is painted as being 'responsible' for the crises in pensions, health care and social care, the latter now especially acute in the UK. There are simultaneously too few people in some places and too many in other places, and whether they stay *in situ* or move, the consequences are often portrayed to be dire. The decline of the traditional family model is lamented and blamed for everything from the growing need for more housing to the lack of decent care provision for both the elderly and the young.

Given how profoundly depressing so many popular demographic views of the world are, it is a miracle that demographers are ever invited out to social gatherings at all. In truth, we aren't invited that often – and we often lie when asked 'so what do you do?' at parties. Believe it or not, the authors of this book find it much easier to be thought of as geographers and sociologists (hardly test pilots or brain surgeons) respectively, rather than as demographers. But in truth, recent demographic change is on the whole far from depressing. In our lifetimes we have seen infant mortality rates plummet; health around the world improve beyond the most optimistic dreams of our forebears; increased freedom of movement; greater freedom to live how you wish to and with whomever you like; and children (on average) treated with ever greater love, compassion and respect. Ageing (which we unduly lament) is brought about by falling fertility and mortality rates, which in turn have been brought about by improvements in health, well-being, education, women's rights and workers' rights (which we rightly celebrate). So why is demography seen as so depressing?

This 'depressing streak' within demography can most easily be traced back to the earlier writings of Thomas Malthus, whose tales of impending doom became so popular at the turn of the nineteenth century. In the classic Malthusian model – which still lurks in the thinking of many writers today – population growth will inevitably outstrip food production. The suggestion is that either the population starts collectively to pull its finger out and apply 'preventive' checks to growth, such as marrying later, or else there will follow a 'positive' check (which should really be termed 'profoundly negative') of famine, war, pestilence and general destitution in order to ensure and maintain a balance. In 1800, when this debate began to gather steam, the world population was around 1 billion. And in fact, Malthus was not quite as grim as he is often portrayed, especially as he aged, but the ideas contained in his earlier writings have long out-lived his later reflections. Ideas can have much longer life expectan-cies than people.

Interestingly, Malthus was not just a demographer but also the world's first salaried economist. Economics is often referred to as 'the dismal science', a term first coined by Thomas Carlyle in the mid-nineteenth century. It is a common misconception that Carlyle coined this phrase in response to the writings of Malthus. This is not true, but the fact that it persists tells us something about how we perceive Malthus and how, by definition, we perceive demography as a close academic relative of economics. Demography can easily be grouped in with the more uncaring and inhuman side of the social sciences. But there is another side to demography that is more opti-mistic, and it is not simply the unscientific side.

Carlyle did have something of significance to say about Malthus. In his 1839 book *Chartism* he wrote that Malthus's world of preven-tive and positive checks presented a view that was 'dreary, stolid, dismal, without hope for this world or the next' (1842: 109). Carlyle was insinuating that Malthus had projected Thomas Hobbes' state of nature, wherein life is 'poor, nasty, brutish and short', and that this was short-sighted.

It is human nature to do as Carlyle did back in the mid-nineteenth century and write a riposte to the most gloomy vision of the future. In general, people tend to have a positive outlook and believe in their community; only a minority are not pro-social. Sometimes these more positive views will be directly based upon new evidence; at other times a different interpretation of the evidence will be in play. Some ripostes, or alternative futures, are based upon serious empirical endeavour. And some take a very long time to materialize. Demography matters because a combination of current and outdated demographic understandings often underlie so much else that we have come to believe. And, as our understanding of our demography changes in future, so too will our beliefs.

It was not until the 1980s, almost two centuries after Malthus began to devise his original dire warnings, that the Danish economist Ester Boserup (1981) was able to convincingly demonstrate that the Malthusian view of the relationship between people and land was over-simplistic, and that food production was far more elastic in terms of labour inputs. Other visions of the future, however, are based more on pessimism than on fact. Stephen Emmott, for example, offers a pessimistic view of the future based upon *his* inter-pretation of recent trends and what they might portend for the future, but others interpret these same trends differently and, as a result, view the possibilities for the future much more positively.

In her recent, excellent and short *No-Nonsense Guide to World Population*, Vanessa Baird (2011) explains how population growth has actually been slowing for some time, and that our real problems concern how we treat and respect one another. It is no coincidence that her other book in the same series was the *No-Nonsense Guide to Sexual Diversity*. In a similar vein, Matthew Connelly's (2010) *Fatal Misconception: The Struggle to Control World Population* tried to place a lid on the scare stories still being told about future demographic dystopias. Those who argue that population is a problem may actually be more concerned about something else that worries them, perhaps something less politically correct, which would explain why repeated recent UN projections showing a rapid population slowdown have little influence on them. The argument can then often deteriorate into a battle between 'pessimists' and 'optimists'.

But even optimists can easily be turned pessimistic by current events. In the UK, the regional distribution of both the population as a whole and its growth rates has become very unbalanced. Parts of the north continue to face depopulation, while London becomes more and more overcrowded. Couple this with decades of under-investment in infrastructure and, ironically, many people in the less densely populated areas are likely to suffer from what might feel like overpopulation. This was a key theme in the 2016 Brexit referendum, but the perceived squeeze on public services was due more to austerity and long-term under-investment than to immigration. Much the same story can be told about the contemporary United States and the 2016 presidential campaign there.

Today in the UK and US the direct and indirect effects of strict constraints on migration could be severe, for both the economy and the labour market. Unforeseen circumstances might transpire that were not raised in the political debates of 2016. At the moment, for example, much migration from the mainland of Europe into the UK and from Mexico into the US is 'temporary', in the sense that migrants come to work for a period of time before returning home. If a shift in migration policy led to higher levels of lifetime migration this could serve to exacerbate the ageing issue in both countries. Repatriation (voluntary or otherwise) of older UK emigrants back to the UK would only add to this, as would a further decline in fertility in the US (one outcome that restricting migration could cause).

Demographers have to consider government policies that could impact on demographic change (Gietel-Basten, 2016a, 2016b).

Perhaps the most immediate issue in the UK is the crisis in the NHS and, more especially, in social-care funding, and in the US the changes being made in 2017 to the Affordable Care Act. These political changes have the potential to increase mortality rates, or at least slow down the improvements that had been seen over recent decades in the UK and which have recently been reported to have halted, or even gone into reverse, in the US (Dorling, 2017a, 2017b).

As with many debates, demographic debates can tend towards the inane ('I am right!' ... 'No! I am right!'), especially when they extend to estimating the potential effects of political policies. This is not least because each 'side' usually offers an equally superficially viable view of the future. It is a curious thing that pessimism tends to be seen as more scientifically 'grounded' or 'realistic', while optimism tends to be associated with the words 'breezy' or 'fanciful'. What is perceived as optimistic when it comes to demographic soothsaying can just as easily be perceived as pessimistic in another sense – usually in terms of a trade-off between economic well-being and the environment. For example, a future of very low birth rates could be looked at 'pessimistically' in terms of population ageing and hence declining economic markets and growth; but it might also be portrayed as environmentally 'optimistic' in terms of the prospect of there being fewer people with a smaller collective carbon footprint.

Compromises are also often viable. It is not impossible that higher economic growth resulting from advanced manufacturing techniques could lead to more resources being made available for better sustainability and climate-change adaptation. Technology and 'robotization' could also offset some of the impact of population decline and ageing on manufacturing – but at what human cost? The future really is unpredictable, especially in times of rapid change, such as is the case today.

If you live in the US or UK it is all too easy to become obsessed with the demographic debates in these two relatively small parts of the world. However, the most significant demographic changes are taking place elsewhere, and it is these changes that will determine the size of the world's human population over the course of the next few decades.

It is not our purpose here to get into the 'optimist' versus 'pessimist' debate about the future of world population – we don't have a position on what would be 'good' or 'bad' when it comes to future numbers. Rather, we want to think about how these visions of the future are arrived at and where demography sits in this process, and to see how our understanding of global demographics can influence local politics and populations. If you are told that we live in a big bad world of ever more desperate foreign migrants, then you are more likely to support policies that would pull up drawbridges and build walls. If you are told that your people are having fewer babies and that this represents a threat to both your economy and your *culture*, then you might become more likely to support pronatalist policies that could be both anti-feminist and bullying in tone, as well as being nationalistic in spirit.

The title of Steve Emmott's book, *Ten Billion*, is important here. While it is all about the disasters to come, it is not titled 'global consumption', or 'environmental degradation', or 'challenges to irrigation systems' or 'issues with the global food supply chain'. Rather, the fundamental problem is seen as the total number of people in the world, just as it was for Malthus. Conversely, for those who study the natural world, i.e. who study species other than humans, it is more often population *decline* that is seen as the dire problem.

The analogy often employed in relation to the future of world human population is that of the 'bomb'. Google 'demographic time bomb' to see the most popular and often heated exchanges on the subject. The notion of a 'population bomb' was popularized by Paul Ehrlich in work relating to environmental degradation written back in the 1960s, and is still widely employed in the same vein. Today there are no shortage of demographic bombs presented as nascent threats, with their fuses already burning: ageing time bombs; migration time bombs; delayed fertility time bombs; you name it, there's a bomb for it. The political potency of these metaphors can be huge; they work like modern-day fairy stories, warning of the dangers lurking in the shadows of the future.

In some ways, the bomb metaphor is quite good, at least if what you have in mind is just an old-fashioned weapon with a long fuse and a bang at some point in the future. Demographic change is often a slow-burn process. While very notable exceptions, such as sudden large migrant flows, famines, wars and so on, occur, the more predictable effects of lower fertility and improved mortality on population ageing, for example, can take many decades to reach their full impact. It is the latter that are usually referred to as demographic time bombs, and that is a problem.

The bomb metaphor is dangerous because it implies something other than a small explosion. The future, so the metaphor suggests, will be determined by the bomb going off. By definition, the bomb exists. It is a fixed 'thing', and the only two choices we have are to deal with it when it explodes, or to defuse it. The clear implication, then, is that it is our *destiny* to confront this 'challenge' at some point in the future. *Ten Billion*, including an ageing population with profoundly negative economic consequences, is our 'destiny' – one which we need to deal with – and even now we may already be powerless to do so. 'We are fucked' if we cannot rise to the challenge, one that has been thrust upon us and that we must reluctantly accept. Such talk is often nonsense.

This leads us to another oft-used expression: 'demography is destiny'. Again, this is fundamentally linked to the metaphor of population 'bombs'. For instance, a perennial favourite of *The Economist* is to compare China and India in terms of the former's low birth rate and rapidly ageing population, and to declare that 'demography is destiny' in terms of how this will shape future economic growth. The profoundly depressing film *Demographic Bomb: demography is destiny* – part-funded by the Family First and GFC (serving God, Family and Country) Foundations – paints a bleak picture of a world characterized by low birth rates and, essentially, economic and societal collapse (see demographicwinter.com). Others have suggested that Africa's future is likewise a dystopian, dysfunctional one of weakening security, poor economic growth and dearth as a result of rapid population growth, again on the grounds that 'demography is destiny' (see French 2013).

The notion of demography as destiny is often deployed in discussions of changes in the voting populations of democracies, and perhaps nowhere more so than in the US. There it is linked to changes in the nature of the population related to age, gender, race (and, perhaps, sexuality), leading some to pronounce that 'demography is political destiny', and that the coming demographic changes will be good news for the Democrats (in the future at least). But people who cannot change their age or gender or race can easily change their political affiliations. It takes only small swings in closely fought elections for changes in political affiliation, or voter turnout, or even voter registration, to be what matters most.

The expression 'demography is destiny' is often erroneously ascribed to the French sociologist Auguste Comte. In fact it probably didn't appear in print until 1970, in a book about changes in the US electorate: *The Real Majority* by Richard Scammon and Ben Wattenberg, in which the authors tried to set out who the voters were and thus by definition who the politicians should be seeking to woo. Chapters 4 and 5 of the book were both titled 'Demography is Destiny', with the subtitles 'Unyoung, Unpoor, Unblack' and 'Middle-aged, Middle-Class Whites' respectively. These two titles essentially present the entire project of the book: to identify who the 'middle voters' were not, and who they were. Indeed, they actually define the 'middle voter' as 'metropolitan ... middle-aged, middle-income, middle-educated, Protestant, in a family whose working members work [more likely] with hands than abstractly with head'. More precisely, the middle voter was 'a forty-seven-year old house-wife from the outskirts of Dayton, Ohio, whose husband is a machin-ist' (Scammon and Wattenberg, 1970: 70). Given that 'demography is destiny', the authors concluded that 'The winning coalition in America is the one that holds the centre ground on an attitudinal battlefield' (1970: 80).

It is ironic, therefore, that the forty years which have passed since this first use of the expression 'demography is destiny' have shown that it really isn't destiny at all. While the housewife in Ohio might still be critical in US politics, this has perhaps more to do with Ohio's current status as a swing state rather than with the housewife's demographic status as white and middle class. Indeed, looking at the electoral landscape of the US today, it is easy to see an entirely differ-ent future having played out than the one anticipated by Scammon and Wattenberg. The Ohio housewife really might not matter at all as her 'demographic' may simply be split between today's two options. It was older, wealthier white men who swung much more for Donald Trump in 2016, while the 'young, poor and black' were not as inspired by Hillary Clinton as they had been by Barack Obama. Again, though, having said all this, when we started writing this book back in early 2016, it seemed that the shifting demographic of the American voting population might have been key to a Democrat victory. How quickly perceptions can change, and how easy it is to get it wrong – for any of us to get it wrong.

We are not blaming Scammon and Wattenberg for being naive. The point is that their mistake was not their fault. They looked at recent trends in voting behaviour, policy formulations and the demo-graphic structure of the country and made a prediction about the future based on that information. Demography turned out not to be 'destiny' for two reasons: first, the demographic future they foresaw did not transpire exactly as they thought it would; second, *every-thing else* transpired differently than they thought it would. What also mattered might have been the Cold War, or Watergate, or the rise of Reagan, or deindustrialization, or further changes in civil rights, or profound changes in the household as a result of feminism, and so on and on. Scammon and Wattenberg painted a rational picture of the future, but it just wasn't the future that transpired. Similarly, no respected commentators writing in 2014 predicted the outcome of US presidential election that was just two years away. Given that, how seriously should we take current forecasts of the world population or economy for 2050 or 2100?

A complementary mistake to believing that current demographic trends will predictably lead to various outcomes, is to believe that various demographic interventions have already had profound effects. This mistake has often been made regarding one of the most famous and notorious population policies in human history: the so-called one-child policy in China, which is widely credited with drastically reducing fertility in the world's largest population from its introduction in 1980 through to the present day. According to the narrative, the policy averted 400 million children being born into poverty (Wang, Cai and Gu, 2011). As such, it is a firm favourite of many who advocate measures to slow population growth in order to limit environmental degradation. But this 'standard' view of the one-child policy is in fact more or less incorrect. The vast majority of the fertility decline in China took place in the 1960s and continued into the 1970s, prior to the full implementation of the one-child policy in 1980 (Basten and Jiang, 2014). That matters, but it is also not really the point here. The point we are trying to make here, and in this book as a whole, is that there is a view that 'policy is destiny', that demographic change is merely a slave to policy changes, whether they be the diktats of Beijing or local family planning cadres, the building of a wall between the US and Mexico, or the UK leaving the EU. In this view, and following the same logic, the recent reforms to the family planning policy designed to alleviate rapid ageing in China should therefore see birth rates increase – but as yet they have not. That has had no great effect on the dominant narrative suggesting that the reform of the one-child policy will lead to a new 'baby boom' (Baculinao, 2016). When these reforms were first hinted at, concerns over a shortage of paediatricians were expressed, while the value of stocks in baby formula and toy companies rose (Steger, 2013).

In the same way that Scammon and Wattenberg didn't foresee *everything else* that happened in America that got between their vision of the future of demographic change and voting behaviour, so the current dominant representation of the relationship between policy and demography in China ignores *everything else* that happened in China between 1980 (and before) and today: urbanization, economic growth, the revolutions in education, health, women's rights, the labour market. As such, changing the policy meant just changing one parameter. Indeed, as we discuss in Chapter 5, there is now strong evidence that very many couples in China are voluntarily choosing to have just one child. Without changes in the other parameters, it is unlikely that a major demographic change will occur in the near future, whether the Chinese state wishes it to occur or not. Similarly, Trump's Mexico Border Wall and Theresa May's Brexit are very unlikely to have the precise demographic repercussions both politicians tell their voters about.

Demographic change is often seen as either completely passive, succumbing to the will of the state, or, in the 'demography as destiny' scenario, as completely active, where everything else succumbs to largely unstoppable demographic forces. These two diametrically opposed positions both represent extremely simplistic views of the world and of how people relate to the society around them. When contrasted with each other it becomes possible to see that neither can be correct.

So, what should we make of the line from Steve Emmott with which we began, about our 'being fucked'? Noting that it worked for him to have a pithy quote summing up the theme of his book, we are shamelessly going to do the same. Even more shamelessly, however, we are going to steal a phrase from someone else:

There is no such thing as destiny. We ourselves shape our own lives.

Which heavyweight thinker did this phrase come from? A classical scholar? An ancient Chinese philosopher? An economist (unlikely!).

No. This is a quote from none other than Giacomo Girolamo Casanova, whose name is now synonymous with 'lover'. Casanova actually informed demography by providing one of the most detailed early accounts of a wide array of innovative contraceptive methods (including an extensive use of lemons), which he utilized in order to minimize his lover-to-child ratio (Quarini, 2005).

The growth of social science came about following the realization that people can exercise control over their destiny, even if the circumstances they start out from can in turn have a great effect on that destiny. This book, therefore, is not about what the future will or won't look like – it is not about being 'pessimistic' or 'optimistic', but about how, by better understanding the role demography has played in recent years and how it might change in the future, we can *take greater ownership* of the future. In other words, we turn 'demography is destiny' on its head. The current vogue, based on this notion of destiny, is to take demography as the fixed variable going into the future, and to suggest that we therefore have to build our future around it: to 'defuse' the bomb, if you will.

On the contrary, as we argue throughout this book, demography is simply too important to be relegated to being a 'constant'. The decisions to move, to marry, to have children, to adopt a healthy or unhealthy lifestyle, to take a job in a city – or to *not* do any of these – are infinitely complex at the individual level. Multiplying these complexities up to the societal level results in an almost infinite array of choices and decisions, each simultaneously determined by – and in turn determining – a multitude of external factors relating to society, economy, politics, religion, culture and a myriad other factors.

In other words, instead of saying 'demography matters' because of its effect on 'x' or 'y', we want to think more about how demography matters in terms of both *reflecting* and *driving* the changes we see around us and how this, in turn, informs our visions of the future. We suggest that only through a better understanding of this interdependence between demographic change and 'everything else' can we move away from what is often a constrained (and dialectically inconsistent) view of the future and towards one that we can take ownership of – one where we can forge our own destinies, and recognize that this is what we mostly do. We say mostly, because demographers have long memories and there are times when events simply overtake us. Plague, disease, famine and war sometimes occur either without our knowing intervention at all, or with the intervention of all but a tiny few, or even despite the attempts of many good people to prevent them. However, in retrospect, we can often say, 'It needn't have been so bad had we behaved differently.' Or we can say, 'It only turned out so well because of the often difficult choices that were made.' Demography frequently gives a firmer basis for planning for the future, by learning both from the past (history) and from other places (geography).

Although we don't like dialectics (it is a clumsy word!), it is inevitable that the end point of our argument entails embracing 'uncertainty' rather than 'destiny'. More so than at many other times in our history we live today in a world where the demographic future is very much up for grabs. To a certain degree, however, our perspective might ultimately lead to a rather agnostic, weak view of the future. We don't know what will happen, and so, er … that's it. This can lead us – and those who think like us – into abdicating our own desires for what we consider a better future. It is therefore tempting to object that if we don't have a more solid view of what might at least be desirable, then 'what's the point?' What's the point of writing this book, or, for that matter, spending a good many years studying demographic change, without a vision of a better future?

What we will do, therefore, is to state throughout the book where *we* believe 'demography matters' – albeit in a slightly different way to how it is usually presented. So far we have mostly related the standard narrative about how demography matters. In the following chapters we will argue more strongly that demography matters because it is used to exploit fears and frighten people; because immigrants may be denied rights and resources; because low birth rates must tell us something about the societies in which we live; because we have a completely outmoded view of what it means to be old; because we are only just learning how often men and women will now choose to live, and to live together, in ways that were until very recently classed as immoral and sometimes criminal (and still are in many places); and it matters because very often demographic stories can give great hope. Who cannot be hopeful when they learn just how rare it is today to lose your baby in its first year of life, compared to just how common that was for almost all of human history, and that infant mortality rates are now improving worldwide even faster than before?

In order to think anew about demographic change in the future it is first necessary to set out the tools we will employ. In Chapter 2, therefore, we introduce some of the key measurements relating to demography, while Chapter 3 considers projections and their methodologies in more depth. These are not dry methodological chapters though. If we believe that demographic change will prove to be a vital component in our global future, and that other interventions will in turn play a critical role in shaping these demographic processes, then it is vital that we get a better idea of how we actually *describe* populations and their changes, *measure* the effect of interventions, and *present* our visions of the future. To that end, in Chapter 4 we attempt to defuse the idea of a population explosion.

In Chapter 5 we ask why so many people are now having so few children. In very recent years there has been a near collapse in global fertility rates. So why has this not drawn more media attention and what does that silence and the trend itself tell us about what is happening? Most importantly, are circumstances stopping people from having children when they might wish to, or are they freer to choose not to have children, with the result that when they do so choose, the children they have are (on average) so much healthier? In countries with almost no family planning or social welfare provision, are people having more children than they would like to simply because the choices they have are so limited? There are so many questions to ask once you no longer consider demography as destiny.

What would a world look like in which people were actually free to have children when they wanted, not to have them if they so choose, and to live in the kinds of families or other groupings that best suited them? We know more and more people are now living alone. Is that out of choice? We need to begin to think about how a world including so many adults with no siblings will function in future. Family gatherings in two generations' time are likely to be much smaller affairs. So will friends come to matter more? And what effect will that have on the future of demography? Perhaps we should start measuring friendship rates as much as fertility rates. And how many real friends can you really have?

In Chapter 6 we take issue with the accepted wisdom that population ageing is problematic, and show how it can be looked at very differently. Do this, as we do, and we face a less cataclysmic future than the one we are usually presented with. The inverse of puberty could be defined as 'doterty'. Doterty is the age at which you start to get into your dotage, when you begin to age rapidly, mentally and/or physically. This is a stage of life that has moved forward over time, but may now occur up to a dozen or more years before death occurs.

Doterty does not necessarily mean a slow decline. Sudden deaths are quite common in the elderly, but rarely cause the distress that they can cause at younger ages. In contrast, deaths from cancer are now hardly ever sudden, and are mostly of people younger than the very elderly. Those in their dotage are not completely incapacitated, just as children are not incapacitated before puberty, but they are in a different stage of life. Is this a helpful way to begin to look at ageing differently? To no longer consider fifty, sixty or seventy as old, but being 'old' as when you begin to feel old?

How might we in future make our dotage something to look forward to, in the way that so many of us now look back on much of our childhood fondly? Until recently childhood was often a time of struggle for most children in the world. They had little power, could frequently be beaten (and abused in other ways), and were made to work long hours for little or no pay. It is possible that people in future will look back at us today and ask how we could have treated our very elderly so badly, in their dotage. There will almost certainly be many kinds of behaviour that we take for granted as normal today which will be looked back on in future as abhorrent.

In Chapter 7 we turn to migration and global economics, the most widely debated demographic issues of our time. We consider trends in the global economy and suggest that the numbers of people moving around the world are still, when compared to the numbers who do not move, very low. We should expect more migration in future. But we should also expect a time when hostility to migration reduces, when migrants are recognized as being innovative, enthusiastic and, except in refugee camps where they are given no choice, rarely staying in places they are not actually needed. Just as most of us in affluent countries no longer worry about people having too many babies (we don't tell our friends to limit the sizes of their families), the time will come when we no longer worry about migrants coming. We will worry if they don't come.

In Chapter 8 we turn to the red meat of political demography and to where politicians and statisticians most often clash. Some politicians wish there were no demographers, as demography encourages planning, and planning (they mistakenly believe) is the road to communism. We have tried to avoid touching on the most contentious issue in demographical history until this point in the book, but it is here that we address eugenics, in both its historical and contemporary manifestations, and then look again at migration and past fertility patterns that may influence it. Throughout the book we present a series of different ways of looking at demographic statistics and introduce some less commonly known measures and concepts that we believe can be used to gain new and better insights. At the end of the chapter we explain the idea of 'net-lifetime-cohort migration' and how it relates to lemons, condoms and the pill.

In Chapter 9 we will state our beliefs with a little less subtlety and more succinctly than we have in this introduction. We have had enough of dismal demography, of a science that forgets that its object of study is us, and forgets that we can have great agency. We have spent too many hours and weeks looking at tables of numbers that treat the (tragic) death of a child as an interesting slight fluctuation in a more general trend, and divide people up by borders that were mostly created to separate the spoils of empire with little thought for those who already lived there. Demography will always be statistical and numeric, but it can become a lot less cold-hearted and careless. It can recognize when politicians are abusing a convenient scapegoat, playing on the fear of or dislike for another group. It is time for this discipline we work in and with to grow up a little as it grows a little older. Demography is about us, and our fellow children, women and men; it is not about 'them', and should not be about fear of others but about concern for all.

As the UN Millennium Declaration so clearly explains: 'We will spare no effort to free our fellow men, women and children from the abject and dehumanizing conditions of extreme poverty, to which more than one billion of them are currently subjected.' As a species we have come a long way in a very short time. A century and a half ago such statements would have been regarded as revolutionary and impossible to achieve because of the then prevailing Malthusian beliefs. Today they are made in the heart of the central chamber of our global politics.

2

Measuring Populations

This chapter offers a short story of what we know, and what we *think* we know.

Understanding demography is very different to understanding how the engine of a car works. We know about the parts that make up demography – they are us. But unlike the components of a car engine, within which we can see what part drives what other part, with us we are very unsure about what determines what. Human societies are like car engines that constantly redesign themselves, and within which every component/person is connected to every other, some much more closely than others; and (unlike engines) people breed. People also try to understand themselves and come with all kinds of inbuilt prejudices, ignorance, failings, imaginative limits and other fallibilities.

Demography: the accessible social science

Opening the bonnet of a car, the majority of people would not know where to start. The names of the parts, the vast jumble of wires and tubes, boxes and plugs, will be a mystery, seemingly unfathomable. Anyone who is able not only to identify these parts, but to understand both how they all work together and which part is not working properly, is rightly lauded as a genuine expert. But, without meaning to undermine the mechanic who will undertake years of careful training and further learning on the job, in essence it is possible to *learn* all of these names and processes and linkages. It is also possible to predict, with a very strong degree of accuracy, what happens to the whole engine, or just to another part of it, when something else happens to one part.

In some ways, understanding demography is the exact opposite of understanding an engine. When you 'open the bonnet' of demography, what you see is actually profoundly *familiar*: statistics relating to births, marriages and deaths; to people on the move; to birth certificates, censuses and surveys; to pensions, schools and hospitals. The reason for this, of course, is that demography – as the study of populations – is about measuring and hence understanding what people do. In this way – *unlike* automobile engineering, quantum mechanics, rocket science and post-modern sociological theory – the 'language' of demography is one that is familiar to everyone. Indeed, it is found in media headlines on a regular basis: 'Divorce rate at all time high'; 'soaring birth rate leading to shortage of school places'; 'population ageing leads to pension crisis', and so on. Already in these familiar headlines we have started to see how, like the engine, a change in one component impacts on another. However, unlike the engine, the mechanisms by which this action occurs are not so straightforward. This is something we will be returning to again and again in this book. It is vital that we now recognize just how little we definitely know about the mechanisms of demographic change.

In this chapter we want to focus first on getting the basics right. Only aficionados talk about the inner workings of a car. Yet everyday ordinary people talk about birth rates, life expectancy and population counts, including their projections, in a much more self-assured way. Frequently people innocently misunderstand them, but some also deliberately misrepresent these measurements. Taking advantage of our collective engagement with these statistics to try to make their arguments sound reasonable, superficially they appear to be addressing sensible concerns about 'demographic facts'.

As demographic measurements form the basis of our understanding of populations, it is worth addressing some possible misinterpretations and misunderstandings of them at the outset. However, please note that this book is *not* a primer in demographic method (see Shryock and Siegel 1993 for that). It, and this chapter in particular, rather serves to challenge a few widely held views on how we measure populations and how we *do* demography. After reading this, the reader might want to take a second look at the news headlines that relate so often to population statistics,[1] the many assumptions that the headline writers are hoping you will make, and those they themselves may not know they are making.

We don't know as much as we might like to think we do

Demography is a social science, and as a science it is grounded in data. In order to calculate *things* – rates, populations, structures – which then feed into other *things* – policies, financial products, housing demand – we need to have data. There is more 'data' today than ever before; there will be even more data tomorrow and a lot more by the time this book is published. A lot of this data refers to people and their behaviour.

The main sources in the demographer's toolkit usually relate to censuses, population registers, the so-called 'vital statistics' of births, marriages and deaths, travel rosters of those entering and leaving the country, and surveys of almost everything you can demographically imagine. These sources form the 'hidden spine' of the rates that are deployed in the press, in policy documents and in academic papers from across the social science disciplines. Yet, how many of us stop to think about how these statistics are created, used and compared to each other? In the UK, for example, there has been much discussion on the value of a population census, a survey of the whole population that takes place only once every ten years (Boyle and Dorling, 2004). Its future in 2021 is not assured. In times of austerity, governments cut back their spending on official data collection, so although we will get more and more ('big') data in future, it may not reflect our populations as accurately as in the past.

In between censuses in countries such as the UK and the US we actually know remarkably little about any changes in how many people are here and how many have been coming and going. While current 'mid-year estimates' of population exist, they are only informed by counts of births and deaths and estimates of migration from doctors' records. At base, the population is not actually counted more than once every decade. In other European countries it is usual to have a continuously updated population register, or at least a census supplemented by a register or five-yearly 'bye-census'. In the past, it was argued that such registers impinged on rights to privacy, but today, when governments, credit reference agencies and the security services already know so much about people, simply not registering every individual does very little to protect their privacy, and results in demographic debate often being very badly informed.

Just consider EU migration into the UK between 2001 and 2011. In 2001, *net* annual migration to the UK from other EU countries was very low, not much above zero in fact. By 2011, however, the figure had risen to around 75,000 people a year. Yet, comparing two points ten years apart does not really reflect the true picture of what happened in between. In 2007, annual net migration to the UK was thought to be as high as 130,000, while in 2008 some 150,000 EU migrants probably left the country (ONS, 2016a). Relying only on census data captures none of this, but it is only in census years that we can be at all sure of the migration figures. Between census years the migration estimates rely on a very small sample survey carried out at a few airports, where people are asked if they intend to emigrate, or what the purpose of their arrival is.

In the UK and the US, as in many poorer countries, the lack of a comprehensive population register greatly hinders demographic analysis. A population register records a wide range of formal information, often originally collected in different administrative systems, but brought together by the register. Where a register is not made we are reliant on cobbling together an understanding of demographic change – technically termed 'estimating' – from a very wide variety of sources which, frankly, were neither designed to work together nor are even fit for purpose. The most striking examples of this, often resulting in great errors, are almost always related to migration, which is notoriously poorly measured in many parts of the world. This means that relatively simple questions, such as 'how many migrants have settled in the UK in the past ten years?', become very difficult to answer. In the US there is even more ambiguity about who lives where and under what residential status. This leads to never-ending debates about illegal immigrants.

There are also important questions around data accessibility to consider. Governments have, quite rightly, generally taken precautions in terms of allowing others access to the information about us that they hold, although there is often strong support for the release of data that might be used for the 'public good', and people are surprised that governments are not doing this more readily, especially in relation to medical research. But they are also aware that governments may withhold data that might reveal inconvenient truths. Similarly, citizens are increasingly on their guard in relation to the protection of the information that is held about them. Gaining access to this basic demographic information, on the basis of which we can 'do science', is often more difficult than is imagined. Further restrictions are often placed on 'foreigners' accessing data, which can hamper international, comparative research. Finally, the data that citizens are increasingly *volunteering* to corporations (from store loyalty cards through to dating apps) is often impossible to unlock because of its commercial value.

There is a substantial literature on the use (and abuse) of surveys as representations of populations and measures of their behaviour (e.g. Sullivan, Bicego and Rutstein, 1990). Issues relating to sample sizes, repeated cross-sections being misleadingly interpreted longitudinally, representativeness, question design, and so on can all compound each other, leading to researchers accidentally (or deliberately) generating a skewed view of society. The reporting of online polls in newspapers represents an extreme version of this. To give just one example:

> Nearly 8,000 people have been surveyed by the Express and Star, Wolverhampton, on the subject [of the EU], with 86% telling the paper they feel the EU interferes too much with the UK. The poll also found immigration was the key issue for 63% of those taking part with a further 82% saying they did not believe that EU membership had benefited the Black Country or Staffordshire. (Greenslade, 2016)

This local poll was clearly conducted in such a way as to encourage a particular reaction, but it was presented as statistically valid research. Is it any wonder that people become so confused about statistics and other facts when the media so often create their own for their own purposes?

Though they rarely are, all statistics should be questioned, including official ones. Official statistics in rich countries can be misleading, even when they come from those few official bodies that have attempted to operate for years at some distance from political interference. Despite all this we tend to accept a statistic and quickly read on, whereas we would usually view a comment made by a politician – without a number attached to it – with scepticism.

This misplaced confidence in figures is, perhaps, nowhere more keenly felt than in the poorer and emerging economies of the Global South. In 2012, the World Health Organization (WHO, 2012) estimated that one-third of births and two-thirds of deaths worldwide were not legally recognized by existing civil registration systems. Of these, three-quarters were in Africa or South-East Asia. Indeed, only four countries in the region (South Africa, Egypt, the Seychelles and Maldives) have mortality registration systems comprehensive enough to allow for proper cause-of-death reporting. In 2010, the UN stated that the demographic data upon which projections for Africa could be made were 'very poor or lacking' in 30 per cent of countries, 'poor' in 18 per cent, 'basic' in 48 per cent, and thus good or excellent in only 4 per cent (compared to 100 per cent in Northern America and

97.1 per cent in Europe). In Asia, Latin America and the Caribbean, more than 20 per cent of countries had either 'poor' or 'very poor or lacking' demographic data.

As a result of the poor quality of the data available, our demographic reconstructions for most countries consist of a series of statistical tricks played out using an array of surveys and other sources that clearly present their own problems in terms of their representativeness of all parts of society. Compare, for instance, how the UN calculates the 2011 fertility rate for Pakistan with how it does so for Norway:

> *Pakistan:* Based on: (a) adjusted age-specific fertility rates from the Pakistan Demographic Survey from 1984 to 2007; (b) births in the preceding 12 or 24 months classified by age of mother from the 1962–1965 Population Growth Estimation Experiment, 1968/69 National Impact Survey, 1976–1979 Population Growth Survey II, the 2003 Status of Women, Reproductive Health, and Family Planning Survey, the 2007/08 and 2011/12 Living Standards Measurement Surveys; (c) maternity-history data from the 1974/75 Pakistan Fertility Survey, the 1979/80 Population, Labor Force and Migration Survey, the 1996/97 Fertility and Family Planning Survey, the 2000/01 Reproductive Health and Family Planning Survey, the 2006/07 and 2012/13 DHS adjusted for under-reporting; (d) data on children ever born and recent births, both classified by age of mother, from these surveys and from the 1968–1971 Population Growth Survey, the 1984/85, 1993 and 1994/95 Contraceptive Prevalence Surveys, the annual Pakistan Integrated Household Surveys from 1991, 1995/96 to 2001/02, the 1998 census, the 2000/01 Reproductive Health and Family Planning Survey, the 2005/06 Living Standards Measurement Survey; (e) cohort-completed fertility from these surveys, the 1981 census, and 1991 Living Standards Measurement Survey. Estimates based on the reverse survival method applied to the annual Labor Force Surveys up to 2010/11 were also considered.
>
> *Norway:* Based on official registration data of births by age of mother through 2011.[2]

We know far more about eighteenth-century Sweden than we do about much of the twenty-first-century Global South (Bengtsson and Dribe, 2006). This represents a huge problem for demographers. In those parts of the world that are currently (as far as we know) changing most rapidly in terms of their society and economy, we lack the ability to properly measure and understand the tremendous demographic shifts that are occurring. More critically, we are generally unable to properly estimate or evaluate the effects of changes in the economy and society on the population. This means that our capacity to develop any kind of theoretical or empirical understanding of how these different processes link up – how the different parts of the 'engine' work together – is profoundly limited.

Much of the explanation for why our demographic statistics are so poor is linked to the incapacity of states to develop and maintain the comprehensive data-collection systems needed, in terms of both cost and institutional structures. Yet, while there are obvious reasons why a government might seek to set up such a system, there are also other factors that might curtail their enthusiasm. For example, there is often a link between 'recording' you as an individual and broader notions of citizenship and rights (Mahapatra et al., 2007). A piece of paper that registers your name can be linked to recognizing you as a citizen with accompanying rights. If there are enough people with their names written down – either in one area, or with one particular shared characteristic such as ethnicity or membership of a tribe – then this can be used to demand collective rights or the recognition of an identity. And that can alter the core politics within a country. All of these features – which are part of the long intellectual history of the process of registration (Higgs, 2011) – represent reasons for governments to *resist* developing decent registration systems.

In Iraq, for example, the region of Kurdistan is clearly capable of designing and implementing a regional census and possibly even a full vital statistics registration system. This is because it has a more developed infrastructure, greater financial and institutional resources, and is much more secure than the rest of Iraq. However, the contested identity of the Kurds in Iraq and elsewhere (in particular in Turkey), as well as the sectarian issues plaguing Iraq as a whole, together with the link between registration and 'identity', means that such a development would be completely unacceptable to the authorities in Baghdad (Al-Hadithi et al., 2010).

The flip side to the argument that population registration is beneficial is that there are equally valid reasons why people might not wish to be registered by the systems put in place ostensibly for their own benefit. In some countries, it is clearly better to be anonymous (see Seltzer and Anderson, 2001 for an excellent review of this). Whether because of your ethnicity, your religion, or for more pragmatic reasons relating to what you own or earn, keeping yourself to yourself is a good reason for many to prefer to stay largely out of the system. This can be seen across the world, from the UK's unique offering of a non-domiciled tax-avoidance status, to people wanting to avoid the police, debt collectors or the taxman, to workers everywhere in the untaxable informal economies.

A short history of error in demography

Perhaps the most extreme case of 'under-registration' has been seen in China in the past three decades (Banister, 1984). In a vast country that has experienced widespread poverty in its recent history, recording the population was always going to be a huge challenge. This was compounded, however, by a series of policies that limited childbearing, with severe punishments for those who had more children than they were 'entitled' to, which meant that the incentive for not registering all your children was extremely high.

One of the biggest problems with under-registration is that by definition it is hard to measure. It is estimated that there are as many as 13 million unregistered people in China, who are currently denied basic rights or the ability to travel legally, marry, get a job, or even open a bank account. These people will be free to become registered following changes in government policy announced in December 2015 (Agence France-Presse, 2015). The implications of this for the total population, the calculation of fertility rates and the sex ratio of the country will clearly be profound, as we discuss later.

The many severe problems affecting even basic demographic accounting mean that our understanding of the recent demographic histories of many countries is still very uncertain. In many cases the countries themselves are very recent creations, often not more than a century old, sometimes having had their borders more recently redrawn following war or economic collapse, as happened after the break-up of the former USSR. It was only at the very beginning of the recent world human population surge that the current political boundaries of Europe were drawn, and by and large they did not stabilize until 1945. And it was only in the century preceding that, as Europeans spread out to colonize much of the world, that most of what we today recognize as geographically defined populations were formed – including states within the Unites States, and countries across Africa, the Middle East and the Asian archipelago.

The very categories we use to count people in, 'states', were themselves the products of profound and recent, sometimes very recent, demographic change. Most states do not become states without enough people living there to undertake the administrative work required in a modern state. There are still people alive today who can remember when many Caribbean islands were not autonomous

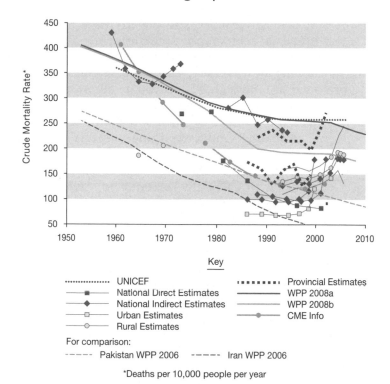

Figure 2.1 Alternative measures of mortality decline in Afghanistan,
1950–2010

Notes: WPP = World Population Prospects. The authors are grateful to David
Coleman for providing the data used to construct this figure.

states; or when Germany controlled most of Europe during the last
World War; or when India included what are now the independent
countries of Bangladesh and Pakistan.

Given how much worldwide demographic history informs our
perceptions of the future, the gaps in our understanding in recent
decades are clearly of critical importance. However, the standard
ways of presenting data often obscure the extent of what we do not
know. Figures 2.1 and 2.2 present just two demonstrations of this,
and show how answering apparently simple questions can actually be
far from straightforward, and how a simple answer can lead to significant misinterpretations.

'What was the mortality rate in Afghanistan between 1950 and
2010?' seems at the outset to be a pretty straightforward question. It's also quite an important one when it comes to seeing how

decades of war, poor governance and poverty have been reflected in that most brutal of demographic measures: the mortality rate. But in a country with no census, no basic universal registration, a barely functioning bureaucracy, sectarianism, rampant corruption and profound instability, how can you go about trying to work it out? Methods include looking at sibling history, the household death roster, and the indirect orphanhood method, all of which can result in substantial under-reporting, especially of female deaths, and produce unlikely results when compared with neighbouring countries. Figure 2.1 shows the various different attempts that have been made to calculate mortality in Afghanistan over recent years. Clearly, while we can get an impression of a 'pattern', we can't really go much further than that in terms of any kind of understanding.

Returning to China, the 'standard' representation of fertility decline in the country – in other words, what comes up if you type 'China Fertility Rate' into Google – is an apparently simple curve. But, as mentioned above, there are some major problems in interpreting the recent history of fertility in China. This means that, depending on the source used to calculate fertility (and some of these sources can in turn be criticized for the reasons given above relating to surveys and so on), the fertility rates you

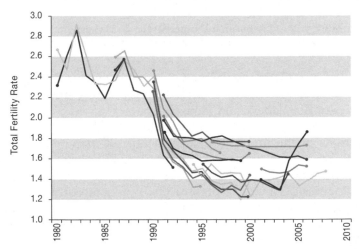

Figure 2.2   Alternative fertility rate estimates for China, 1980–2010

Source: Authors' calculations based on Gu and Kai, 2011; Lutz et al., 2007; and other sources.

are left with can again be profoundly different, as Figure 2.2 shows.

For the year 2000, for example, Lutz et al. (2007) identified no less than thirty-one different fertility rates published in various articles regarding China, ranging between 1.23 and 2.3. These are not shown in Figure 2.2, but if they were included they would show even more uncertainty for that year. Indeed, there is even much uncertainty around the fertility rate in China today. This links not only to concerns about the state of registration, but also to accusations that sections of the Chinese state have systematically misrepresented the country's fertility rate in recent years (e.g. Zhao and Chen, 2011). China is far from unusual in terms of all this uncertainty. Figure 2.3, for instance, shows the confusion that currently prevails over estimates of fertility rates and trends in Nigeria.

In China, the recent trends in fertility are important in terms of telling us how rapidly the country might age and see its population decline. But in other countries the question is far more

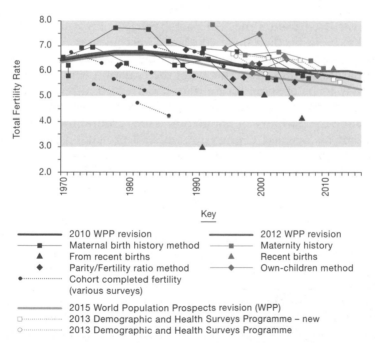

Figure 2.3 Alternative fertility rate estimates for Nigeria, 1970–2015

Source: Drawn by the authors using data published by the United Nations Population Division, 2015.

about the extent to which rapid population growth will continue. Consider Nigeria (Figure 2.3), for which the UN's World Population Prospects estimates that the population will more than double from 182 million to just short of 400 million by 2050. As one of the so-called MINT (Mexico, Indonesia, Nigeria and Turkey) 'emerging economies',[3] Nigeria is often proclaimed to be one of the economic powerhouses of not only West Africa, but of the continent as a whole. Clearly, then, understanding its demography is critical to a better understanding of future global demography, as Africa is predicted to see rapid population growth in the decades ahead. However, no one knows precisely how rapid that growth currently is.

While Nigeria has had its fair share of challenges over recent decades, it is certainly no Afghanistan. Yet, look again at the various fertility estimates for Nigeria since 1970 from which the UN try to ascertain what actually has happened and what will happen. Those who devised the UN demographic methodology use the word 'cloud' for such an assortment of data. The smooth lines drawn in Figure 2.3, sloping gently down from over six children per woman in the 1970s, 1980s and 1990s, to under six today, heading soon to under five, are constructed from a mess of past estimates, most of which have tended to be lower than these combined best-guesses.

To an extent we can disentangle why this all matters. For a start we can separate our need to know what the situation is now from what it is likely to be at some future date if current trends continue.[4] In the next chapter we will talk about population projections, and how they define the narrative of population issues around the world. Both the recent history of a country for which a projection is performed and the histories of other countries can be critical when it comes to shaping the track that is modelled for the future. But just as important is the so-called 'baseline' – or what the circumstances are today.

In the case of China, for example, if you are projecting a population of 1.4 billion by the end of the century, and there is this much uncertainty about recent and even current fertility rates, then that uncertainty will inevitably carry over into the projection. This is why the numbers in Figures 2.2 and 2.3 above *really matter*. The numbers in Figure 2.1 are a little less important because Afghanistan is a less populous country and we would expect uncertainty in the estimates given the many wars there involving foreign powers since at least the 1980s. We will return to this point later on in this chapter. But it should by now be clear that we generally know much less than one might expect about most populations around the world, even in its more politically stable regions.

The use (and abuse) of the measurements we use

In the first section of this chapter we set out the inherent 'accessibility' of demography in terms of its measurements. To a certain degree, this general familiarity with the demographers' toolbox is quite unique within the sciences. These rates feel intuitive: birth rates, death rates, divorce rates, population growth rates. Yet they are often misunderstood – sometimes innocently, sometimes deliberately. Developing a 'demographic literacy' in terms of some of these measurements will, we think, empower the reader to better see where demography matters and, perhaps more importantly, where it should not be relied on as much as it is at present; where facts are just estimates, and where estimates are little more than 'guesstimates'; and where the statistics may not show what you think they are showing.

Divorce is a classic example. Much is made about the demise of marriage as an institution, which is in turn linked to a conservative narrative surrounding the integrity of the (traditional) family as a whole and, at one rhetorical extreme, to 'the collapse of family life', as the *Daily Mail* put it a few years ago (Chapman, 2011). All of this can feed into a 'moral panic' of sorts. In 2013, there were 114,000 divorces in the UK compared to about 250,000 marriages. This has led to the frequent claim that 'half of all marriages end in divorce'. Despite the ease of counting the numbers of registered marriages and divorces in a particular year, there is no direct relationship between the two figures because they are entirely different populations (save for those tiny few who divorce within twelve months of marriage); there is no common denominator. We can use the 'divorce rate', which compares the number of divorces to the entire married population, but this can still present something of a misleading picture, because divorces are not evenly distributed across either generations or the length of marriages.

Just as calculating divorce rates can be confusing, there is also a lot of confusion around how fertility and childbearing is measured. Some of this is related to the general presentation of statistics and a (deliberate) misunderstanding or misapplication of context. And this confusion is not simply statistical; some of it is also overtly political. Take the stories in 2015 in the UK claiming that 'Muhammad' had become the most popular name for new baby boys (Dearden, 2015). The original story came not from the Office of National Statistics (ONS) and their list of the most popular names, but from 56,577 users of a website called babycentre.co.uk who had had a birth in 2014. As it happens, Muhammad was the fourteenth most popular name for boys in England and Wales in 2014, with 3,588 babies registered under that name (ONS, 2015a). That anomaly was widely reported, but this was not the end of the story.

An article in the online *Spectator* objected to 'various left-wing "fact-checker" websites who denounced the survey as an abuse of statistics' and led with the headline that 'Muhammad really *is* the single most popular boys' name in England and Wales' (Clark, 2015, emphasis added). Underlying all the arguments is that there is more than one way to spell Muhammad – and if all the different spellings are added together that does then inflate the total number. Taken together, Muhammad (3,588 births), Mohammed (2,536) and Mohammad (1,116) do, indeed, total 7,240, making it the most popular name in England and Wales, followed by Oliver trailing in second place with a count of 6,649. But, the story should not be allowed to end there. If we are counting multiple versions of the same name, then adding together Oliver and Ollie (7,749) would put them back in first place. This was dismissed by the *Spectator* with the claim that 'Oliver and Ollie are not really the same name ... The latter is a shortened, bastardised version of the former.' That excuse does appear to be a little harsh.

The semantics of baby names in terms of shortenings, regional variations and so on are not what is at the heart of this debate. One of the main reasons why Muhammad (however it is spelled) *may be* the most popular name for boys in England and Wales – and, indeed, in other parts of Europe (Waterfield, 2009) – is because Muslim parents (especially those hailing from Pakistan, Bangladesh and India) disproportionately call their baby boys Muhammad. Indeed, as the *Cambridge Companion to Muhammad* points out: 'Muhammad is the world's most popular boy's name ... If there is a Muslim family in the world that does not have a brother, grandfather, or uncle named Muhammad they almost certainly have a relative who has been given one of the Prophet's other names: Mustafa, Ahmad or al-Amin' (Brockopp, 2010: 10). The cultural propensity to choose certain names is therefore critical to the total number of names we see. The Muslim population in England and Wales was under 5 per cent at the 2011 census. Quite possibly first names are becoming more varied among non-Muslims, which by itself would cause Muhammad and other names to go up the rankings. Muhammads actually totalled just 3.8 per cent of the ONS's top 100 (and 2 per cent of all) boy's names in 2015, which also contained no other obviously Muslim boy's name (ONS, 2016d).

Why, though – we have to ask again and again if we are to get to the heart of *why demography matters* – does this story about babies' names matter? It matters because we all know that this is a story not about names, but about Muslim fertility; a story which ties into a demographic counterpart of a religious or political 'Islamic threat' to society. In some places this is made explicit. For example, the point about Muhammad being the most popular name in England and Wales (as well as in a number of other European cities) is rehearsed in a recent book by William Kilpatrick (2012) entitled *Christianity, Islam, and Atheism: The Struggle for the Soul of the West*. What matters most is that this discussion came immediately after the following passage:

> 'Israelis might have nuclear bombs but we have the children bomb and these human bombs must continue until liberation.' Thus said the supposedly moderate imam Yusuf al-Qaradawi. Even without the nuclear bomb, Muslims still have the advantage of a population bomb. The world as a whole is not experiencing a population explosion. Quite the opposite; the world's population is in decline. (Kilpatrick, 2012: 20)

Similarly, an article in the *Daily Telegraph* (Waterfield, 2009) on the 'fact' that Muhammad had become the 'most popular boy's name in four Dutch cities' juxtaposed this announcement with the statement that

> Geert Wilders, leader of the far-Right, anti-Islam Freedom Party … has demanded a government investigation following the *Daily Telegraph*'s Aug 8 report that over a fifth of the European Union's population has been forecast to be Muslim by 2050. Dutch cabinet ministers will on Friday discuss 79 parliamentary questions tabled by his Freedom Party concerning levels of 'non-Western immigration' and its impact on Dutch society.

In 2015, following the migrant crisis in Europe, the Pew Research Center estimated that by 2050 the Muslim population of Europe will be 10.2 per cent (Masci, 2015).

This, then, is why *understanding* demography can matter so much. As Imran Awan, a criminologist at Birmingham City University, noted, 'some Islamophobia is perpetuated by fear and a sense that Muslims are taking over and polarising society … Little issues such as the name of Muhammad are turned by the far right into vitriolic hate against Muslims' (quoted in Khaleeli, 2014). This debate then links into a pervasive narrative about rapid population growth among Muslims and a globally high fertility rate. And this, again, is not quite so straightforward as it may look. According to the Pew Research

Center, the aggregated total fertility rate of Christians around the world is 2.7, while for Muslims it is 3.1 (see Lipka and Hackett, 2015). Furthermore, while very high fertility rates can be seen in Muslim-majority countries such as Afghanistan, Yemen and Sudan, the total fertility rate (according to latest World Bank estimates) of the country which is home to the largest number of Muslims in the world – Indonesia – is only 2.3. Finally, when Muslim countries are compared to non-Muslim countries with similar levels of affluence or poverty, it is usually the Muslim country which has the lower fertility rate (see Dorling, 2013a).

To be sure, there are also important differentiations *within* European countries in terms of different ethnic groups. But, again, this story is far more complicated and strongly related to other characteristics such as income, education, country of birth, number of generations since average time of arrival in the new home country and so on. Demographers have spent decades refining these measurements, but often it is the very simplest 'fact' – such as the prevalence of the name Muhammad – which is the one that is heard the loudest, regardless of its 'true' value.

Baby booms and baby slumps

In the foregoing section we have discussed how a 'non-demographic' measure such as the popularity of babies' names can present a misleading view of population trends – or at least a greatly oversimplified one. But what about the other way around – when demographic measures, improperly applied, can present a misleading view of society with potentially negative consequences? Again, returning to fertility, there is often a degree of confusion about how we measure childbearing. In recent years in the UK, for example, there has been a 'panic' about a so-called 'baby boom', which will have consequences for school places, public services and so on. Before looking at this in more depth, however, let us recall that there was a mirror-image panic about a 'baby bust' in the UK during the 1990s, when the total fertility rate fell from 1.80 in 1992 to a record low of 1.63 in 2001. The links to concerns about population ageing were made explicit at the time. Remarking on 'historically low birth rates', one tabloid referred to Scotland as 'the granny flat of Europe' (Scotsman, 2004).

Even trying to understand the vicissitudes in patterns in childbearing in just one country is actually rather more complex than at first sight. It can be annoying to hear a social scientist say 'it is all very complex'. Often things are not that complex and one simple reason will explain most of what has occurred; but when it comes to demography this is rarely the case. In order to understand both the UK 'baby bust' of the 1990s and today's 'baby boom', we need to understand how fertility is usually measured. Firstly, just taking the number of births is clearly very important in terms of planning for the number of school places or houses and so on. Yet, just because the number of births is increasing, that doesn't mean that individual people are having more children. The number of births will be strongly affected by the number of women of childbearing age at the time.

Because of historical changes in the pattern of childbearing, especially baby booms, and changes in mortality and migration patterns, individual women might have the same (or even fewer) children on average than a decade previously, but because there are more women, there are more children. This particular phenomenon is sometime called a 'baby boom echo'. The so-called 'birth rate' is most frequently used to measure it, not least because it is the most simple to explain, being the average annual number of births per 1,000 people (both male and female combined). But, again, this can be disproportionately affected by the age structure of the population; a population with many young adult women in it should expect to see more births. In response to these critiques, an alternative measure was developed – the total fertility rate.

We have referred a few times in this chapter to the 'total fertility rate', beginning with Figure 2.2. This is generally used interchangeably with 'average number of births per woman', but that is not entirely correct. The total fertility rate (TFR) is actually a very unusual, synthetic measurement that is the sum of many different *age-specific* fertility rates.[5] Crucially, though, the TFR is usually represented as a 'period' measure rather than a 'cohort' measure. This means that it represents a 'snapshot' of a cross-section of behaviour across all women of different ages, *including those who have yet to have (more) children*; as opposed to a 'cohort' measure which can be used to tell you (on average) how many children women born at a particular time had *in total* in their lifetimes. Clearly, then, if we want to know about total childbearing by generations of women, the *cohort* TFR is best. But to calculate that we would have to wait until the cohort has reached the age at which reproduction is no longer common (normally given as either forty-five or fifty). So, instead, we usually use the *period* TFR – but that does not account for children not yet born.

The reason why all our caveats are important is that a decline in the fertility rate can actually just reflect the impact of *postponing* child-bearing and then having children later on in life. This postponement (and then recuperation) can occur for a number of reasons at both national and household levels. Some reasons are more short-term, being related to economic circumstances or child-friendly policies being implemented. Others reflect more broader societal changes, such as cultural revolutions resulting in greater female participation in higher education and the labour market.

Of course, different factors can act together to produce a result that would not have occurred had they operated independently. To return to the recent patterns in UK fertility, for example: it has been shown that the decline in fertility in the 1990s – the much-decried 'baby bust' – was actually largely driven by women postponing their child-bearing until later (ONS, 2015b). As such, it is these women, born in the 1960s and 1970s and having children later on in life, who have become an important driver of the recent upturn in fertility. This, however, is not the only answer as to why UK fertility has recently risen. Indeed, the Office of National Statistics is clear that 'there is no single explanation underlying the rise in fertility in England and Wales', citing several factors including more women again having children in their twenties, increases in the number of foreign-born women (with different typical fertility schedules), and 'government policy and the economic climate indirectly influencing individuals' decisions around childbearing' (ONS, 2015b). What government statisticians cannot explain at all is why the fertility rise was so similar in so many different local authority districts between 2002 and 2009 in the UK, places which each had very different population profiles.[6]

This whole discussion on fertility is important in the British context because it feeds into the narrative regarding immigration. It will be just as important in most other affluent countries in the world today. The recent increase in fertility in the UK is often ascribed to immigrants. However, on closer inspection and with the help of a 'demographic deconstruction' we can see that the situation is (and apologies for our repetition) rather more complex. Indeed, the story is often contradictory. In 2014, for example, the total number of births to foreign-born women reached 27 per cent, a record high. Yet, at the same time, the estimated TFR for foreign-born women was 2.09, *the lowest recorded since 2004* (ONS, 2015c). The reason for there being more children in this group, therefore, is based around the *number* of non-UK-born women having children, and their age profiles, not their individual fertility rates. These figures on children born to mothers who were not themselves born in the UK are certainly important, but it is of course critical to bear in mind that the increase in UK-born women's TFR over the past decade was largely driven by the so-called postponement effect. In other words, to say that immigrants drove the recent UK baby boom is not true; their contribution is just a minor part of the story.

The example of fertility in England and Wales shows us how a partial representation of demographic measurements can present a misleading view of national trends when placed within a political discourse relating to immigration. However, the way in which these measurements are presented can have a profound effect on how we understand changes in the economy, and thus on what policies end up being proposed. This is why *understanding* demography really matters. When demography is misapplied it can give an impression that is often, at best, only a very partial picture of reality. It can result in people arguing that immigration needs to be restricted because, firstly, it is resulting in a great rise in fertility, which it isn't, and secondly, because such a rise would be a problem, which given the generally low fertility in the UK and Europe more widely, it wouldn't.

In Chapter 3, we will return to the question of measuring fertility in terms of the 'low fertility crisis' in Europe, and the 'hope' that that crisis is now largely over. In Chapter 7 we will examine global projections and suggest that current evidence of baby boom effects might well be being missed, effects that could result in there being far fewer people alive in 2050 and 2100 than is currently assumed to be likely. But before we can get to those arguments there is a lot more to consider. Next we offer a few illustrative examples of why measuring is paramount. Figure 2.4 gives an example for Sweden. The TFR line shows the period total fertility rate, which reveals tremendous fluctuation. This fluctuation has been the focus of various news stories in the Swedish media, trying to understand why people are sometimes having fewer children than before and at other times having more. Swedish demographic data is amongst the highest quality data in the world, so now we can worry solely about interpretation rather than error.

The 'cohort fertility rate' line in Figure 2.4 shows the cohort fertility rate for women aged 40 according to the same scale as the 'total fertility rate' line. Clearly, the difference is that the cohort fertility trend is almost completely flat. What the difference between these two lines shows us is that the age at which women chose to have children in Sweden changed dramatically, but the total average number of children remained the same. What it does not show, however,

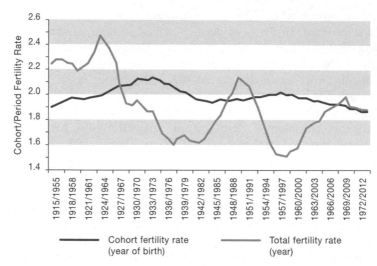

Figure 2.4   Period total fertility rates and cohort total fertility rates
at age 40 in Sweden

Source: Drawn by the authors using data from the Human Fertility Database, 2017.
Max Planck Institute for Demographic Research (Germany) and Vienna Institute
of Demography (Austria). Available at www.humanfertility.org.

is *how* this 'average' fertility rate is arrived at, taking into account
changes in childlessness and so on. The timing and other choices
that resulted in these two trends reflected conditions in the Swedish
economy, policies to support families and several other factors, some
of which we may never identify.

In 2016 we saw the first dramatic moves towards a national two-
child policy in China (see Gietel-Basten, 2016c, 2016d). While this
reform was widely hailed as the 'end of the one-child policy', the
reality is that the majority of parents in China were already entitled to
have a second child (Basten and Jiang, 2014). In 2007, 59 per cent of
couples were allowed a second child if the first was a daughter, and a
major reform in November 2013 had entitled all couples with an only
child to have a second child. We will discuss the context of low fertility in China in the following chapter, but here suffice it to say that
these reforms were broadly aimed at increasing fertility in the setting
of a transition towards a rapidly ageing society. In this context, of
course, the very simple question to ask in a few years' time will be
'what impact did this change in policy have?' We can get some sense
of this now from looking at what impact the earlier 2013 reforms
might have had, and various news outlets have sought to do just that.

Singapore's *Straits Times* led its coverage of the news one day in January 2016 with the headline 'China in shock: why no baby boom?' (Wee, 2016). The evidence for this was simple. In 2013, the total number of births in China stood at an estimated 16.40 million, which rose to 16.87 million in 2014. However, while it was forecast that as a consequence of the changes the estimated total number of births in 2015 would be 18 million, the actual figure was just 16.55 million, representing a *fall* in the total number of births. So were the reforms a failure?

Again, closer inspection reveals a more complex picture. As we have already demonstrated, the total number of births is a function that starts with the total number of women and their age structure. As such, the simple metric is a very unreliable one. Secondly, the Chinese zodiac year is often an important consideration in the context of childbearing in China, and the year of the Goat (as 2015 was) is not considered to be an especially auspicious one. Thirdly, of course, it is just too soon to know. While there will be some couples for whom time is not on their side, who wish to have another child and will try very soon or have been trying already, the majority of couples may not, in fact, be in any great rush. Only after some years, and following more in-depth research, will we be in a position to see whether these earlier policy reforms had any noticeable impact. And the same can be said of the 2016 reforms introducing a national two-child policy in China.

The need to wait in order to be sure will inevitably compromise our ability to use contemporary fertility evidence to decide whether these changes in policy have been a success or not. This, again, comes back down to how we measure fertility, and to issues of postponement and the difference between our period and cohort measures. Firstly, if Chinese fertility spikes in 2016–17 it does not necessarily mean that this increase will continue and translate into a change in *cohort* fertility. Secondly, it is possible to anticipate that the period total fertility rate in China will increase anyway in the near future, again largely driven by a generation of women disproportionately postponing childbearing but then having a child later in their lives. Rapid social and economic transformations have pushed the mean age of first marriage and childbearing up to record highs in recent years in China (Wei, Jiang and Basten, 2013). If the 'natural' repercussion of this occurs at older ages, as it has in many other countries, then this will lead to an increase in the period TFR. Disentangling people's *ability* to have a second child from their *willingness* to do so will probably be only a background consideration; the political narrative will be that the policy has been a success and the state will take the credit for a positive intervention.

Perhaps the best recent illustration of a government taking rather too much credit for its interventions comes from Russia, where, after hitting a historically low TFR of 1.16 in 1999, fertility remained below 1.3 until 2006 (World Bank, 2016). In 2001, however, in his last speech as the then prime minister, Vladimir Putin stated that 'The state, society, religious institutions, public education, and culture should jointly endeavour to generate a strong, happy family with many children', thus indicating his intention to increase fertility through government policy during his upcoming presidency (Zakharov, 2016). He did not disappoint. Putin introduced one of the most generous and far-reaching pronatalist policies in the world, with a specific focus on supporting families to have a second child, as well as significant increases in parental leave and a wide variety of pregnancy and child benefits that could be 'topped up' by regional administrations. The centrepiece of the programme was the so-called 'Maternity Capital'. This was money granted to mothers of second-born children and above and was valued at over US$13,000 in 2013. The money could only be spent on household improvements or children's education, or be put towards the mothers' pension provision.

There is no doubt that over the course of the programme the period total fertility rate in Russia has increased by a not insignificant amount, to the extent that, in 2015, ROSSTAT (the Russian Federal State Statistics Service) estimated that the TFR of Russia was just short of 1.8. There is also no doubt that the policies have had an appreciable demographic impact, especially on the speed of transition to having a second child. This has been presented as a major coup for the Russian government and for Putin personally.

Again, however, if we are to understand what happened here, the devil is in the detail, and especially in the timing. Firstly, it has been argued that the sharpest increases have been seen in the poorer areas of Russia, where the 'Maternity Capital' simply offsets other problems of poverty. Secondly, what might happen in the future? Have women and men in Russia been rushing to take advantage of the policy quickly before it disappears – which is what is forecast to happen given the total cost and Russia's economic travails (especially after the drop in oil prices)? Thirdly, the issue of timing also relates to the past. Russia's recent history is one of political and economic turmoil – especially in the period immediately following the collapse of the Soviet Union. In Russia, as elsewhere across Central and Eastern Europe, fertility then took a nosedive – for good reason. But, as with the other cases outlined above, there is a difference between not having any (or any more) children, and waiting for a better time to have them. This can be shown in Figure 2.5, which compares the cohort fertility rate with the period TFR and what is called the *tempo-adjusted* TFR (adjTFR), a measure which tries to take account of these ongoing changes in the age of childbearing. As Figure 2.5 shows, just looking at TFR exaggerates the *decline* in fertility and, hence, can exaggerate the increase too. As Sergey Zakharov (2016), one of Russia's leading demographers notes:

> The period of 1999–2006 can be characterized as a period of compensatory growth of fertility rates (recuperation) for generations born in the 1970s after they reach very low levels in the 1990s when they were at the beginning of their fertility career ... At the heart of this growth lay the realization of births delayed during the most difficult years of economic and political transformation of the Russian society ... The fundamental socio-economic changes in the Russian society initiated the transformation of the age pattern of fertility: the rejection of early family formation in favour of a later marriage and parenthood.

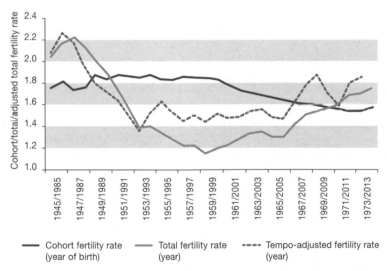

— Cohort fertility rate   — Total fertility rate   ···· Tempo-adjusted fertility rate
(year of birth)   (year)   (year)

Adjusted Fertility Rate is an adapted version of the traditional Total Fertility Rate that takes into account the effects of changes in tempo, usually postponement of births.

Figure 2.5   Cohort and period total fertility rates, Russian Federation, 1985–2013

Source: Drawn by the authors using data from the Human Fertility Database, 2017. Max Planck Institute for Demographic Research (Germany) and Vienna Institute of Demography (Austria). Available at www.humanfertility.org.

Again, therefore, we see multiple factors working in interaction with each other to shape the fertility rate, including postponement as a consequence of social and economic upheaval; general trends in developed countries related to fertility transition and women's changing roles as feminism strengthens and sometimes wanes; and large-scale policy interventions. Suffice to say that such intricacies are often side-lined in favour of a simple 'policy up, fertility up' presentation of the demographic 'facts'. In the words of Putin himself, 'the demographic programs enacted in the past decade are, thank God, working' (see Keating, 2014).

Finally, just in case you thought you were getting to grips with fertility, consider that these same issues of taking into account denominators and timing variations plague all demographic measures. To take the simplest one, consider how mortality is measured. It is supposedly simple because live births and deaths only happen once to any individual. You might, for instance, think you know what life expectancy is, but this, according to Chin-Kuo Chang et al. (2011), is what it actually is:

> Life expectancy at birth is a demographic index which is a feature of overall mortality emphasizing the impact of deaths occurring in younger age groups. It is estimated from the age-specific mortality of a specific cohort over a given period of time using the life table method and is calculated from the accumulated person-years contributed by the entire cohort divided by the total population number at birth.

Contrast that with the definition given to undergraduate students of the social sciences in the most recent *Dictionary of Human Geography* (fifth edition): 'life expectancy: The additional number of years of life that individuals who reach a certain age can anticipate. It is calculated by using current data on mortality and making assumptions about future trends in growth rates within the framework of the life table.' Both definitions cannot be 100 per cent right. So, if you are confused, don't worry, that is what you should be. It is far better to be confused about demography and its most basic measures than to presume it is all obvious and straightforward.

The simplest demography is about the past, a place where every relevant person is now dead. The inescapable difficulty is with living people, not knowing what they might do in the future, not knowing whether they might emigrate, when they are going to have children or when they will die. This is compounded with the difficulty of collecting data, which varies from country to country. Our problems to date have been caused by far too many people being far too sure of themselves and not appreciating the limitations of so many statistics that are so freely bandied about. There are many social problems that it is far too easy to put at the door of recent demographic changes, such as the lack of adequate services, the inadequate provision of housing, or the dearth of well-paid jobs. Our problems are compounded by people who don't like a particular aspect of society, to whom even the changing variety of shops selling different kinds of food on the high street, or the number of babies that they see as being unlike their babies, can cause offence. These individuals then try to use simplistic demographic arguments to shield their actual prejudices, claiming that everyone else is just ignoring the statistics. Remember that if you can't get a doctor's appointment, this has less to do with (tax-paying) migrants 'swamping' the NHS, and more to do with investment in public services being cut (Gietel-Basten, 2016a).

Conclusion

To some extent, this chapter was born out of a degree of frustration that the authors, like many other demographers, feel when asked about recent trends in fertility. There is always an answer that the interviewer or reporter 'wants', whether it be related to immigration in some countries, or the impact of policy in others. Undoubtedly, these factors form a crucial part of the puzzle. But, as we have seen, a sizeable part of the complete answer often lies in rather more complex issues relating to measurement. Frankly, opportunities to explain the tempo effect and the finer points of measuring fertility are few and far between.

Start telling someone that the definition of life expectancy is not what they might expect it to be and they soon glaze over. Yet, we would argue again that this is where 'demography matters'. The measurements we use can serve to hold a mirror to popular opinion, policymakers and the media, can give us a deeper understanding of the processes that we see changing around us, and can help us to develop a better sense of how to evaluate those changes and their effects on our societies.

As we said at the start of this chapter, demography is an inherently accessible subject. We can easily picture a 'birth rate' or an average number of children per woman, or the idea that we have, on average, a certain number of years left to live. That is why such figures are used in newspapers, on TV, on the Internet and in everyday parlance. Yet without a more critical approach to these measurements, many misleading conclusions will be drawn – either accidentally or deliberately. As such, we felt it important to set out the 'ambiguity' of these core measurements at the outset of this book – not just to inform the reader doggedly progressing through it, rather than skipping to its conclusion, but also to contribute towards developing a demographic literacy more generally.

Having covered how little we know, and how difficult it can be to present what we do know adequately, in the next chapter we move on to discuss how projections are formulated and presented, and what it is possible to know – especially what unknowns can be known. The future is not determined; it is largely up to us, including how we choose to measure and describe our recent past, and what an extrapolation of that might lead us to next.

3

Destiny and Determination

In this chapter we move beyond the simplistic idea that 'demography is destiny'. We discuss projections and the idea of taking responsibility for the future, rather than believing it is in some way preordained. Taking responsibility does not mean introducing particular prescriptive state policies to affect demography. It means realizing that *people* make choices about their lives and lifestyles, about whether to migrate, or if and when to have children. The ways in which we choose to treat and think about others affects all these factors and our own behaviour. We make our own history within the constraints of our societies; but although we know more about the circumstances in which we make it than we have ever done, our knowledge is far from complete. However, if we are more careful about what we think and choose wisely between the various truths offered to us, we can determine a far better destiny than the one many people fear is our collective fate. Taking responsibility also means respecting other people's demographic choices, understanding them, and helping to accommodate them.

Projections versus forecasts

There is no doubt that population projections are a central part of the way in which demography is presented in the media, in policy documents and in academic articles. In some ways, projections offer an insight into the future, with all of the attendant challenges that are currently feared and opportunities that are hoped for. How many headlines or newspaper stories have included a population projection, with some concern attached to it about what the numbers imply?

As we said in Chapter 1, and will expand on at length in Chapter 4, the word often grafted onto these projections is 'bomb', or 'time bomb'. The implication here is usually that some ongoing process (which has cleverly been spotted by the author) will grow and grow until the consequences become devastating. The classic statement of this was Paul Ehrlich's 'population bomb', whereby population growth would threaten the (human) world's existence by putting an insufferable strain on natural resources. Bomb metaphors can be seen across almost all demographic realms, but perhaps the one most frequently employed is the 'ageing time bomb', which will apparently come as a result of low fertility and increased longevity – a phenomenon that we unpack in Chapter 6.

In March 2016, the British tabloid newspaper *The Sun* referred to a 'migration time bomb' about to explode, meaning the UK would struggle to cope with projected rapid population growth driven largely by immigration (Woodhouse, 2016). Such changes are regularly equated to the UK 'growing by a city the size of *x*' (often Newcastle, sometimes Sheffield) for dramatic effect – even though, of course, any population increase from immigration is largely dispersed around the four countries of the UK. Even UK countries that receive few immigrants from overseas, such as Wales, get many internally from England, but that too tends to be dispersed. However, pointing out that this is equivalent to every local neighbourhood getting one or two extra people fails to sound so frightening. In reality, of course, some places receive no migrants and are shrinking in size. Other places, particularly in central London, have a few streets in which almost everyone living there was born in another country.

Strangely, population projections do seem to be inextricably linked to bad news. This seems justifiable when the population is falling and 'everyone is leaving' – such as the forecast (but very unlikely) extinction of Japan and South Korea (Gietel-Basten, 2016e) – but less so when it is rising. Historically it has been the countries that grew in size that did better economically. It is even stranger when we consider that immigrants tend to be attracted to areas where there is a growing demand for their labour, often due to economic good news. Projections revealing that young adults are finding it increasingly hard to start a family, and may even be choosing to emigrate to be able to do so, are rarely presented as being devastatingly bad news, despite the implications for those affected.

Juxtaposing the current rapidly rising population projections for many countries in Africa – which in recent decades has at times filled the airwaves with laments over the state of its agriculture, governance and economic growth – means it can appear intuitive to paint a disastrous future of want, hunger and misery, wherein life will become 'nasty, poor, brutish, and short' as 'things fall apart'. On the flip side, as we discuss in Chapter 7 (on Population Economics), the standard narrative would suggest that in the UK it is difficult to see a positive future for either the National Health Service or an economy based on cheap labour if there were to be a population decline coupled with population ageing in a UK receiving fewer immigrants. All of these scenarios can engender hopelessness, or helplessness, as we gaze into the future, and as we consider our profound uncertainty about how countries, systems, institutions and resources will cope with the often striking demographic changes projected to soon be on the horizon.

In this chapter we take the opportunity to think a little more about what projections are, how they are designed and how they are deployed. Again, this is not a methodological diversion; rather it goes to the very heart of how demography is used to present the challenges of the future. It is about how, through either idleness or intent, too many people have both misunderstood what a projection actually is and, worst of all, believed that demographers have a kind of crystal ball through which they can see into the future.

We don't.

By showing how projections are made, and by thinking more profoundly about what they actually *are*, we can better see why 'demography matters'. We can move beyond the paralysing influence of a 'demographic destiny', a pessimism which we will have to struggle with, and move towards a view of the future which is profoundly uncertain but also optimistic, one in which demographic changes influence, and will be influenced by, a plethora of choices which we can all make and for which we are all responsible.

Firstly, let us think about the very words we use. Projections and forecasts are often considered interchangeable. Yet there is something of a subtle difference between them. Strictly speaking, projections are a statistical extrapolation of past trends. They can rely upon data from a place itself, or, if using more sophisticated models, data from elsewhere. The models of demographic change used by the United Nations in its global population projections broadly follow this pattern of 'borrowing strength' from information about what has happened and is happening in other areas, not just the area under consideration. In this sense, a population projection *has to be correct*, by definition. The reason for this is that it is simply an application of statistical rules; in other words if it is 'out', that is the fault of the population, not the model!

To put it another way, projections are based on the current trend, and if a particular projection does not transpire, that is because the population has stopped following the trend. The crucial word here is *current*. It is always the trend only since a specific date, which might be the earliest for which reliable data is available. No current trends last for ever, and very often it is possible to find other times when, or other places where, the current trend has not persisted for very long at all.

Forecasts, in contrast, differ in the sense that they involve a degree of more subjective and obvious human intervention, usually based on assumptions about the future. In reality, of course, there are very few forecasts that do not take into account recent data (and its extrapolation), and few projections that do not involve an element of human forecasting. These factors all matter in how projections and forecasts are usually performed.

While forecasting is often a rather opaque process, experts in demography usually define the assumptions behind their forecasts. Despite this, how various demographic experts come up with their assumptions is often, in hindsight, difficult to determine – although a recent forecasting exercise sought to explicitly integrate the design assumptions in a transparent way (see various chapters in Lutz et al., 2014). Indeed, in later chapters we will talk about the general paucity of social-scientific theory within demography, and how this can make forecasting even more difficult. Without doubt, though, assumptions about the future are usually arrived at through a combination of understanding what is behind recent trends in the specific process you are trying to forecast, and a wider understanding of the demographic process you are forecasting, including evidence from elsewhere, as well as from readings in sociology, economics, biology and other relevant disciplines.

The dented crystal ball

Sometimes our assumptions about the future are just wrong. Take life expectancy, for instance, which we defined at the end of the previous chapter. The 'longevity revolution' has undoubtedly been one of the most remarkable developments in recent human history. With more and more of us living for longer and longer, the recent apparently linear increases in life expectancy will have profound impacts upon society and the economy (as we discuss in greater depth in Chapter 6). Here, Figure 3.1 shows the highest recorded retrospective figures for life

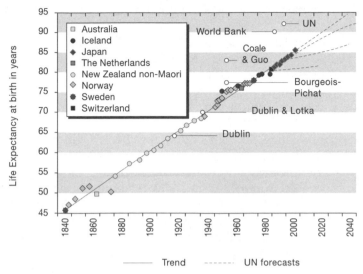

Figure 3.1 'Broken limits to life expectancy'

Source: Oeppen and Vaupel, 2002. Reproduced with permission from AAAS.

expectancy at birth from 1840 to the present day and reveals just how linear this trend has been (Oeppen and Vaupel, 2002). Given this, however, it is reasonable to ask just why so many countries currently find themselves in the grip of a 'crisis' relating to pensions, health and social care, since we've been able to see this regular increase in life expectancy coming for many decades. Why, you might well ask, wasn't something done earlier to prepare us for this?

Looking at Figure 3.1, we can see why. Each of the horizontal lines represents an influential study or report that asserted that the level reached at that point would be the end of increases in life expectancy. Consider Louis Dublin, writing in 1928 and basing his analysis on data from the United States, where life expectancy was at that point around 57. Dublin supposed a maximum average life expectancy of 64.75 years. This was based on 'present knowledge and without intervention of radical innovations or fantastic evolutionary change in our physiological make-up, such as we have no reason to assume' (quoted in Oeppen and Vaupel, 2002). To be fair to Dublin, the medical advances of the twentieth century that occurred after he wrote those words were pretty 'radical innovations'. But, as Oeppen and Vaupel also point out, if Dublin had been able to access the data from New Zealand at the time, he would have known that his calculated maximum life expectancy had already been surpassed by non-Maori females there, who attained a life expectancy of 65.93 in 1921!

While Dublin had access to only a very limited amount of data in the 1920s, more recent researchers have had far more and better information at their disposal. So what should we conclude when we consider the maximum limits to life expectancy that have been pre-sented – and quickly surpassed – much more recently? What should we think now? In Figure 3.2 we focus in on the much more recent history of forecasting life expectancy for the UK. In each forecast from 1980 until 2001, the assumptions regarding future life expec-tancy were significantly lower than the actuality. Clearly, then, the forecasters expected mortality declines to diminish, and hence the pace of life expectancy increase to slow down. While this might seem a rather arbitrary decision to make, it can be explained by the fact that the most dramatic declines in life expectancy over the twentieth century were driven by improvements in early-age mortality and by effectively combatting infectious diseases; any future improvement would have to be largely driven by improvements in older-age mor-tality, and in tackling diseases such as cancers and cardiovascular disease more effectively.

We should be cautious when looking at the future assumptions of yet more linear rises in life expectancy in Figure 3.2. It is surely tempting to say 'we have now got it right' because the assumptions for the future implied in the graph are based on a neat extrapola-tion from the past. However, this future is far from assured – at least according to many current discussions within academic demogra-phy. Again, these assumptions about the future can be drawn from a number of sources. If we look at Japan, we can see current life expectancy of 86.8 for females and 80.5 for males (WHO, 2017). Similarly, female life expectancy is above 85 years in many countries including Spain, Singapore, Australia, Italy and France, and each of these have seen near linear increases in recent decades. The tempta-tion to assume this increase will continue is great.

It is equally tempting for demographers in many countries, includ-ing the UK, to forecast increases at least to the levels currently attained by the 'best-performing' countries, and beyond. Looking at changes in lifestyles, and recent improvements in the prevention and treatment of heart disease and stroke, supports this 'optimistic' future outlook. On the other hand, a significant group of demographers counsel against such a view of the future (see, for example, Carnes and Olshansky, 2007), citing the possibility of a law of diminishing returns to older-age mortality improvements as well as questioning

Past projections of female life expectancy at birth and actual figures, 1980–2030

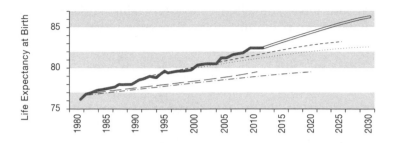

Past projections of total fertility rate and actual figures, 1980–2030

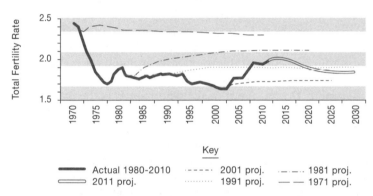

Figure 3.2   Past projections of female life expectancy at birth, total fertility rates and actual figures, UK, 1980–2030

Source: Basten, 2013b.

the extent to which healthy lifestyles can or will be adopted by the majority of the population – at least on the scale of current 'world leaders' such as Japan (see Tokudome, Hashimoto and Igata, 2016). Indeed, the so-called 'obesity crisis' has been cited as a potential major check on future life expectancy, especially in the United States (Olshansky et al., 2005).

Taken as a whole, therefore, the forecasting of life expectancy tells us a number of salutary tales: about the availability of data; about the appropriation and extrapolation of patterns of change from elsewhere; about the conservative nature of forecasting the future; and about the levels of great uncertainty and disagreement among experts which are often concealed in popular descriptions of what is known. In Chapters 4 and 7 we will talk more about the forecasting of fertility, and how this can present a very skewed view of the future in places currently characterized as having both rapid and slow population growth. Firstly, though, it is worth making a brief point about the design of assumptions on a more conceptual level.

The failure to foresee falls in fertility

Let's take a look at the past projections of total fertility rates in the UK compared to the actual figures shown in Figure 3.2 above. Firstly, it was clear that the 1971 projections did not foresee the transition of fertility rates to below the so-called 'replacement rates' (around 2.1 in the UK). In the previous decade, only a handful of countries had seen fertility fall to below 2, and these could be 'dismissed' as outliers from Communist Europe or, interestingly, Japan. We have already mentioned the paucity of well-developed theories relating to much of current demography, and will return to it again in Chapters 5 and 9. Suffice it to say here that one of the cornerstones of demographic 'theory' from Malthus onwards is the notion of some kind of self-compensating mechanism between fertility and mortality. This is most eloquently outlined in Demographic Transition Theory, which posited in the mid-1940s that the 'end point' of the declines in fertility and mortality rates seen around the world would be a kind of equilibrium, a 'steady state' operating between the two. Below-replacement fertility was not part of that foreseen future – even though it *had* already been seen in the interwar period (Van Bavel, 2010).

Figure 3.2 further represents the 'other side of the coin' and shows past projections of fertility in the UK. As well as not being able to foresee a future of below-replacement fertility, the ONS (then the Office for Population Censuses and Surveys, or OPCS) forecasters clearly assumed that this would be a temporary phenomenon, forecasting an increase back to 'the safe zone' both in 1981 and, to a lesser degree, in 1991. Perhaps, ironically, the forecasters did not foresee the increase in fertility that occurred in the 2000s for the reasons outlined earlier in this chapter. They then took the usually safe path of extrapolation without too much consideration. Indeed, this view was not just confined to the UK. Figure 3.3 shows actual fertility and the assumptions about it that were made for Austria from the 1980s onwards, and demonstrates how neither the Austrian National Statistical Office nor the United Nations foresaw that low fertility might be here to stay.

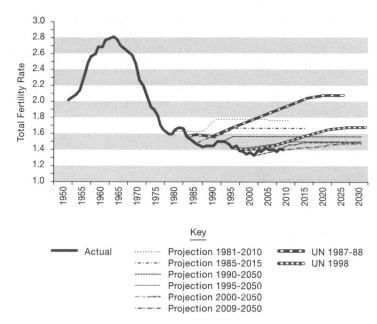

Figure 3.3   Past projections of total fertility rate in Austria

Sources: Statistik Austria and United Nations. The authors are grateful to
Ina Jaschinski of the Wittgenstein Centre for Demography and Global Human
Capital for providing the data.

It is clear that our colleagues got it wrong. This is really the most
important lesson of this chapter. As demographers we do the best
we can with the data we have and the available empirical studies and
existing theories. Despite this, things can happen that we just cannot,
or do not, foresee. To return to Louis Dublin, he based his projection of future life expectancy in the United States on there being no
'intervention of radical innovations or fantastic evolutionary change
in our physiological make-up', but to a certain degree there was, with
the former (revolutions in medicine and public health) affecting the
latter in terms of our future general health and well-being.

The projections of fertility discussed above were partly based on
the working hypothesis that fertility below replacement was somehow
'unnatural', perhaps being based on the supposedly constant 'two-
child norm' which is reflected in fertility preferences (see Chapter 5
below). More particularly, very low fertility has been interpreted
as a *new phenomenon*. As such, that assumption makes it very difficult to predict how it will develop. This is not to say, however,
that projections that fertility will rise again should be disregarded.

Rather, they can serve to inform the projections of other countries further down the line, either through formal statistical modelling, or through the process of theory building, which means thinking more carefully about what you believe to be happening. It is now becoming commonplace for demographers to look back at past projections to see what trends there are within their errors (Goldstein et al., 2011).

So demographers get projections wrong. Indeed, it goes without saying that all projections/forecasts should be taken with a pinch of salt. Demographers have sought to integrate the inherent uncertainty in projecting the future by designing probabilistic (stochastic) projections, which show various confidence intervals around a particular future (see O'Neill et al., 2001). At the very top of the demographic hierarchy, the UN demographers have moved towards employing this method in their highly influential global population projections, the World Population Prospects. So is that really the best we can do? Can we not incorporate a better kind of uncertainty into our assumptions? In Chapter 7 of this book we provide an example of how more uncertainty can be included by providing some very different forecasts of the global future, but before we get to that we should think again about how much of that future is in our hands or out of our control.

From 'showing' the future to 'shaping' the future

In 1970, Singapore was a newly independent, poor trading post in South-East Asia. Figure 3.4 shows the 1970 forecast for the number of expected births over the next thirty years versus the actual number of births. Compared to the projections presented earlier for the UK and Austria we can reasonably chuckle at just how wrong the Singapore government of the time was. While they were projecting a rapidly continuing growth in the number of births, Singapore actually saw a decline to one of the very lowest human fertility rates on earth. Yet again, demographers just didn't foresee what was going to happen. Other societies had seen their fertility fall before 1970, so why did the Singaporeans not anticipate that?

'They should have tried harder' is not quite the right way of interpreting the huge forecasting error that Figure 3.4 reveals. Though Singapore was certainly 'in the right place at the right time', there was certainly no guarantee that its population – and economy – would see the kind of revolutionary change that it did. Many

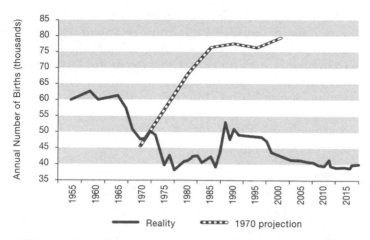

Figure 3.4   Singapore projections of births versus reality

Sources: Arumainathan, 1973: 35, 45; Department of Statistics, Singapore,
Table M810081.

other societies did not. Furthermore, at the time the Singaporean government placed the following caveats on the projections: 'There will be some social factors that could act as a depressing influence on [birth rates], as well as government activities towards promoting family planning programs and reducing the size of families' (Arumainathan, 1973: 45).

The caveats were realized, but *critically* the projections were also vital in driving the policy changes. So the projections became *active agents* in proving themselves wrong. In other words, the projections presented a *scenario* of future population change *without* the changes noted above actually happening. This scenario was deemed to be one that was less desirable, so an alternate course was set upon. In Chapter 8, where we turn to politics and demography, we will ask whose fertility was seen as most problematic in Singapore in the past and why such high forecasts were made; but even without such potential political bias (in this case racial prejudices about which group would have the highest fertility) it is easy to forecast incorrectly and for incorrect forecasts to themselves influence the future. Indeed, this kind of situation is not unique: the population explosion of the late twentieth century in many countries fed into forecasts which in turn prompted policymakers to design, or redouble their efforts in, family planning programmes. And it turns out that often they did have in mind particular social, ethnic or religious groups whom they thought should plan to have fewer children than others.

This, then, is the true value (and both the true danger and hope) of population projections, and it is another way in which demography really matters. Rather than showing us what the future will be, and therefore being something that we plan around, projections just show us *one vision of the future*, one *scenario* which will only play out under certain circumstances. In other words, there is no such thing as 'demographic destiny'; rather, we make our own future as societies (and individuals). Projections then become a spur to action.

Consider the following quote from a recent article in *The Sun*:

> BRITAIN'S population will be almost three million larger than official predictions by 2039 if immigration continues at runaway levels, a Home Office minister was forced to admit today.
>
> As migrants trying to reach northern Europe used a battering ram to smash through border fences in Greece, Lord Bates confirmed current rates of net migration would swell the population by 500,000 a year.
>
> Official projections say the UK's population will rocket from 64.6 million in 2014 to 74.3 million in 2039.
>
> But that assumes immigration will add just 185,000 each year from 2021 – and last week damning figures showed net migration is currently running at 323,000. (Woodhouse, 2016)

At the heart of this story are the official ONS projections for the total population, which do, indeed, project a growth in population to 74.3 million by 2039. These projections, as already noted, will be based on a series of assumptions relating to fertility, mortality and migration, assumptions that are published, along with a justification for them, in official ONS reports (for the latest projections at the time of writing [May 2017] see ONS, 2014). Of course, these assumptions are already relatively fragile and could fluctuate in terms of the future of mortality, possible downturns in fertility, and, critically, in terms of the relationship between Britain and the EU.

Brexit is one extreme scenario that could alter migration flows – even if the UK were to remain in the free movement of labour area, along with Switzerland and Norway (which as we write in early 2017 appears to be unlikely). That is because migrants from the rest of the EU would become second-class citizens, and so the UK would be less attractive as a destination, especially if the Brexit negotiations were to alter the rights of EU nationals already living in the UK. The referendum result has already made many people feel unwelcome and deterred others from thinking of coming. And, again as we write, almost no consideration has been given to how it will affect the numbers of 'ex-pats' who might want to return. Much more importantly, the economic effects of the referendum result, which were an almighty shock, could be expected to drive many young people to emigrate while discouraging immigration if being in the UK is suddenly so much less advantageous. Others might rush in to try to gain a foothold while they can, as occurred in the 1960s when the UK took away the rights of British passport holders from the Empire to come to the 'mother country'.

In general, in recent decades in the UK, the most likely sources of uncertainty have always tended to lie in its economic performance relative to its European neighbours, as well as in possible EU expansion and rates of *emigration* out of the UK. In the economic recessions that occurred in the 1970s, 1980s and 1990s, the UK was a net emigration state. However, following the global financial crashes of 1929 and 2008 it received more immigrants than it lost emigrants. In all cases, short-term economic events have had no more than short-term effects on migration, but if that is not noticed then what is temporary can be forecast as the 'new normal'.

Building uncertainly into the model

The ONS 'base' projections have been rightly criticized for not taking into account many economic and political factors and for failing to fully identify the degree of uncertainty involved. Because of this, the ONS now produces a series of 'variants', or alternative scenarios, based upon higher or lower fertility, more or less improvement in mortality, and three alternative migration assumptions ('zero net migration', 'no change' and 'long-term balanced net migration' – eventually falling to zero). These alternatives – all of which are, in our view, quite possible, and none of which encompass the extreme economic and political scenarios that have occurred – are presented in Figure 3.5.

Note that even without including these extreme scenarios, within a relatively short period of time (i.e. to 2039) the difference between the largest and smallest projected population is around 10 million people. This is part of a wider issue concerning the failure to acknowledge uncertainty in all our statistics – including past estimates, not just forward projections – and the policy implications of that unavoidable uncertainty. As such, the *definitive* statement that the population '*will rocket*' needs to be tempered somewhat. Returning to *The Sun* newspaper story, however, we see that it actually goes beyond these official projections to include the opinion of both the newspaper and,

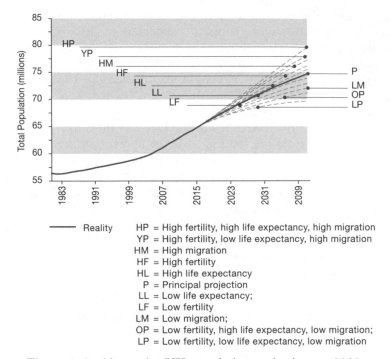

—— Reality	HP = High fertility, high life expectancy, high migration
	YP = High fertility, low life expectancy, high migration
	HM = High migration
	HF = High fertility
	HL = High life expectancy
	P = Principal projection
	LL = Low life expectancy;
	LF = Low fertility
	LM = Low migration;
	OP = Low fertility, high life expectancy, low migration;
	LP = Low fertility, low life expectancy, low migration

Figure 3.5 Alternative UK population projections to 2039

Source: ONS, 2015c. National Population Projections: 2014-based Statistical Bulletin.

to a degree, the minister, in terms of projecting *current* rates of migration into the future. This, of course, is just one particular scenario and one which for many reasons, not least those given above, may very well not transpire.

The fact is that ONS projections are being taken as representing *the* future, but the reality will almost certainly be different, and potentially very different. Not only do the projections represent just one vision of the future, they are also deliberately deployed (by *The Sun*, and in effect its proprietor Rupert Murdoch) precisely in order to *change* the future, and ultimately in the hope of proving the projections wrong. They were deployed to set out and justify a particular political course; in this case, in the cause of anti-immigration and an anti-EU/pro-Brexit agenda. Ironically, the very latest ONS estimates of the population and of immigration, which showed a slowdown in population growth due to very high numbers of deaths among the elderly, did not influence the result of the Brexit referendum because they were released on the day of the actual vote (ONS, 2016b).

Consider this quotation from Chris Grayling, at the time Leader of the UK House of Commons, and subsequently campaign manager for Theresa May in her successful bid to become prime minster:

> If immigration carries on at this current rate, it is going to put increasing pressure on public services – health and education … It is going to mean that we have to build over very large amounts of green belt land to provide extra housing for people moving to the UK. It means we are going to have to build far more roads to cope because we will have gridlock otherwise. It is going to change the face of our country. It is going to make the United Kingdom a very visibly different place – much more built up, much less green space around our cities. If you live on the edge of a city or the edge of a big town and there are some nice fields down the road, there is a strong chance they will end up being built over in the next few years. And you, the citizen of the United Kingdom, have no say over that. (Ross 2016)

The headline for this article?: 'Britain's green fields will have to be built over to provide new homes for migrants, warns Chris Grayling'. Again, we see the use of a projection into the future – in this case the scenario of constant immigration – in order to frighten people into taking an alternative course. It worked. Mr Grayling supported the Leave campaign, and immigration fear was its most powerful political weapon. Projections, then, are incredibly important political tools, which can be used as a stick to coerce people into making particular electoral choices. Indeed, they have been a valuable recruiting tool of the far-right across Europe – and of the not yet so far-right. In the US, President Trump's anti-immigration promise to build a wall and make Mexico pay for it did appear to help him become just popular enough to win just enough votes in just the right places. He also promised to help stem the immigration of Muslims into the US, possibly partly influenced by European anti-Muslim propaganda: 'Trump describes a country under siege from refugees and immigrants, Mexicans, and Muslims' (Foran, 2016). However, once he tried to introduce his anti-Muslim travel ban in late January 2017, mainstream European political leaders reacted in horror.

As we mentioned in Chapter 1, a number of books predict Europe's demographic collapse and its imminent takeover by Islamists of a more or less radical hue (see Coleman and Basten, 2015, for an overview of these). *The Telegraph*'s Adrian Michaels is especially adept at presenting a 'grim' future for the paper's readers, supposedly justified by what he would claim was a more open and frank

conversation. 'Europe's low white birth rate, coupled with faster multiplying migrants, will change fundamentally what we take to mean
by European culture and society' says Michaels, under the less than
'innocent' headline 'Muslim Europe: the demographic time bomb
transforming our continent' (Michaels, 2009a). In this particular
piece Michaels suggests that Muslims will account for 20 per cent of
the European population by 2050. Another article by Michaels published in the same newspaper in the same year states: 'Although some
polls have pointed to a lack of radicalisation in the Muslim community, little attention is being given to the integration of migrants,
it is claimed, with fears of social unrest in years to come' (Michaels,
2009b). Clearly, then, the implicit link of Muslim immigration to
radicalism is made, and made often.

It should not matter what proportion of people in any area
adhere to any particular religion or ideology, or have no religion
at all. Maybe one day we will escape from the constant cycle of
fear of them: first Catholics, then Jews, then Communists, and
now Muslims? As ever, any projections cited can be disputed –
the respected Pew Research Center in Washington estimates that
Muslims will actually account for 10.2 per cent of the European
population by 2050, while the 20 per cent figure used by Michaels is
drawn from a report by Major Leon Perkowski for the US Air Force
(Perkowski, 2006). The demographic future view of Islam in Europe
appears now to have been solidified in the narrative: 'Europe will be
Islamic by the end of the century', as Princeton's Professor Emeritus
of Near Eastern Studies Bernard Lewis told *Die Welt* in 2006 (Die
Welt, 2006).

So projections can be used to present a future that allows politicians, and those who seek to influence both them and us, to put
forward a narrative expedient for what they want to achieve. A better
understanding of *what* these projections are, *who* makes them, and
how they arrive at their final numbers – as well as a more critical view
of *why* they are being presented in this particular way – would certainly be of benefit to society. Remember: if you wouldn't trust the
politician, don't trust the projection. In fact, don't trust the projection anyway.

This rather gloomy, cynical way of looking at projections is,
however, only one part of understanding them – they are to be
feared, but they can also give us hope and be a force for good. As
we saw in Singapore, projections can be used to usher in more 'positive' policies (although, as we discuss in Chapter 8, we can certainly
question whether all of Singapore's population policies were quite as

'enlightened' as one might have hoped). But projections – and different population scenarios – can spur us into thinking about alternative views of the future and, ultimately, might even set us off along a better pathway or, conversely, on paths of inaction that might in themselves be highly beneficial. What would happen if we just allowed people to do what they want to do? Help those who want fewer children to have fewer and those that want more to have more? And why do we never ask questions such as these? This book does.

Live and let live, and famine

In Chapter 5 we discuss the low fertility future of many countries in Europe and East Asia, as well as some locations, such as Thailand, which are not often associated with very low birth rates. These low rates are of great concern for governments worried about rapid population ageing and, in some cases, population decline. As we argue in Chapter 5, however, the real concern comes from the fact that people generally have fewer children than they say they would like to have. This suggests that there are things going on in society and in the lives of many people that are preventing them from realizing their aspirations. These, we argue, are related – differently in different places – to gender roles, fragility of employment, the provision of housing, high costs of living, unrealistic expectations (and costs) of education, and much else. In other words, they are related to many areas which policymakers very much need to address. Demography can be used as a tool for understanding human well-being. If you want to influence future population levels, then you should attempt to influence what most affects people's demographic behaviour. If you want them to have more children, then make it easier to start a family. If you don't want more migrants, don't expand the number of low-wage jobs on offer.

In its 2010 World Population Prospects, the UN introduced a new means of designing assumptions for fertility forecasts. This was based upon the experience of some European countries that had seen their fertility rates increase, or 'recuperate' from falling to levels that had been well below replacement. This increase in fertility therefore became seen as a 'standard' pathway for countries to progress along – even though we know much of the increase was driven by the so-called 'tempo effect' as discussed in the previous chapter. We now also know that the increases in many countries either stagnated or declined again in the wake of the post-2008 financial crisis.

Nevertheless, this increase in fertility was assumed for all countries with very low fertility, hence the forecast that their fertility rates would rise to around replacement rate, often within the first few decades of the twenty-first century. This produces very uniform projections and ones which can easily be called into doubt – very possibly we are now over-projecting future numbers.

One of the authors of this book took great exception to this statistically driven way of designing population projections (see Basten, 2013a). Although the sociological and empirical reality of these settings made it feel like an imminent increase in fertility was unlikely, this was not really the main reason for criticizing the projections. Projections can, after all, be based on a wide number of subjective ideas about recent trends and the future. The concern was that if these (supposedly most authoritative) population projections predicted a fertility increase, then that could be interpreted by policymakers as suggesting that demographers thought their countries would follow a North-western European low fertility transition and that very low fertility would 'go away' naturally. Of course, the context in North-western Europe is very different from that of East Asia in any number of ways, as we discuss in Chapter 5, and as such the context of supporting families and broader issues relating to gender roles, the welfare state and the labour market – all of which impact upon childbearing – are also at variance. The great concern was that presenting a future of fertility increase would be a 'spur to *inaction*', just at a time when governments were beginning to recognize the need to tackle some of the root causes of low fertility.

Undoing this perception required explaining to policymakers the nature of the new projection model employed by the UN, backing up our claims about the variance by performing in-depth research on the contemporary context of childbearing in low fertility Asia, and then working with the UN to alter their model. All of this was due to the application of a naive and far too simple statistical model to make a projection and present it as a plausible forecast.

But just as projections can be spurs to inaction, they can also be spurs to action. Indeed, there is the potential for projections to be truly transformative in terms of the ways we envisage the future of our societies. Generally, today, the 'nightmare' population projections tend to hail from sub-Saharan Africa, where the 'population bomb' meme seems to still resonate most strongly, and where the Malthusian disaster scenario of population growth massively outstripping resources, leading to immense poverty and hunger, is still often being presented as being most likely. In 2011, commenting on famine relief to the Horn of Africa, the environmentalist Jonathon Porritt (2011) said that 'if the population of the four countries most seriously affected by the current drought (Ethiopia, Uganda, Somalia and Kenya) continues to grow at the same pace, then this particular begging bowl will become a near-permanent feature of the international scene'. That passage is from a blog post glibly entitled 'Who would have thought it? Population growth and famine would appear to be linked!' The fact that the US population has tripled over the twentieth century and now has some of the highest obesity rates on earth suggests that Porritt's assumptions about this link are not as straightforward as they might at first appear to be. Again, population growth is presented as the 'bad guy' rather than the systems in which this growth operates.

If we take Somalia as an example, the demographic future can indeed look pretty bleak, but it always looks bleak in the aftermath of disaster. The terrible famines that repeatedly hit Somalia still resonate in the memory of most Somali people alive today. As recently as 2010–12 more than a quarter of a million Somalis perished as a consequence of a severe drought, the effects of which were exacerbated by civil conflict.

However, compared to some other countries in sub-Saharan Africa, the total population in Somalia both today and predicted for 2050 is relatively small. In Uganda, for example, the population is 'expected' to rise from 39 million in 2015 to 101 million in 2050; while in Nigeria an increase over the same period is anticipated from 182 million to 398 million (UNPD, 2015). But the orders of magnitude seen in Somalia are relatively similar. The main UN projection for the country suggests an increase from 10.8 million in 2015 to 27 million by 2050 and 58.3 million by the end of the century. Looking at Somalia now – at the state of the economy, the climate (and the direction of climate change), the agricultural systems, and at the state of institutions and governance – it is hard to see how these numbers can be sustainable without either further disastrous Malthusian checks or huge levels of out-migration. However, that does not mean that the future demographic destiny of Somalis is not largely or at least partly in their own hands, and to not believe that requires having a very low opinion of them. We must not forget how in the past populations have recovered from all kinds of disasters and then not spiralled out of control in their numbers following an initial post-crisis baby boom (as the UK experienced as recently as 1919 and 1946).

Instead of taking fright at the current UN projections, and holding our heads in our hands in dismay at the impending doom, we can actually take steps to alter the future. Firstly, remember that the UN projection for Somalia is not a *will happen* but a *might happen*, and a *might* only under certain circumstances. The scenario, for example, implies a future decline in fertility. But what if this decline was rather faster than the model anticipates? In the main model upon which the numbers quoted above are based the total fertility rate in Somalia is assumed to decline from 6.6 children per woman in 2010–15 to 3.54 by 2050–5 (resulting in the total population growing from 10.8 million to 27 million). However, if fertility fell by just 0.5 more, i.e. to 3.04 by 2050, then the total population would be 25.5 million. This is clearly not a negligible drop. On the other hand, if fertility stayed the same in Somalia, the total population in 2050 is projected to be 35.7 million, close to 10 million more. What this indicates, therefore, is that we are presented with a *choice*. We broadly know the 'recipe' for lower fertility: decent family planning programmes coupled with health provision and improved availability of education; female empowerment both within and outside the home; better general education; and possibly out-migration to places where lower fertility is the norm. If Somalia *chooses* – or is able – to go down this route at a greater pace, then it is likely that fertility will decline more rapidly than current projections forecast. In other words, the 'main forecast' presented by the UN is just one scenario with one outcome based upon one set of parameters. If we change those parameters, we can envisage a different outcome. We can prove the projection wrong, and as Somalia becomes more quickly connected to the outside world, the influence of global norms of much lower fertility may well impact far faster than is currently forecast.

Projections have always been wrong, especially close to the home country of the two authors of this book, where our forefathers have been making them for longer than most in other parts of the world. In the nineteenth century it was Ireland in particular and the higher fertility there that concerned the Malthusians. Ireland's population was projected to grow and grow, possibly making the UK (of which it was then a part) a majority Catholic country at some point. What actually happened, however – a famine that was not in the least tempered by the actions of the British (Anglican) landowners, and subsequent continual mass emigration – meant that Ireland is today the only country in the world to have a lower population than it did a century and a half ago. It is not impossible that Somalia, through out-migration, famine and benign neglect, could suffer a similar fate and prove the current projections tragically incorrect, but for political, not deterministic reasons. However, far brighter scenarios exist which dramatically reduce population growth without that reduction having to be a result of disaster.

Adding education to population forecasts

Demographers have recently begun integrating other parameters for projecting change. One such parameter is *education*, which could be considered to be truly transformative both in terms of demographic futures (linked to improved health and lower fertility in poorer countries) and the general economic and political vitality of a country. Figure 3.6 shows the population pyramid for Somalia in 2015 with each age group divided by educational attainment. Clearly, the population is characterized by very high proportions of people having no education, especially at older ages and among women. Indeed, the improvements in the number of primary and secondary educated younger people have been disproportionately benefiting young men

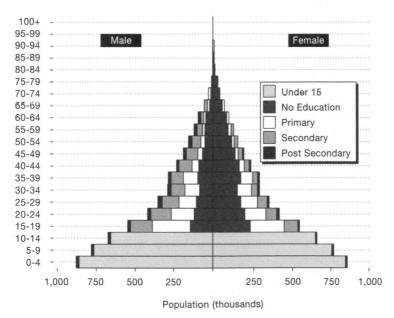

Figure 3.6   Population pyramid with education, Somalia

Source: Drawn by the authors using data from the Wittgenstein Centre for Demography and Global Human Capital (WIC) Data Explorer.

(shown on the left of the population pyramid) rather than women – something which could impact upon short- to medium-term fertility.

Turning to 2050, however, Figure 3.7 presents not just one view of the future for Somalia but six. Each represents a different scenario, or more particularly, a different 'Shared Socioeconomic Pathway' (SSP); each posits both alternative futures of development and educational attainment and links both of these back into alternative models of demographic behaviour. The precise details of each SSP are covered in more depth elsewhere (KC and Lutz, 2017). In brief, though, each of these different pathways assumes an alternative future for education and development. SSP2 is based upon countries following a 'global trajectory' of other countries' improvements in educational investment. For SSP2-CER, the attainment shares at age 30–34 of future cohorts are fixed at the levels observed in the base year; while in SSP2-FT the most rapid country-specific expansion parameters are applied to all countries throughout the projection period. In other words, all countries follow the educational development paths taken in the past by the frontrunners in East and South-East Asia.

SSP1 represents a 'rapid development' scenario, whereby 'educational and health investments accelerate the demographic transition leading to a relatively low world population', implying low mortality, high education and low fertility for countries such as Somalia. SSP5, entitled 'conventional development' is somewhat similar to SSP1, but also assumes higher levels of migration. SSP2, meanwhile, represents a world characterized by stalled demographic transition, with low investment in education, higher mortality and fertility, and lower migration as a consequence of an emphasis on security and less international exchange between countries of people, remittances and trade in goods. Finally, SSP3 represents a scenario of high levels of inequality, where investment in education in poorer countries is polarized, resulting in an unequal distribution of educational attainment and, consequently, higher fertility rates.

Figure 3.7 shows both the total population size as well as the educational achievement level of males and females aged 20–29 – a crucial part of the population in terms of both work and reproduction. The differences between the various scenarios are immediately apparent from the figure. The total population in Somalia under the different scenarios ranges from only a modest growth to 11.8 million under the conditions of SSP5 through to more than doubling to 22.6 million under the 'stalled development' scenario (SSP3). But the total population is only one component of these alternative futures. The total number of children is, of course, dramatically different

Population (thousands)

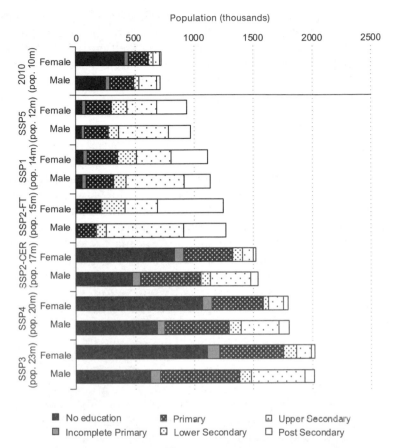

Figure 3.7   Alternative futures for Somalia, males and females
aged 20–29, 2050

Source: Drawn by the authors using data from the Wittgenstein Centre
for Demography and Global Human Capital (WIC) Data Explorer.

under different pathways – more than three times more between the
two most extreme scenarios. Some pathways are marked by much
more mortality than others – ironically meaning, of course, that lower
fertility will eventually lead to substituting one perceived 'problem',
namely population growth, for another, namely population ageing.
But really, the key difference lies in education – and this is a theme
that we will be returning to throughout the rest of this book. It is not
just the total number of people that matter, but what their characteristics are, how they are empowered to make choices, and how they in
turn behave in terms of consumption, reproduction and mobility. See

how, potentially, a population largely characterized by very low educational attainment can be transformed into a much more educated society where men and women are equally well educated. Imagine how this might translate into other areas of life. On the other hand, imagine if nothing is done. Then the young population in Somalia by mid-century will have quadrupled in size and, being largely bereft of training and education, may be even less well equipped to deal with the attendant challenges of this rapid population growth.

The scenarios for Somalia that represent better investment in education do indeed translate into lower levels of overall population growth. But that is not all. A society with better education is (generally) likely also to be more productive, more innovative, more likely to adapt to climate change, more healthy, more amenable to women's rights and less susceptible to malign political manipulation. All of this means that we can look at these alternative scenarios for Somalia – or any other country for that matter – and *choose* the future we want to have. Again, as Casanova himself advises, 'There is no such thing as destiny. We ourselves shape our lives.' We have to set about altering the parameters and changing the conditions so that we can move towards the future that we want. By doing so we move far away from the defeatist, pessimistic projections of apocalyptic futures.

Embrace the uncertainty, and shed the fallacy that 'demography is destiny'. That assumption is – to put it simply, but not too rudely – rubbish. But none of this is ever easy. Even in the affluent US, access to good education is poor relative to almost all other comparable countries. This may partly explain why people in the US might be more susceptible to malign political intervention. The US scores lowly when its 16–24 year olds are tested for their problem-solving ability, numeracy and literacy. However, we should not be too smug. The country that is most often ranked second to the US in terms of educational inability is the UK, where both the authors of this book were educated (see Dorling and Tomlinson, 2016).

Demography affects, and will be affected by, many of the biggest decisions that different societies will have to take in the near future. Of course, one might object that 'it's ridiculous to assume that Somalia could develop so rapidly in such a short period of time, and have so many people in higher education'. But such doubts are based upon looking at Somalia today. Indeed, one of the reasons why these gloomy predictions of the future are so misleading is that they are usually based upon changing just one parameter – namely population. It's odd that we can conceive of a world with 10 billion people easily, but picturing a world characterized by fairness and investment in education, health and sustainable technology seems to be somewhat harder, if not impossible, to imagine. This is why it's not surprising that some people think 'we're fucked' (Emmott, 2013). It takes a great deal of imagination to see how we might not be, but it is not impossible to be that imaginative.

Alternative scenarios are not just important for very poor countries such as Somalia that are struggling with high fertility, famine and poverty. The interrelated futures of education and population will play a critical role in shaping the future of the global economy. We will discuss this in greater depth in Chapter 7, but here by way of example it is worth mentioning the alternative futures for one of the world's great economic powerhouses: India. KC and Lutz (2017) consider three different scenarios for India that produce very different outcomes, summarized by the total population in 2050 varying from 1.55 billion in SSP1 to 1.97 billion in SSP3 – a difference of more than the combined present-day population of the US, Canada and Mexico – depending on what happens now and in the next few decades to come. Given India's core infrastructure (not least relating to education), its current rapid economic growth (which could be translated into further investment in health and education), and its current levels of urbanization, any of these three futures can now be imagined as possible without having to stretch your imagination too far. Firstly, as just noted, there are the huge differences in the total population that could result from following one of these three pathways. But, again, beyond total population, there is no doubt that the India under SSP1 is going to be completely different from the India under SSP3 – in terms of the health and the skills of the population, and how this could be translated into productivity and further economic development.

These three alternative futures are in the hands of policymakers and populations themselves. However, we must temper this point by observing the roles played by global capital, which we elaborate on in Chapter 7, and international migration, which we turn to in Chapter 8. The outcome of these projections are especially important in terms of the future fight for economic and political supremacy, both regional and global, between India and China, including skirmishes in the pages of *The Economist*. What *The Economist* never imagines is that the peoples of both countries could win. That is because its writers have no vision of winning which does not create losers, where winning is not simply synonymous with 'becomes the richest'.

As we saw in Chapter 1, the phrase 'demography is destiny' is used regularly in the media. There has been much debate about its origins, but the most convincing attribution is discussed by John Weeks (2013), who traces it to Scammon and Wattenberg's 1970 book *The Real Majority*. Scammon was director of the US Census Bureau from 1961 to 1965, while Watternberg was a speech writer for President Johnson. The main claim of their book was that the future of American politics was destined to be a centrist one. Their thesis was that 'middle voters' would come to dominate the US electorate in the future, resulting in more Democrat majorities, and that those voters' centrist tendencies needed to be reflected in the posturing of any given political party or politician. Looking at the electoral landscape in 2016 and 2017 ... how wrong they were!

It is ironic, therefore, that Scammon and Wattenberg were mistaken not only about the future landscape of both American politics and the US electorate as a whole – something we discuss below in Chapter 8 on population and politics – but also in the very concept of demography being destiny. Their analysis was based on a narrow projection of both recent trends but also on one politically expedient vision of the future. It was ultimately wrong precisely because they could neither foresee the profound demographic and social changes to come in the US (and beyond), nor identify the inter-relationship between these changes and policies, economic development, geopolitics and voting behaviour.

However, as we have tried to show in this chapter, most users of projections do broadly the same thing as Scammon and Wattenberg did, but in a rather more subtle way. The unquestioning use of projections to suggest that populations *will* do this or that, over the next however many years, gives the impression that future population is the fixed parameter, and that we will need to build our world around that parameter. But that is just another way of saying that 'demography is destiny'. We have argued that this way of presenting the future can result from a naivety regarding the formulation of projections, but it can also be a deliberate attempt to shape the current narrative around a 'threat' in the future from an ongoing or imagined trend.

But demography is *not* destiny. This should be obvious from the fact that we are so uncertain about future demographic trends. Consider the earlier examples of how we got things wrong in the past by not adequately envisaging continuing improvements in mortality or sub-replacement fertility; and, indeed, we continue to be uncertain about the future directions of both these factors as well as other large-scale demographic processes. For instance, future researchers may be amazed that we did not foresee much higher rates of international immigration given how much cheaper travel now is, and despite border controls appearing to be tightening in many countries. But to imagine something very different to what we see today is always hard, and to imagine what might take us there is even harder.

The real reason why demography is not destiny, as we have identified through the presentation of different scenarios above, is that there is simply no one-way interaction between population and everything else. Rather, the interaction is profoundly two-way (or, more likely, multi-dimensional). Demographic change can spur changes in policies, the economy and society; but changes in policies, the economy and society can spur demographic change.

Conclusion

The key thing to remember is that projections, in setting out one particular vision of the future, can give us some indication of what that future might look like under a certain set of parameters. The idea that a population projection should stay constant while everything else changes is pretty ludicrous, but the principle also holds in reverse. The future is what we make it. Inevitably it will be different from the present, possibly very different. All projections do is give us a subjectively defined, and probably inaccurate, indication of what might happen if we do certain things. In this way, therefore, the best projections can push us into action to do everything we can to make the world a better place. This, then, is where demography really matters. Not in terms of presenting a simple, hegemonic view of future challenges, often unhelpfully based around the idea of a 'time bomb', but in showing us just how uncertain the future is, and how much the decisions we take now will guide the development of humanity over the next century.

Before leaving the subject of projections it is worth briefly returning to some of the points we made in the previous chapter about the data we have. Of course, a projection – or a series of scenarios – will only be as good as the data being input and the level of understanding we have about the relationship between various parameters such as levels of education, health care provision, and social and cultural changes. Yet the state of our knowledge is frequently parlous, not least in terms of the data upon which we base all our projections. Consider the example of China given in the previous chapter, and the uncertainty around projecting education-specific futures for a population of more than 1.3 billion people when we have no precise idea of what the current fertility rate is, or of how it has changed over recent years. Estimates of infant mortality rates in China vary wildly as well: in urban areas they may now be very low (even lower than in urban areas in US), but in rural areas they may still be quite high. Since the sources we have contradict each other, we find it hard, as yet, to know quite what to believe. By extension, our projections of the populations of many poor countries are similarly built on sand because of the lack of both adequate demographic data and in-depth research on the mechanisms by which demographic change occurs in relation to other drivers.

We certainly need to improve demographic literacy around projections, both in terms of what they are presenting and, indeed, what they actually represent. But, at the same time, we also need a revolution in the way we understand population dynamics, in terms of both their measurement and how they relate to other drivers. We will never fully understand the engine, but we could do a much better job of guessing how the various parts interact, or what most influences what, than we currently achieve.

4

Population 'Explosion'

This chapter focuses on the explosion that has occurred, and the implosion that is beginning. The population bomb exploded some time ago – around 1850. The fuse may have been lit much earlier than that. Many people put the date as 1492, due to the social, political, economic and finally demographic repercussions of joining up humanity's Old and New Worlds.[1] The explosion began in Europe, and then triggered further population explosions in other continents as Europeans moved out around the world. What had been relatively stable social systems were first disrupted and then almost entirely overthrown through colonization, imperialism and the imposition of so-called free trade. Before such disruptions, population levels were usually very stable, other than in times of war, plague or infrequent famine.

By the 1960s the effects of what had been a series of explosions in population growth from the 1500s to the 1900s worldwide were at their greatest. It is no surprise that the 'population bomb' phrase was coined at the end of the 1960s, in 1968. But it is hugely ironic that 1968 was the very point at which the threat began to abate. The population bomb had gone off long before. There are no new bombs. No fuses are being lit today. From the early 1970s onwards natural population growth began inexorably to slow down. Today in many parts of the world it has ceased. Each year there are now more deaths than births in the places where growth has already stopped. Elsewhere, the aftermaths of past smaller explosions continue to be felt, but there are none that compare to the crescendo reached shortly after 1968. When we discussed future scenarios for Somali in the previous chapter, we were distinguishing between continued growth (not explosion), a slight slowdown or a rapid slowdown. No country in the world is currently experiencing rates of fertility that are expected to rise in an explosive manner, but the overwhelming narrative ignores this vital truth.

The overwhelming narrative

Population explosion remains the dominant narrative in the global population debate, despite the sudden rapid rises in population due to rising fertility having ended. But 'there are already too many people on the planet', or so we are told. We apparently know this because there are so many more people than there used to be. But if that were the measure then there have been too many people in every decade since the time of the Black Death, or at least since shortly after 1492. But people are 'flooding' in from the countryside, rapidly increasing the size of cities. Is that not an explosion? It may in fact be the opposite, since when people move to urban areas they tend to then have fewer children. More people does not necessarily mean too many, especially when more of us live in high-density cities, which means overall pressure on land is abated.

So many cities are now megacities that you would not recognize the names of most conurbations in the world with even 5 million inhabitants. For most people, only the very few largest cities, those that contain at least 10 million people each, are familiar. However, they may well not be that familiar to you. By 2030 none of these cities other than New York are fully in Europe or the US. And only a tiny fraction of the people in the world will have had much experience of living in more than one or two of these cities. The vast majority have never visited a city of this size, probably including you. If you are reading this book, then Europe or the US is most likely to be where you are now. Two of these megacities are on the borders of Europe. Only one is in the US and only one is in the rest of the Americas. Table 4.1 gives the full list.

The numbers in this table are very approximate because no one can agree on the precise boundaries of cities. Many of the 2015 population estimates will have already been revised by the time you read this because population numbers keep changing, very rapidly in the case of a few of these places, but much more slowly in others. (There will also be errors in the 1950 estimates, but few would try to correct those now.) It is very important to recognize that the populations of these cities can't be counted precisely at any one time. This is not just because of errors in counting but because some people

Table 4.1. The largest cities in the world, 1950, 2015, 2030

1950			2015			2030		
City	Country	Population (millions)	City	Country	Pop. (mil.)	City	Country	Pop. (mil.)
New York	US	12.3	Tokyo	Japan	38.0	Tokyo	Japan	37.2
Tokyo	Japan	11.3	Delhi	India	25.7	Delhi	India	36.1
London	UK	8.4	Shanghai	China	23.7	Shanghai	China	30.8
Osaka	Japan	7.0	São Paulo	Brazil	21.1	Mumbai	India	27.8
Paris	France	6.3	Mumbai	India	21.0	Beijing	China	27.7
Moscow	Russia	5.4	Mexico City	Mexico	21.0	Dhaka	Bangladesh	27.4
Buenos Aires	Argentina	5.1	Beijing	China	20.4	Karachi	Pakistan	24.8
Chicago	US	5.0	Osaka	Japan	20.2	Cairo	Egypt	24.5
Kolkata	India	4.5	Cairo	Egypt	18.8	Lagos	Nigeria	24.2
Shanghai	China	4.3	New York	US	18.6	Mexico City	Mexico	23.9
Los Angeles	US	4.0	Dhaka	Bangladesh	17.6	São Paulo	Brazil	23.4
Mexico City	Mexico	3.4	Karachi	Pakistan	16.6	Kinshasa	Democratic Republic of the Congo	20.0
Berlin	Germany	3.3	Buenos Aires	Argentina	15.2	Osaka	Japan	20.0
Philadelphia	US	3.1	Kolkata	India	14.9	New York	United States of America	19.9
Rio de Janeiro	Brazil	3.0	Istanbul	Turkey	14.2	Kolkata	India	19.1
St Petersburg	Russia	2.9	Chongqing	China	13.3	Guangzhou	China	17.6
Mumbai	India	2.9	Lagos	Nigeria	13.1	Chongqing	China	17.4
Detroit	US	2.8	Manila	Philippines	12.9	Buenos Aires	Argentina	17.0
Boston	US	2.6	Rio de Janeiro	Brazil	12.9	Manila	Philippines	16.8
Cairo	Egypt	2.5	Guangzhou	China	12.5	Istanbul	Turkey	16.7

Source: Data from the UN World Urbanization Prospects, 2015.

may live for part of the year in a city, or even just part of the week; others commute inwards daily but sleep outside the city boundary. In Chapter 2 we discussed the basic problems of counting people, why and how so many can be missed or sometimes double-counted; but for now let's not worry about those errors and believe the numbers we are given and the projections that are made. Short-term projections and estimates are much more likely to be reliable than long-term ones because small errors of assumption can magnify greatly, as we illustrated in Chapter 3.

Some cities, such as Tokyo, Moscow and possibly Istanbul, will probably have lower populations soon or within a few decades. Others, especially those in China, are not expected to grow much larger in size than their 2030 projections because the young urban population is surrounded by much older rural populations, and very few people are having families of more than two children any more, while many have no children or just one (despite the recent relaxation of child policies). However, many other 'megacities' are not as yet showing any signs of growth slowdown because the rural depopulation around them is still accelerating and more and more people are moving into urban areas, or to their edges. It is this continued rapid growth of some of the largest cities in the world, due largely to internal migration from the countryside, that is the current most obvious manifestation of the abating population explosion.

Defining the populations of cities is notoriously difficult, much harder than defining the population of a country.[2] Not only are the functional (real) boundaries of each city hard to determine, as well as the daytime, night-time and weekly population norms, but also many people living in cities are often not there officially, whether because they lack the necessary permit to do so, or because they live elsewhere for several months of the year. The UN population estimates given above can be compared to alternative estimates crowd-sourced by the contributors to various Wikipedia pages that compete as an information provider.[3] One problem with Wikipedia as a source is that, if you look at the web-page referenced as the source today, you will often see significantly different numbers for each city, and often a different ordering of them than what was there a year ago. UN bodies make estimates, but they have to rely on various sources that are also of often-dubious quality. To try to estimate recent population changes, demographic researchers even resort to satellite data showing the changing extent of built-up areas and slums.

The populations of states are easier to estimate than the populations of the cities within them. We use the word 'countries' here interchangeably with states, but it is worth noting that some states such as the UK contain more than one country, and also that state boundaries can change over time, although not as constantly and fluidly as city boundaries expand. Sometimes groups of states, such as those within the Schengen area of the European Union, and the states of the US, have free movement of people laws that in effect make their boundaries far more fluid. In the past, cities had walls and if you were not within them you were not within the city; today these old walls often mark the historic heart of a city.

Although cities can grow very fast, some smaller countries have experienced equally as dramatic population growth in recent years. The populations of entire countries have quadrupled in just a few generations. In such places the 'bombs' went off decades ago. But to many people, the world as a whole looks out of control. What will this population growth lead to? Population growth may be decelerating, as we explain later, but the global population is itself still growing and will do for some decades to come, mainly due to ageing. A substantial rural population will also likely continue to grow for some time to come. So, if you are standing in the middle of a megacity today it can easily feel as if population growth has never been as fast – because for you, where you are standing, that is the case – but you are standing in a very unusual spot.

Just a century ago London was the largest city in the world with a population that only just exceeded 1 million people. The rapid urbanization of the planet is one way in which population can grow significantly without the pressure on the land also rising. In fact, that pressure can fall if population densities rise faster than population numbers. Space can be much less of an issue if horizontal space is substituted for vertical, as in the tower blocks of the growing megacity. But just how many more people can we squeeze in? You can read story after story about how there are too many people and how the population explosion is out of control; you will rarely read about the population slowdown because it is not news. As noted earlier, it has been ongoing worldwide since the 1970s.

Extremist politicians use images of crowds of people – especially of younger men with darker skins than the politicians usually have – to try to stoke up fear of a potentially endless flow, as if they were pouring from an always open tap. Images such as that in Figure 4.1 raise questions in the minds of those who view them. If there are already too many people, how will we cope with even more? And often this results in the reaction 'we must put up border fences'. They can even make others wonder whether we need to begin to plan to

Figure 4.1 Nigel Farage, then leader of the UK Independence Party, and the launch of his 'Breaking Point' campaign poster in June 2016 in the run-up to the UK's referendum on membership of the European Union

Source: Mark Thomas/REX/Shutterstock.

colonize the moon or other planets. If there are so many people on the move, what hope is there? Those who fear these migrants most are particularly fearful of the children yet to be born to the migrants. Maybe it is already too late? But few people mention how low migration across international borders currently is, or how small a fraction of humanity now lives in a country they were not born in. And few people worry about the harm that is caused by not allowing more migration. In fact many cannot *imagine* that there is any disadvantage in *not* having migrants arrive. They cannot imagine living in a city that is emptying out, rather than still receiving people. Glasgow in the 1960s, Liverpool in the 1970s, Detroit in the 1980s, Rostock in the 1990s, and many more remote Chinese cities in the 2000s are all places in which people can testify to what happens when migrants no longer arrive in decent numbers (see, for example, Richardson and Nam, 2014).

It is common to hear laments about human overpopulation. And it is certainly true that there are an awful lot of us, especially if you take into account that we are larger-than-average mammals. Large concentrations of people need to be fed and watered, need sewage systems to cope with their waste, and pest control to deal with the vermin they attract, but that is all often harder to provide in a city that is shrinking in population and seeing its tax base fall. In general it is not our total numbers but *how we live* that matters, especially when it comes to the sustainability of large populations. We need to look at how many other animals we are responsible for, breeding, feeding and slaughtering them. A global population of 7 to 10 billion cannot eat as much meat sustainably as a smaller population could, but we are now trying to eat more meat per person than ever before.

When the world population reached 7 billion in 2011, humans weighed, in total, about 350 million tonnes (Chappell, 2011), each of us weighing on average just under 8 stone each (around 2 billion of the total population are children and more people are underweight than overweight worldwide). By total weight we are the heaviest animals on the planet, except for the cattle we farm to provide us with food (1.4 billion of them, 520 million tonnes worth at any one time). We weigh more than the 1.1 billion sheep (65 million tonnes) and the 18.6 billion chickens (40 million tonnes). If we ignore the fish in the oceans, and the insects, which both weigh more than us, then the vast majority of animal life on earth *by weight* is us and what we farm to eat. We have taken over the planet.[4]

The issue this chapter focuses on is the mushrooming of global human population numbers over the last century, and the perceived futures that various extrapolations of that growth suggest. These extrapolations could have included the nightmare Malthusian scenarios with which we began this book, recently reiterated in Emmott's *Ten Billion*, in his earlier stage play, and possibly soon in *Ten Billion: The Movie*. But long term, even large-scale population growth is far from guaranteed, and we now have plenty of examples of shrinking cities and even shrinking countries. Feedback effects could limit the incredible projections seen in many of the countries currently expected to grow in population the fastest (see Chapter 3). Human endeavour and technology, not least that driven by huge changes in human capital accumulation, female empowerment, and rising environmentalism, mean that the population context of the twenty-first century is very different from that of the twentieth.

Emmott famously suggested that it makes sense to teach your children, and in particular your sons, to learn to use a gun, because war and anarchy appear to be the most likely consequences of our current population growth and the future collapse of civilizations he foresees. However, if the scenarios he projects were to develop it would make more sense to teach your children to shoot bows and arrows, since the world would quickly run out of bullets and the means to mass produce modern weaponry in the apocalyptic conditions he describes. Often those who foresee apocalypse have not thought through their imagined futures in enough detail. They completely miss other possibilities that are far more probable than the end of the world being nigh.

One of the worst effects of worrying about growing populations is not worrying enough about shrinking populations. There are political, economic and sociological implications to the population explosion potentially fizzling out earlier than expected. Demographers have long insisted that demographic changes – longevity, lower fertility and the consequent changing age structure – have sociological impacts that hugely affect politics. For example, in most of Europe we now rarely experience deaths within our family households ('at home') because reproduction is so much more 'efficient' than it was 100 years ago (most deaths were of babies and children), and this mass ageing requires that we view support in older age in new ways, for example by recognizing that older people now have far fewer younger relatives than was the case in the past.

The images of streams of young men heading for affluent countries are misleading in another way. The year 1990 saw a peak in births worldwide. The population born since includes fewer and fewer people each year. Continued global population growth is caused not by fertility but by people living longer. Perhaps the real image used to scare us should be that of an endless stream of old people in wheelchairs rather than fit young men?

There are many differing viewpoints to consider here and no single settled 'worldview'. A world with less untimely mortality is, in some ways paradoxically, likely to be a more demographically stable world. The paradox is that fewer deaths can result in fewer people. So let's develop this story further with the help of a press release concerning a small species of the Anopheles mosquito, of which just the females transmit the parasite that causes the disease – malaria.[5]

Malaria and the good news that is so often ignored

In November 2015 the United Nations issued a press release, quoting the then UN Secretary-General Ban Ki-moon: 'Today, we celebrate major advances in our fight against malaria.'[6] The challenge of malaria reduction had been set out in the Millennium Development Goals (MDGs) in 2000. By 2015 the goals had been achieved.

You rarely hear good news reported. This is not because there is no good news around. It's because good news doesn't sell newspapers, doesn't have people glued to TV screens, and doesn't agitate politicians and pundits. Nevertheless, good news abounds. Six weeks before the Christmas deadline, the UN was able to announce that every one of the six MDG targets to reverse the incidence of malaria by 2015 had been met. Some had been more than met – they had been greatly surpassed. And when you reduce malaria, you also help to begin stabilizing human numbers, as people have fewer children once they realize that their children have become much less likely to die before themselves.

In the fifteen years from 2000 to 2015, UN agencies were able to show that malaria prevention interventions had contributed to a 60 per cent decline in malaria mortality rates around the world. They claimed that this had averted some 6.2 million deaths that would otherwise have occurred, primarily in young children in the poorest parts of the globe. That is a number similar to all those murdered in concentration camps during the Second World War. It is a huge number of lives.

A cynic might say that while they understand that such an achievement is to be welcomed, won't those children go on to have children of their own? Will this achievement not result in an ever-larger world population and more destitution, hunger and disease in the future? Thankfully, that cynic would almost certainly be wrong. It is worth saying it again and again, when fewer children die in childhood, parents have fewer children overall. The rapid curtailment in infant and childhood mortality taking place today could well be the key factor in not just the ending the population explosion, but in seeing it become an implosion.

The UN went on to report that in Africa, where 90 per cent of all malaria-related deaths are estimated to occur worldwide, there had been a 69 per cent reduction in malaria mortality among children under the age of five between the years 2000 and 2015 (Ki-moon, 2015). This was an incredibly rapid and sizeable recent fall. Figure 4.2 shows the world with countries sized according to the number of malaria deaths occurring in each country around the year 2000, when possibly 1 million people a year died of malaria, mostly very young children. It shows the concentration of these deaths then in Africa. Not only is the number of deaths and cases reducing rapidly, but the concentration within the African continent is also reducing. In 2003, 92 per cent of malaria cases and 94 per cent of malaria deaths worldwide were recorded as being in African territories.

The term malaria comes from the medieval Italian *mala aria*, meaning bad air. The disease was identified long before people

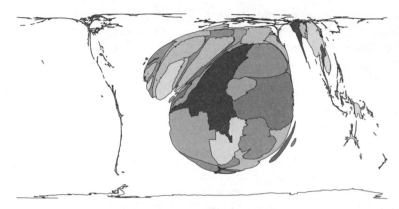

Figure 4.2 The world reshaped according to the 1 million malaria deaths recorded in the year 2000

Source: www.worldmapper.org. Data derived from various UN estimates

realized that the mosquito was the common carrier of the disease. In 1999 malarial deaths were described as an unmitigated public health disaster. Malaria is preventable and treatable, but people cannot seek treatment if it is not available or available but not affordable. In 2004 one man explained it thus: 'My wife died a few months ago, very probably from malaria because she had a lot of fever and was also vomiting. But she never went to a health centre. Because of the lack of money.' It was as simple as that.

Preventing malaria is even more important than treating it. The disease can be prevented by reducing the mosquito population, and by giving people bed nets so that they are not bitten by mosquitoes at night; drugs can also help, as can improved nutrition and sanitation, which make a population more able to cope. But above all, there has to be a commitment to seeing malaria deaths as preventable and seeing that prevention as being hugely worthwhile. This is not just for the sake of those affected by the disease, but is also in the interests of entire countries and people everywhere – because classical demographic theory holds that when fewer children die people don't need or want to have as many, and are also more likely to know how to achieve that. Figure 4.3 shows where the 133 million children born in the year 2000 were born. Birth rates are highest where child death rates are highest. Malaria deaths have never fallen in number before – as far as we know – in the entirety of world history. Today over 100 countries that had previously experienced malaria are free of the disease.

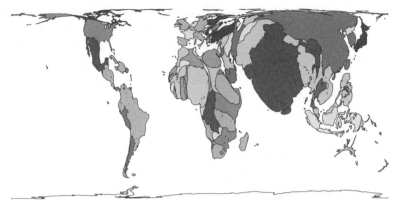

Figure 4.3   The world reshaped according to the 133 million births
recorded in the year 2000

Source: www.worldmapper.org. Data derived from various UN estimates.

If even malaria can be controlled then there is much more that we can also achieve together. The President of the 70th session of the UN General Assembly, Mogens Lykketoft, explained that 'the world's success in rolling back malaria shows just what can be achieved with the right kind of determination and partnerships. It provides bold inspiration to all nations that seek to create a healthy environment for their children and adults.' And he went on to say: 'We can and we must eliminate malaria by 2030. This will require full implementation of the new strategy developed by the Roll Back Malaria Partnership and the World Health Organization. In it, we have the path forward – I urge all member states to fully support implementation of this strategic plan.'[7] If we are going to live well with a large human population, we are going to have to plan better. Reducing childhood mortality is just one of the many things we will have to plan for.

The plan Lykketoft outlined included a commitment to reduce global malaria cases and deaths by 90 per cent and to eliminate the disease in an additional thirty-five countries by 2030. But he then went on to explain that to achieve this over 100 billion dollars would be needed, with an additional 10 billion required to fund more malaria research and development. And he was more explicit: 'annual malaria investments will need to increase to 6.4 billion dollars by 2020'. That is more than double the investments being made today of 2.7 billion dollars a year, and which are decreasing.

In the same press conference, representatives of the World Health Organization (WHO) explained that if these 'investments' were made then more than 10 million lives would be saved by 2030 and over 4 trillion dollars of additional economic output would be generated. Reducing the incidence of malaria would also contribute to goals to reduce poverty, improve educational enrolment, and increase equity and women's empowerment – all of which are then related to lower fertility. However, the WHO did not point out that final link. Perhaps they should have? They also did not mention that it could become much cheaper to reduce malaria deaths even further in future. Genetically engineered mosquitoes raise the possibility of eradicating malaria in an area within a single breeding season – although of course that might turn out to be a pipe-dream. Instead, they ended with a blunt message:

> In 2015, 214 million cases of malaria infection were reported, leading to the deaths of over 470,000 people. The majority of those perished were African children under the age of five. Malaria, a major cause and consequence of poverty and inequity, hinders economic development, damages food security, inhibits participation in education, and weakens national health systems.[8]

Without due diligence malaria could return again to the UK (Chin and Welsby, 2004). The world could be malaria-free by the end of the twenty-first century, or a lack of coordination and empathy, coupled with global warming, could spread the Anopheles mosquitoes northwards. Nothing is set in stone.

The algae bloom of human beings, 1800–2000

Before 1851 human global population experienced relatively slow growth. This had been the case for most of human history, with the exception of the period known as the Neolithic revolution. That revolution occurred independently in at least four parts of the world and is thought to have taken place around 11–12,000 years ago in some of those areas, later in others. The global population of humans alive in the world just before the Neolithic revolution has been estimated at around 6 million people, with a huge amount of error associated with that estimate. For every person alive then, there are now well over 1,000 people alive today. The rise during the Neolithic revolution was roughly six-fold, to 36 million in the space of many dozens of generations. And then population growth slowed again and it took many hundreds of human generations for a further six-fold rise in global numbers to take place between 1800 and 2000. The last time such a rapid rise in human beings occurred was before the ancient Greeks were refining their myths and even before the Buddha was contemplating whether there was more to life after death.

According to estimates from the United Nations Population Division (see Table 4.2), the global population in year zero, just over 2,000 years ago, was around 300 million. Other estimates vary between 170 and 400 million, so there is a huge degree of uncertainty. The first semi-reliable estimates of the population of England are derived from the recording and publication of the Domesday Book in 1086, calculated by academics as being between 1.1 and 1.9 million at that time, but it could have been over 4 million.

Up to the end of the first millennium (current era) the world's average population growth rate was under 0.1 per cent a year. During the second millennium population growth rates were slow and, at times of plague and the spread of diseases to the New World, they were temporarily negative. Despite such setbacks, the global human

Table 4.2. World population, year 1–2011 (in billions)

Year	Billions
1	0.30
1000	0.31
1250	0.40
1500	0.50
1750	0.79
1800	0.98
1850	1.26
1900	1.65
1910	1.75
1920	1.86
1930	2.07
1940	2.30
1950	2.52
1960	3.02
1970	3.70
1980	4.44
1990	5.27
1999	5.98
2000	6.06
2010	6.79
2011	7.00

Source: Data from the United Nations Population Division, 1999; Population Institute, 2011.

population reached 1 billion by 1820. It had reached 1.3 billion by the early twentieth century and then rose rapidly to a staggering 6 billion by 1999. On 31 October 2011 the United Nations declared that the global population had reached 7 billion. Table 4.2 shows our best estimates of how the population levels on the planet have changed over the last 2,000 years.

The population growth rates varied between different regions of the world. Since we obviously cannot use nation states, we categorize the world into regions, or geographically contiguous territories. Figure 4.4 presents a series of cartograms highlighting the changing geographies of population growth over the last 2,000 years by these regions. The territories are drawn in proportion to their population at the different moments in time. In year one CE, the combined population of what is now China, Mongolia and Korea was the same as the population of the UK in 2014, which by that year numbered around 62 million.

Two millennia ago the population of what is now India, then at the centre of the 'known' world, was, at 78 million, less than that of Germany today. Across the rest of the planet, the remaining 90 million humans were very unevenly spread out. As can be seen in the first cartogram, the largest territories are mostly China (coloured in light grey) and India (medium grey). In these two modern-day territories an estimated 135 million people, more than half of the then total global population, were thought to live. At that time there were 40 million people in Europe, 18 million in the Middle East and 11 million in Northern Africa. North and South America as well as the Pacific-Asia region were very sparsely populated. Generally the colder areas in Northern latitudes tended to have lower populations, whereas the territories that now encompass the Ganges, Tigris, Yangtze, Nile and Po rivers were the most populous.

The second cartogram in the series (4.4b) shows the distribution of the population in year 1500, the time of the Spanish conquests in South America. Although the global population nearly doubled from year 1 to year 1500, its geographical distribution remained largely the same, with Southern and Eastern Asia remaining the most populous world regions. It is also interesting to note that at this time the combined population of Mexico and Peru was greater than the total population of the land now labelled as 'all other American countries'. This pattern was about to change very quickly in the following centuries. In particular, the invasion of the New World in 1492 was accompanied by the exposure of its inhabitants to germs and illnesses

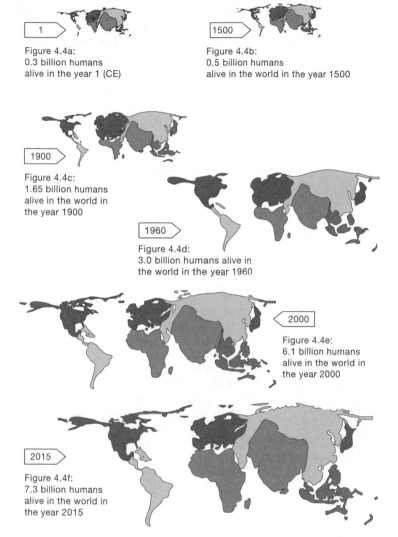

Figure 4.4a:
0.3 billion humans
alive in the year 1 (CE)

Figure 4.4b:
0.5 billion humans
alive in the world in the year 1500

Figure 4.4c:
1.65 billion humans
alive in the world in
the year 1900

Figure 4.4d:
3.0 billion humans alive in
the world in the year 1960

Figure 4.4e:
6.1 billion humans
alive in the world in
the year 2000

Figure 4.4f:
7.3 billion humans
alive in the world in
the year 2015

Figure 4.4   Distribution of humans alive in the world in the last
2000 years

Source: www.worldmapper.org. Data derived from estimates by the Angus
Maddison Project.

to which they did not have immunity. This had a devastating effect
upon the indigenous populations, who died far faster from those
diseases than from the colonial wars and atrocities committed by the
Old World powers.

Across the Atlantic, the shock of discovering what was virtually a new planet – the New World – was so great that the economy of the Old World was transformed. The riches plundered from the New World turned the previous social order of the continents on its head. The then relatively underdeveloped far west of Asia (Europe) suddenly became the economic centre of the world. Before then only the Greeks (Ptolemy) had defined Europe as a separate continent. A little more slowly, China became peripheral. Trade flows altered, colonization began, the taking of slaves accelerated in Africa and within a few centuries everything had changed for most people in most parts of the world. From continent to continent human populations began to multiply rapidly as the established social orders were overturned. The first, fastest and most destabilizing population explosion was within Europe itself. Africa was depopulated through both slavery and 400 years of forced migration, mostly to the New World. India was colonized (twice). Chinese empires were destroyed, partly through the British Empire-orchestrated opium trade. A nascent North American empire was conceived. Between 1500 and 1900 the global population tripled to 1.5 billion and the geographical distribution changed significantly, as shown in the cartogram for 1900 (4.4c).

During this period, which was characterized by imperial rule and territorial expansion, the populations of Britain and North America increased more than ten-fold. The next cartogram in the series, 4.4d, shows the geography of the global population in 1960, when it reached 3 billion. The proportion of the world's population living in South America had increased rapidly since 1900. In contrast, the Western European proportion began to decline in relative terms from 15 per cent in 1900 to 11 per cent in 1960 and then 6 per cent in 2000 (4.4e). The cartograms in Figure 4.4 (very roughly) scale the total map area to the total population size to illustrate the overall growth since 1900. The final cartogram, 4.4f, is of the 7.3 billion in 2015. It shows much of Africa and India are now growing faster than the global average.

Figure 4.5 includes the 120-year period between 1851 and 1971 known as the era of global population acceleration. It is the era in which most of the rapid algae-bloom-like expansion of the human population occurred. After 1851 the population was not just growing, but *the rate of growth itself was accelerating*. It continued to accelerate throughout this period, with the notable exceptions of the periods associated with the two world wars. Despite those setbacks the world's average population growth rate rose from 0.1 per cent a year to over 0.5 per cent between 1851 and 1870 and went up to over

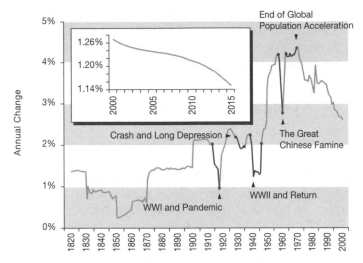

Figure 4.5 World annual population growth, 1821–2015

Source: Drawn by the authors using data from the United Nations' World Population Prospects: The 2015 Revision.

1 per cent by 1900, with the brief drop to 0.3 per cent during the First World War and the influenza pandemic that followed (1918–19).

After the First World War, global population annual growth rates rose to 1.3 per cent during the 1920s, before falling again to 0.8 in the era of the Great Depression from 1929 to 1936. The growth rate then briefly rose to just over 1 per cent again in the late 1930s, before falling dramatically during the Second World War. After that first truly global war there was a further and rapid acceleration to 1.8 per cent by the mid-1950s, briefly interrupted in the three years of the Great Chinese Famine. That famine occurred between 1958 and 1961, when up to 45 million premature deaths occurred. Human worldwide growth rates peaked just ten years after the end of the Chinese famine at 2.1 per cent in 1971. The period of acceleration ended in that year and annual growth fell to 1.6 per cent in 1982, jumped to 1.9 per cent in 1983, following the great Eastern Africa famine, and has been falling continuously since then.

The insert in the figure shows the trend since the year 2000. Note the rapid deceleration in population growth subsequent to the financial crash of 2008. It should be noted that all these increases get compounded and therefore a continuous growth of 2 per cent annually means that the world population doubles every 35 years (not 50). It is also very important to realize that events such as famine, war and epidemic actually result in the long term in greater population growth, in response to the deaths and destruction. So, in future, the more disasters we avert and avoid, the faster we should expect the population decline to be.

Censuses, surveys and scenarios

The analysis of past trends in population growth can be used by demographers to try to project what the future population growth rates might be in different places. In Chapter 3 we discussed the many problems with forecasting, here we look at the variety of global forecasts on offer. In countries without population registers, such as the UK and US, the population census, which records demographic and socioeconomic information at specific points in time and is normally carried out every ten years, is an essential instrument for obtaining reliable estimates of population numbers. In Chapter 2 we lamented the poor quality of data for many parts of the world. At the global and long historical scale, only in relatively recent decades and still only in a few places on earth have we had really good quality population enumeration. This is despite a very long history of census taking.

Censuses were taken in ancient times by kings, pharaohs and emperors to estimate the size of the population they had to keep suppressed and the number of soldiers they could raise, as well as to estimate their tax base. However, the first modern-day, regularly repeated censuses started in Prussia in 1719 and in the US in 1790. The first ten-yearly census in Britain was not held until 1801. Census datasets describe the state of the whole national population and are extremely relevant for the analysis of a wide range of socioeconomic issues and related policies. In addition to the census, there is an increasingly wide range of administrative and private sector sources of suitable socioeconomic data that can be used for demographic research, but much of it is not greatly reliable, as discussed in Chapter 2. All this matters when it comes to defusing the 'population bomb', because the downward trend in the inset in Figure 4.5 could be an error of enumeration, but might be a sign that the deceleration itself is accelerating.

The data collected from censuses can be used to provide estimates of past population sizes as well as projections into the future. In particular, it becomes possible to calculate birth and death rates which in turn allows one to project population numbers both backwards and forwards in time, including estimates of future and past migration flows. Those estimates are useful for making global population forecasts because when people migrate from poorer to rich territories they tend to adapt to the norms of the richer territory and have fewer children than they otherwise might have had.

On the basis of the past demographic trends reviewed above it is expected that in the next few decades global population growth rates will continue to decline, as they have for the last four decades, but possibly even faster. In particular, the United Nations predicts a fall in growth rates to below 1 per cent by around 2020, declining further thereafter to 0.3 per cent by 2050. That would be the lowest growth level recorded since the mid-eighteenth century. However, even these more modest growth rates will see the world's population grow by over 35 million a year. Even such slowed growth will result in an overall population of 9.5 billion by 2050, 2.5 billion more than present, unless the slowdown accelerates.

Given the compound nature of population growths it takes only small changes in fertility/death rates to have major consequences for population totals over a long period. However, we already know that it is population ageing that will be responsible for most population growth in coming decades, although high fertility would alter this. As Figure 4.6 shows, the UN produced (in 2012) a range of global population predictions for 2050 ranging from 8.3 billion to 10.8 billion, based on different fertility rates. Note that if current fertility

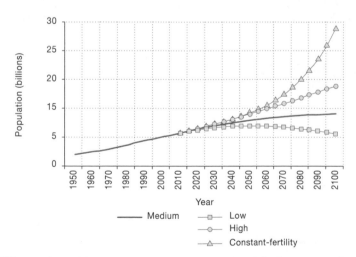

Figure 4.6 How changes in fertility rates might impact on future population growth

Source: Drawn by the authors using data from the United Nations' World Population Prospects: The 2012 Revision.

rates remained constant, the projected total population would be very much higher by 2100.

It is instructive to see the breakdown of the UN estimates and predictions by country and world regions. One of the classifications used by the UN is to divide world regions and countries into 'more developed countries' and 'less developed countries'. This is problematic, but we will nonetheless use these terms are here, as they are routinely and widely employed by organizations such as the UN and the World Bank. The second figure below, Figure 4.7, shows the official UN estimated past and projected future growth rates in so-called more developed and less developed countries. As can be seen, population size in the 'more developed countries' has remained relatively stable since the late 1950s, at around 1 billion. In contrast, the total population of the 'less developed countries' has increased rapidly from approximately 1 billion to 5 billion since 1950.

This difference in growth rates between richer and poorer parts of the globe is depicted starkly in Figure 4.7, which shows that the rates of population growth in the latter, although declining rapidly, will continue to be far above those in the former for the foreseeable future. Within the category of 'less developed' there are further variations, some reasons for which will become more apparent below. The forty-eight 'least developed countries', according to UN data, experienced the greatest increases in population growth. This group had only 8 per cent of the world's population in 1950, but in

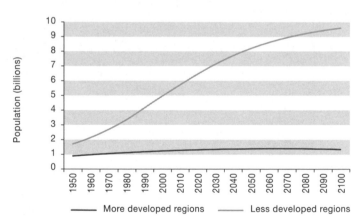

Figure 4.7 Population growth by more or less developed countries (in billions)

Source: Drawn by the authors using data from the United Nations' World Population Prospects: The 2012 Revision.

the subsequent half-century they contributed around 15 per cent of the overall global growth. Such differences in population growth rates have altered the relative distribution of the world's population. For example, the 'more developed' countries in 1950 combined amounted to approximately a third of the world's population; by 2010 this had fallen to around 18 per cent.

As Table 4.3 below shows, this has meant that significant changes have occurred in the overall population share by region. Europe's share fell from approximately a quarter to around an eighth of the global total between 1900 and 2000, with Africa being the biggest continental gainer in percentage terms. What is most significant here is how quickly this has happened, with most of the changes taking place since 1950.

By 2050 Europe's share is likely to have fallen to 7 per cent, while Africa's is expected to be nearly three times that. Over the period 2003–50 Africa's population is projected to grow by around 1 billion people, representing over one-third of all the global growth (36.4 per cent) compared to only one-sixth (16.6 per cent) previously for 1950–2003. Meanwhile, Asia seems destined to remain the main contributor in absolute terms, adding a further 1.4 billion by 2050, but this is a marked reduction in the pace of growth compared to its 2.4 billion gain between 1950 and 2003.

Table 4.3. Changes in overall population share (%) by region

Major area	1950	1975	2010	2050	
				Low	Medium
More developed regions	32.2	25.7	17.9	13.8	13.6
Less developed regions	67.8	74.3	82.1	86.2	86.4
Least developed countries	7.7	8.5	12.1	19.1	19.0
Less developed regions, excluding least developed countries	60.1	65.7	69.9	67.1	67.4
Less developed regions, excluding China	45.9	51.3	62.0	71.4	71.5
China	21.9	23.0	20.1	14.8	14.9
Africa	9.1	10.3	14.9	25.4	25.1
Asia	55.3	58.6	60.2	53.7	54.1
Europe	21.7	16.6	10.7	7.5	7.4
Latin America and the Caribbean	6.6	8.0	8.6	8.1	8.2
Northern America	6.8	6.0	5.0	4.7	4.7
Oceania	0.5	0.5	0.5	0.6	0.6

Source: Data from the United Nations World Population Prospects: The 2012 Revision.

A combination of factors has resulted in a dramatic fall in global fertility rates. In the 1960s the average was around five children per woman, but it has now fallen to below half that figure. The fertility rate today by country worldwide ranges from 1.2 children per woman in the Republic of South Korea to 7.6 in Niger, and the world average total fertility rate is now estimated to be 2.5.

In Asia and South America the average fertility rate is still rapidly falling and in almost all cases is below 2.5, often below 2.1. In sub-Saharan Africa the majority of countries currently have fertility rates of above 3 or in a few cases 4, but many are beginning to see fertility decline more quickly than before. Figure 4.8 shows how the average fertility rates were falling up to 2010 and were predicted to continue to fall. In Europe and North America they are now well below the population replacement rate of 2.1, which is the minimum needed for a population not to decline over the long term; and they are projected to reach that level in most regions in the world before 2100. The highest fertility rate predicted by the UNPD for 2100 is 2.13 children per woman in Africa, the lowest is 1.93, and that is not very low at all. Many demographers suspect that the lowest rates will be much lower than 1.93 simply because they are lower than that already in many countries.

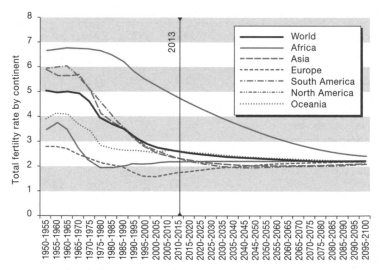

Figure 4.8   Total fertility ratio by continent, 1950–2100

Source: Drawn by the authors using data from the United Nations' World Population Prospects: The 2012 Revision.

Demographic transition or population explosion?

Traditionally a gradual demographic transition model was used to try to help with the analysis and understanding of past trends and demographic processes. However, one of the key limitations of this model was that it did not take into account the inter-dependencies of cities, regions and countries, which need to be considered when analysing past and future world population growth. In this section we draw on recent relevant work presenting an alternative approach to the analysis of global population growth, adapting punctuated equilibria ideas from biology (Dorling, 2013a).

Figure 4.5 (p. 87) showed that the period from 1851 to 1971 can be described as an era of global population acceleration, barring the four epochal events annotated in the figure. The year 1851 can be described as a global minimum for recent population growth rates. Looking at our recent past in relation to what our near future is projected to be, in the inset in Figure 4.5 we can clearly see that we have been living through a major demographic transformation.

Currently the population growth line in Figure 4.5 is still dropping almost as quickly as it did between 1971 and 2000, although you can see a slight 'hump' of baby boom just around 2010 if you look carefully (the inset shows that to have been an aberration as fertility falls so quickly after 2010). Annual global population growth was 1.27 per cent a year in 2000, fell to 1.22 per cent by 2009, and is probably at 1.12 per cent in 2017. That is a continuous rapid decline in growth rates. It is made up of many slightly greater decelerations and a few slower ones. Over the 2000 to 2009 period, the Netherlands saw its growth rate fall from 0.67 per cent a year to 0.42 per cent; the United Kingdom rate fell from 0.39 per cent to 0.28 per cent; in Spain it fell from 0.16 per cent to 0.08 per cent and was negative in 2015; in Italy growth of 0.2 per cent in 2000 has declined so fast that it became a fall of 0.03 per cent by 2009; in Germany a 0.14 per cent rise turned into a fall of 0.5 per cent; and in Japan a 0.19 per cent rise became, in just ten years, a fall of 0.16 per cent. All this occurred before the greatest economic slump since 1929 had set in, curtailing fertility even more quickly. United Nations data published in 2015 still refers to estimates revised in 2012. As yet we do not have a full picture of how much the global economic recession has impacted on fertility and mortality. By the time you read this we should know. At some point during 2017 revised UN figures will be published.

In biological theories of evolution, the concept of punctuated

equilibria is used to describe the phenomenon of many species suddenly dying out and new ones quickly emerging. This usually occurs
following a period of general stability and little evolutionary change.
After the upheaval and realignment, another period of quiescence
and stability establishes itself. Most of the time there is relative
equilibrium. What changes during the quiescence are largely the
mechanisms that tend to operate to preserve the status quo, to bring
events back into line. However, occasionally and very rarely, that
equilibrium is punctured and there is great and rapid change. That is
what has happened to human beings: there has been a rapid change
in our numbers since 1492, a change so great that it has only been
seen once before – a very long time ago in the Neolithic era, which
itself also began slowly.

We are now in the second human population explosion period.
At first the effects of humans regularly crossing the Atlantic hardly
impacted on world population statistics. The global population had
fallen slightly in the years immediately after 1492, as deaths in the
Americas spread with the introduction of infectious diseases from the
Old World. Then, globally, annual population growth rates rose by
about a quarter of a per cent yearly from 1500 to 1600, next falling to
just 0.08 per cent on average from 1600 to 1700, but then rising by
just under half a per cent yearly, on average, between 1700 and 1850,
after which the slow puncturing of the equilibrium finally resulted
in all human groups in every continent growing quickly. Different
groups were influenced most strikingly by events outside of their
control and at different times. For example, the populations of the
Americas were decimated many times over, starting shortly after the
first Atlantic crossing was made.

It is hard to tell what occurred around 1851 to cause that date to be
the global minimum for recent population growth. It may well have
been a combination of factors. Some may have been technological,
including the slow and benign spread of electricity that aided people
to read and learn after dark, although the spread of sewer systems
almost certainly mattered more in helping more children to survive
as infectious diseases were reduced. Some were political, such as
the immediate and dramatic effects of the 1848 revolutions across
Europe, which led so many of those in power to realize that they
could not continue to treat those beneath them as virtual slaves.

The nineteenth-century population acceleration was clearly partly
related to the understanding and control of diseases stemming from
overcrowding, poverty and unsanitary living, as well as the introduction of condoms. Condoms became widely popular in North America

in the 1840s before they were widely used in the UK. It is not impossible that just as later on it took a great deal of birth control to apply the brakes, earlier just a little birth control had created the conditions for (what was then) more sustainable growth to become established.

This discussion of the possible reasons for the rapid acceleration that began in 1851, with its potential source as early as 1492, provides an outline of just one possible explanatory framework for demographic transformations. Similarly, we can consider the possible reasons for the slowdown beginning in 1971, which in retrospect we now see clearly as a turning point rather than a blip. Those reasons might include the gradual, benign spread and multiplication of vaccines that has greatly reduced infant mortality; the control of malaria through bed nets, treatment and the draining of swamps; right through to the culture of the 1967 summer of love and the immediate and dramatic effects of the 1968 uprisings across the rich world. Many came to see that there were limits to endless growth, which included limits to desired family size. Other potentially very important reasons include the work that was done in spreading education, especially to women (and as forecast forwards for India at the end of Chapter 3); the invention and increasing availability of the contraceptive pill, widespread use of which began in North America in the 1960s; through to the iconic effect of seeing, for the first time, the earth from the moon in 1969. Why might that have mattered? It may have helped people worldwide to begin to think and act a little differently and a little more quickly than they otherwise would. As a Chinese premier famously commented with regard to 1968 and the small revolutions of that year – 'as yet it may be too early to know what their significance might be'. There is some speculation that he thought he was being asked about earlier events and thought it still too early to tell, but clearly something fundamental did change around the years 1968 to 1971.

Most of the possible reasons why the slowdown began then cannot be even roughly quantified. However, it is highly likely that without new, effective and widespread forms of contraception, human beings would not have managed to limit their numbers once the great change began in 1851, and there could have been demographic developments similar to those predicted by Thomas Malthus (discussed in Chapter 1), who, in his 1798 *Essay on the Principle of Population*, forecast a never-ending cycle of population growth, war and famine. It turns out that Thomas should have been more doubting and less deterministic.

Conclusion

One of the most crucial questions that demographers need to try to answer, and one that we keep returning to in this book, is what the level of fertility is likely to be in the near future, since it is this that will matter most to the speed at which the population explosion fizzles out. Overall, fertility rates tend to fall, but they do not always do so, and within the last decade there have been some intriguing developments. If we really want to know whether the population explosion is coming to an end, then we should look at the most recent numbers available on fertility.

Table 8 of the 2015 United Nations Human Development Report reveals that in some of the most affluent countries of the world total fertility rose between 2000–5 and 2010–15. It rose slightly (by 0.1 on average) in each of the five countries heading the UN's Human Development Index: Norway, Australia, Switzerland, Denmark and the Netherlands. These five countries now have total fertility rates per woman of 1.9, 1.9, 1.5, 1.9 and 1.8 respectively. Over the same period, the fertility rate rose by an average of 0.2 in Canada, New Zealand, Sweden, the UK and Belgium, which now have total fertility rates of 1.7, 2.1, 1.9, 1.9 and 1.9 respectively. If a similar rise were to occur in the next decade then all would have surpassed fertility replacement level. New Zealand already has. However, what the total fertility rate calculations do not take into account are the effects of recent migration of young adults into these countries, or of fertility being delayed due to rapid university expansion, which affected women more than men (the tempo effect described above in Chapters 2 and 3). It is possible that, in favourable circumstances, with continued in-migration for many years to come, fertility rates of 1.8 to 1.9 children per couple might become the norm, but that would represent a slowdown since without that in-migration of people into low fertility territories, fertility elsewhere and globally would be even higher.

Other less affluent but very highly populated countries are moving upwards a little too. Over the same very short time period fertility in both Spain and Italy rose from 1.3 to 1.5, and in Poland from 1.3 to 1.4, but in Argentina it fell from 2.4 to 2.2. In Russia it rose from 1.3 to 1.5 (see our comments on Putin unfairly taking credit for this in Chapter 3); however, in Malaysia it fell from 2.5 to 2.0; in Iran from 2.0 to 1.9; in Venezuela from 2.7 to 2.4; in Turkey from 2.3 to 2.1; in Mexico from 2.5 to 2.2; and in Brazil from 2.3 to 1.8 – in every case fertility rates in these countries are converging towards 1.8 or 1.9, not 2.1. And these are not a randomly chosen set of countries. They are the next most affluent countries after Belgium with populations of at least 30 million.

The largest countries are also moving towards convergence to below fertility replacement level. Over the same period China moved from 1.6 to 1.7; Indonesia from 2.5 to 2.4; the Philippines from 3.7 to 3.1; India from 3.0 to 2.5; and Bangladesh from 2.9 to 2.2 – all in just ten years. These are all countries with a population of between 100 million and 1.4 billion. And they are all moving very rapidly indeed towards a new steady state, a state that looks as if it will be below 2.1.

But what of the world's poorest countries – are they seeing fertility falling as fast as in the middle-ranking countries? The answer is: often faster! In Kenya fertility in just that one decade, 2005–15, fell from 5.0 to 4.4; in Pakistan 4.0 to 3.2; in Myanmar 2.2 to 2.0; in Tanzania 5.7 to 5.2; in Nigeria 6.1 to 6.0; in Uganda 6.7 to 5.9; in Sudan 5.3 to 4.5; in Afghanistan 7.4 to 5.0; in Ethiopia 6.1 to 4.6; and in the Congo 6.9 to 6.0. These are the poorest countries with at least 30 million people. All are seeing the fertility rate fall rapidly, apart from Nigeria, but even there it is still falling. Furthermore, the reliability of figures for Nigeria have been of concern for some time: since health workers are incentivized to find babies to vaccinate, more babies are likely to be recorded.

Worldwide, total fertility rates fell from 2.5 to 2.4 in the ten years to 2015. At that accelerating slowdown rate, within just forty years the planet as a whole will be below fertility replacement levels. Where and whether population continues to rise for a few more decades will depend almost entirely on where and whether life expectancy continues to increase. By 2014 average global life expectancy was already 71.5 years, with the highest in Japan at 83.5 (for both sexes combined). The population explosion is ending.

5

Why No Children?

Human demography currently presents a confusing collection of contradictions when viewed worldwide. The number of people living on the planet is rising rapidly as we write, because fewer and fewer are dying young. It has never risen so fast in absolute terms: there are roughly 2 million more of us each week. Yet the rate of growth is slowing rapidly. It has slowed as rapidly before, but then only in times of pandemic and world war. In a few parts of the world people continue to have as many children as most people had just two generations ago. But in most of the world they now have far fewer. This chapter tells the story of why and how this has happened and what it might lead to.

A polarized world

In the previous chapter we talked about the narrative of a 'population explosion' and how that results in demographic change being perceived as a profound threat to the future of humanity – derived by naively extrapolating forward from an often oversimplified vision of the present. This 'threat' comes not only from a perceived challenge to natural resources, but also from a learnt cultural attitude of 'them versus us', relating to who should or should not be having more children, and the imagined future geopolitical roles of different groups of people or regions. In the last chapter – and indeed in Chapter 3 when discussing projections – we argued that the concern about our growing numbers represents only a very partial view of the future of humanity and its relationship to the world we all inhabit. We also suggested that there is good reason to be more optimistic than the doom-laden projections offered by various authors would currently suggest.

But, of course, the future of global population features in the popular press not only as a bomb likely to explode in the near future; it is also characterized as a bomb which is set to 'implode' as a consequence of low fertility rates. In fact, in many cases, particularly in the UK and other European countries, populations are predicted to both explode *and* implode simultaneously, with the emphasis on either depending on the intentions of the journalist writing at the time – usually wanting fewer of 'them' or more of 'us'.

When juxtaposed to the 'population explosion', especially as presented in exaggerated form, the transition to low fertility is usually considered to be a very strong, positive development. In most countries where fertility is high, the number of children that people say they would like to have is (on average) slightly *lower* than the number they actually end up having. This 'gap' between the two figures is sometimes referred to as reflecting an 'unmet need' for family planning (Peterson et al., 2013). Meeting this unmet need has, of course, been a huge part of population policies around the world for the past five decades (Ross and Mauldin, 1996). Also, as we briefly touched upon earlier, other drivers generally associated with 'improvements in society' will impact on and reinforce each other's effects, reducing fertility where it is higher – often mediated through a further lowering of the perceived ideal family size referred to above. These drivers include improvements in education, health and women's empowerment, as well as broader structural changes related to economic development, urbanization and social infrastructure (Basten, Sobotka and Zeman, 2014).

Perhaps the most influential theoretical model used in this regard is the Demographic Transition Model (DTM) – indeed, the concept has been referred to as 'the central preoccupation of modern demography' (by Paul Demeny, quoted in Kirk, 1996). The DTM, first postulated in the mid-1940s, is concerned with the relationship between fertility and mortality rates, and the 'transition' from high to low rates in both. In the first phase, both rates are high, cancelling each other out and so leading to broadly low overall population growth. In the second phase, mortality falls dramatically, while fertility remains relatively high. The reasons for this decline in mortality are contested (by different authors and/or for different places), but they tend to revolve around improvements in nutrition, medicine, sanitation, public health measures and so on. During this second stage, the gap between declining mortality and sustained high fertility means that overall population growth increases rapidly. During the third phase, mortality continues to decline, and fertility begins to fall rapidly. Population continues to grow, but at a slower pace. In the classical interpretation of this stage, the changes in mortality directly impact upon changes in fertility: because more children survive, fewer are needed. As the economic resources of societies grow, infrastructure is laid down: roads, railways, sewage systems, schools, hospitals and so on. Parents in the succeeding generations supposedly respond to all this by having fewer children. (This broadly economically determin-istic approach has been strongly challenged in recent years, not least by Cleland and Wilson, 1987). Finally, in the fourth phase, it is sug-gested that fertility and mortality rates will be broadly aligned, and that a stabilization in population growth rates will somehow occur.

There is, of course, some empirical evidence that backs up the broad outlines of the DTM, particularly from historical and recent trends in England and Sweden. Despite this, there has been much criticism regarding the validity of the model and both its empirical basis in historical and contemporary data as well as its theoretical power in predicting future changes. We will not get into this discus-sion here (see the work of Kirk 1996 for an extended discussion), but simply note that the DTM is now widely seen as being discredited. So why does it keep coming up time and again in discussions of pop-ulation trends? Perhaps because it is highly intuitive and represents a world where things 'balance out', both in terms of the relationship between fertility and mortality and, ultimately, in terms of homeosta-sis and modest levels of population growth.

Returning to our discussion of fertility rates in Chapters 2 and 3, the relative 'sanctity' of a replacement rate of around 2 is expressed as an 'ideal' or 'optimal' fertility rate. If we look at the global aggregate fertility rate for 2015–20, as produced by the UN, we see that the total fertility rate (TFR) is 2.47, down from 4.96 in 1950 (UNPD, 2015). Moving forward, the medium variant of the UN estimates suggests that global TFR will steadily fall to around two children by the third quarter of the present century. It is tempting, therefore, to conclude that this is the end of a great human success story: the result of 'controlling' fertility to achieve equilibrium, with no more decline and no more growth. In reality that can only be a fantasy scenario.

That scenario is based on the erroneous assumption that somehow there is a *natural* desire of all people, everywhere, under optimal circumstances, to want to have on average 2.1 children. But there is no way that such a desire can be 'in our genes', because for most (99.975 per cent to be a little more exact[1]) of our existence as a species we have mostly had far more children than two. Moreover, in 2010–15, eighty-seven of the 201 countries for which the UN makes projections reported a fertility rate of below 2.1. Once population sizes are accounted for, this amounts to more than half of the world's population. By 2050–55, it is forecast that 141 of 201 territorial units will have fertility of below 2.1. The *range* of fertility rates below 2.1 is significant too. In 2010–15, the world's lowest fertility rates were seen in places as diverse as Taiwan, Hong Kong, Singapore, South Korea, Moldova, Bosnia and Portugal – all places with aggregate population fertility rates below 1.3. Ever more evidence is accruing that low fertility is likely to be part of the global demographic architecture for years to come (Basten, Sobotka and Zeman, 2014). There is no reason to assume that population growth will end with stability; it could easily be replaced with continuously falling levels, or yet more instability than that.

Because these falls are much greater than was previously anticipated, in recent years low fertility has come to be seen as a problem. The 'population implosion' narrative has been closely linked with fears about population ageing and the implications this will have for national and global economies, social welfare and health systems, and perceived threats to cultural identity arising out of a growing fear of others – Muslims, Christians, the poor and the rich, even the 'old'. According to some scenarios, the transition to low fertility has suddenly transformed from being one of humanity's greatest success stories into being one of its greatest threats. This applies especially if what you hold most dear is an idea of Europe as one of the top dogs – because it was in Europe that the sudden fertility decline was first noticed.

In Chapter 6 we will consider the implications of population ageing, and how it is often (mis)represented as a threat. Chapter 7 will focus on how the future of fertility interacts with other drivers – especially migration – to affect the ways in which the global economy is currently shaped, and is likely to be shaped over the next fifty years. Finally, in Chapter 8, we will show how low fertility rates are tied into the political dimensions of demography, not least through narratives of cultural identity, nationalism and population decline. In this chapter, though, we want to explore in a little more depth the context of low fertility in different parts of the world, and to consider how the 'problem' might have been misrepresented. As is becoming a theme in this book, unlike many others we do not see low fertility as a major demographic problem but more as something that requires understanding and investigation. However, we are greatly concerned that too little attention is paid to what most people, or at least many, actually *want*. Do they really want to have fewer children, or more? Are some of us becoming afraid of a fantasy scenario that is very unlikely to be realized? Firstly, however, we explore in a little more depth just where low fertility is occurring.

The low fertility world

As mentioned in Chapter 3, demographers and forecasters working in the UK in the early 1970s failed to foresee a decline in fertility rates to below replacement rate. Their assumption that fertility would never fall much below two children was based on previous trends but also on demographic notions of stability derived from the DTM, as well as perhaps more ethereal notions of what the 'ideal' or 'normal' family looked like, drawn from both the sociological literature and the dominant thinking of the time. In Britain a series of books called *Peter and Jane* were published to teach children to read. They featured the (then) ideal family: white, with two children, an older boy and a younger girl.

Such memes can be counterproductive. One of us was once advised against having a third child because 'no one will want to know you'. From the 1970s onwards, more and more settings in Europe followed the lead of some Communist states and Japan and saw their fertility fall to below two children per woman, often well below. By 1980–85 most countries in Europe (all except the former Yugoslavia, Albania, Ireland, Iceland, Slovakia, Romania, Moldova and Poland) had fertility rates of under 2. These declines were driven by a variety of factors of varying importance in different parts of the continent, not least the role of explicit policies in the Socialist states (Frejka and Gietel-Basten, 2016), as well as broader changes in the economy and society, especially in relation to women's roles and, of course, in the use of contraception. The overall dynamics of fertility transition are covered in greater detail elsewhere (Basten, Sobotka and Zeman, 2014).

During this same period, fertility started to decline very rapidly on the other side of the world. In 1960, TFRs in Hong Kong, Taiwan, South Korea and Singapore were all between 5.1 and 5.6 – roughly the same as Guinea in Africa today. By 1990, however, fertility in Taiwan, South Korea and Singapore had fallen to around 1.7, while Hong Kong's was one of the very lowest in the world at just 1.24. Again, a substantial literature covers these changes, but they were broadly associated with dramatic changes in both the economy and society bolstered by highly effective (and more or less prescriptive) family planning programmes.

During the 1990s, when sub-replacement fertility was still a relatively new phenomenon, it soon became apparent that the widespread falls were not abating. Indeed, during this period a new category was created for countries where fertility fell below 1.3 – they were called 'lowest-low fertility' (Billari and Kohler, 2004). Elsewhere in East Asia, the phrase 'ultra-low fertility' was also coined to represent the extremely low levels to which rates had fallen there. This 'lowest-low fertility' was often represented – admittedly beyond the scope of the originators of the phrase – as being irreversible and reaching the point at which irreparable harm would be done to both economic growth and the functioning and financing of public services.

Looking at Figure 5.1, it is easy to see where the moral panic about low fertility in both Europe and Asia came from. By 2003, sixteen territories in Europe (encompassing around 400 million people) and a further five territories in Asia were reporting fertility of below 1.3 (Goldstein et al., 2009). During this period, concern was rife about the future of Europeans and the European continent. The Rand Corporation penned a report in 2005 entitled *Population Implosion? Low Fertility and Policy in the European Union*, while in the same year the European Commission claimed that the low birth rates were a 'challenge for the public authorities' and that a 'return to demographic growth' should be the first of three 'essential priorities which Europe had to face up to regarding demographic change' (Commission of the European Communities, 2005). Also during this period, the world was treated to a new literature on 'demographic suicide', with books such as Philip Longman's *The Empty Cradle: How Falling Birthrates Threaten World Prosperity and What to Do About It* and Jonathan Last's *What to Expect When No One's Expecting: America's Coming Demographic Disaster*, each portending an apocalyptic future (see Coleman and Basten, 2015 for an overview). As mentioned in Chapter 2, other books and newspaper articles took more pointed approaches, linking the lower fertility of 'Europeans' and the higher fertility of Muslims (often forgetting, of course, that the two categories might not be mutually exclusive). Perhaps the most striking quotation from the time came from Pope Benedict XVI (2006), who said that 'the problem of Europe, which it seems no longer wants to have children, penetrated my soul ... To foreigners this Europe seems to be tired, indeed it seems to be wishing to take its leave of history.'

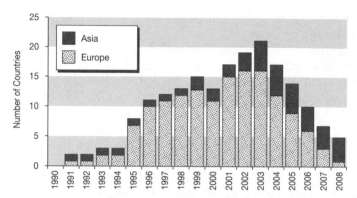

Figure 5.1   Number of countries with total fertility rate below 1.30,
1990–2008

Source: Goldstein et al., 2009. Reproduced with permission.
Notes: Excluded: territories below 1 million (includes Cyprus, Macao and Malta)
and territories with low-quality data (includes Albania and Bosnia Herzegovina).
East and West Germany and Hong Kong are counted as separate territories.

By 2008, however, this picture had changed dramatically – at least
in Europe. The total fertility rate had risen steadily across the continent, leading to the presumption that Europe had seen the 'end of
lowest-low fertility' (Goldstein et al., 2009). We now know that to a
large degree the fall to very low levels, and the subsequent rise, was
due to the so-called tempo effect (discussed in Chapter 2), where
many women (and men) postpone childbearing and then 'recuperate' later on in life. Given the economic and social upheavals of the
1990s, especially in post-Socialist states, such a transition is hardly
surprising. In 2007, the usually rather gloomy *Economist* was able to
pronounce that 'Suddenly, the old world looks younger: Reports of
Europe's death are somewhat exaggerated.'

In 2007 it did indeed seem as though very low fertility was likely to
be a passing phenomenon. As mentioned in Chapter 3, in the UN's
World Population Prospects 2010, the projection model assumed
that fertility in all countries where it was currently well below 2 would
increase back up towards 2, as had been seen to occur in Europe
(UNPD, 2011). This 'optimism', however, was somewhat short-lived.

As Figure 5.2 shows, in the years immediately following the onset
of the economic crisis in 2008, the earlier increases in fertility either
stagnated or reversed. Furthermore, the projected increases in East
Asia – which were supposed to be driven largely by the so-called
tempo effect – were muted (Frejka, Jones and Sardon, 2010), while

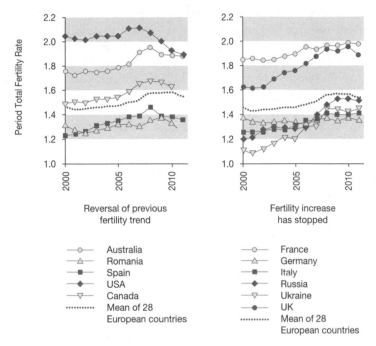

Figure 5.2 Recent trends in period total fertility rates in Europe
and other selected low fertility countries

Source: Drawn by the authors using data from Eurostat and national
statistical offices based on Figure 3.3 in Basten, Sobotka and Zeman 2014.

fertility still remains extremely low in the sixteen European territories
mentioned above.

In addition to the post-2008 trends, it was becoming apparent that
low fertility was no longer a feature only to be associated with either
Europe or the richer countries of East Asia. By 2000, fertility well
below 2 could be found in many other parts of the world, including
Vietnam, Iran and much of the Caribbean (in Cuba it was just 1.6).
By 2012 the TFR of Thailand was identical to that of Japan, at just
1.41. If sub-national counts were used, then five Indian states could
be identified as having fertility of 1.7 or less (Säävälä, 2010), as well
as much of Western Turkey. The most significant new entrant to the
'low fertility club' was of course China, which, numerically at least,
sets the global scene for concerns over low fertility and its implications. These features of the new global low fertility pattern, and how
they might affect economies in the future, will be discussed in greater
depth in Chapter 7.

All of these very recent empirical developments have forced us to completely rethink our models of demographic change, and especially how we thought the future of fertility might develop. Indeed, it is tempting to state that in this rather unprecedented period of demographic history we are 'flying blind'. To put this another way, as Wolfgang Lutz stated in 2006 (and published in 2007, well before the economic crash): 'The social sciences as a whole have yet to come up with a useful theory to predict the future fertility level of post-demographic transition societies' (2007: 16). We do not even know whether the trend will be up or down. As a consequence, while earlier projections sought to identify very low fertility as a passing trend, contemporary models now increasingly see it as a more intransigent part of the future global landscape. This can be seen both in some of the more recent UN projection models, but also in a recent large-scale international survey (Basten, Sobotka and Zeman, 2014).

Once again demography has generated a moral panic in the popular and the policy media, this time relating to low fertility in different parts of the world. In 2015, *The Observer* headed an article: 'Europe needs many more babies to avert a population disaster. Across Europe birth rates are tumbling. The net effect is a "perfect demographic storm" that will imperil economic growth across the continent' (Kassam, 2015). Elsewhere, *The Telegraph* sought to show 'How Europe is slowly dying despite an increasing world population' (Akkoc, 2015). These headlines can sometimes appear rather measured when compared to recent stories in the press about countries in East Asia, such as: 'Why Taiwan's single people are a national security threat' (Ketels, 2015). In February 2015, Beatrice Lorenzin, the then Italian health minister declared that 'We are at the threshold where people who die are not being replaced by newborns ... That means we are a dying country' (quoted in Squires, 2015).

In 2016, Paul Demeny, one of Europe's most respected demographers, was explicit in identifying two demographic crises for Europe, one visible, one unrecognized. While the migration crisis was the visible one, low fertility was the unrecognized one – unrecognized because 'time horizons are short'. He explains:

> Politicians are immersed in the here and now, their attention span extending at best to the next election. Public opinion has a similar limitation. In that short-term outlook the processes of population shrinkage and population aging are virtually imperceptible. From year to year population size and age distribution seem to be much the same.

The road leading to what may in effect amount to collective national and civilizational suicide is taken unhurriedly, step by step. (2016: 111)

When one looks at the *cohort* fertility rates – which measures *completed* childbearing for women – rather than just the period rates which provide a cross-section and are subject to more fluctuation, we can see a much clearer picture. Looking at Figure 5.3, it appears that there are really three kinds of patterns emerging in the 'classic' countries which are seen to generally characterize the 'low fertility world'. In English-speaking countries and Nordic and Baltic Europe, fertility overall is still relatively high (at an *average* of around two children per woman) and relatively stable. In Continental Europe – with the notable exception of France – cohort fertility is also relatively stable, but at a rather lower rate of well below 2. In Eastern and Mediterranean Europe and East Asia, however, the trends appear to be much stronger, now moving down towards some of the lowest fertility rates in the world (Basten, Sobotka and Zeman, 2014). What this means is that for cohort fertility to change in these countries there needs to be something of a dramatic turnaround in the entire concept of who has children – when, why and how they manage to, and equally why many people don't try.

Pushing parents, supporting parents

So what have governments done in order to try to 'turn things around'? We can see them becoming more and more active in encouraging people to 'do their bit', to procreate more in order to 'fix the problem'. From the extremes of Iran's President Ahmadinejad suggesting that those who advocate family planning are 'thinking in the realm of the secular world' (Associated Press, 2010), and Turkey's President Erdoğan describing contraception as a 'treason' which prevents the 'multiplying of our descendants' (BBC News, 2016), through to far less overt attempts – ever more governments around the world have been making various efforts to encourage people to have more children. Some of the more blunt policy instruments can be found in Iran, where new mothers have been given gold coins and other incentives, while government financing of family planning schemes and vasectomies have been cut (PBS, 2014).

In Turkey, the health minister Mehmet Müezzinoğlu declared in 2015 that 'Mothers should not put careers other than motherhood at the centre of their lives. They should make raising good generations

Why Demography Matters

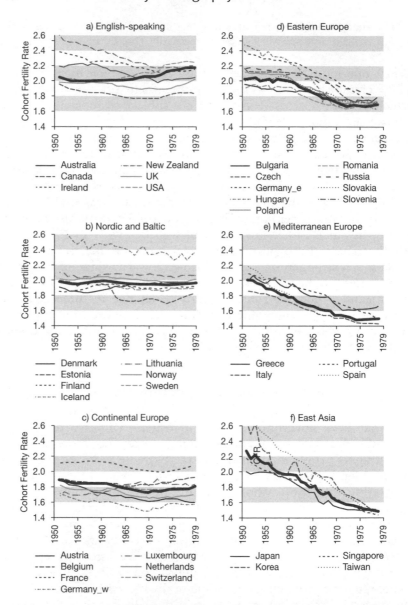

Figure 5.3 Cohort fertility rates [CFR] (and forecasts): thirty-seven
countries divided into six groups

Source: Myrskylä, Goldstein and Cheng, 2013, reproduced with permission.
Notes: Years denote mothers' year of birth, not when their children were born. Bold
lines show the average for each group. East and West Germany are treated separately.

the centre of their attention.' To this end, the Turkish government put in place far-reaching pronatalist policies, including a remarkable offer to students who married before leaving university of a US$4,000 grant, their student loans wiped out, and free hostel accommodation. If these lucky couples go on to have at least three children then a dowry account will be opened and gold coins given to the family, with yet more such coins added as more children are born (Al-Monitor, 2015). As Erdoğan himself exhorted women, 'Don't delay your marriage. Decide quickly and marry while you are studying or immediately after graduation – the minute you find your destiny [kismet]. Don't be too selective. If you are, you won't achieve it' (Cumhuriyet, 2014).

Elsewhere, other policies have been implemented which have sought to promote childbearing more or less explicitly. These can be seen primarily in Central, Eastern and Southern Europe, as well as in East and South-East Asia. We say more or less explicit, because while some are grounded in a clear pronatalist framework, others are based in a much more broadly based family policy system. There are overviews of these policies for the OECD (Thévenon, 2011), the post-Socialist countries of Central and Eastern Europe (Frejka and Gietel-Basten, 2016), and in East and South-East Asia (Jones, Straughan and Chan, 2009). They range from the payment of a baby bonus through to extended periods of parental leave with more generous pay; from tax breaks and mortgage relief through to improved access to childcare and so on. Perhaps the most famous recent examples include Russia's 'Maternity Capital' programme, as discussed in Chapter 2, and Singapore's package of policies designed to encourage childbearing, which include both very generous financial packages as well as government-sponsored dating (Yap, 2003). These policies apply so long as you are not a female migrant worker in Singapore, in which case you have compulsory six-monthly pregnancy tests and are repatriated if pregnant (Phua, 2012). In addition to national efforts, local governments in both Europe and in East Asia are developing policies to support childbearing. The exception is the UK: the former chancellor George Osborne announced that no additional benefits would be received for the third or subsequent children in any family receiving tax credits or Universal Credit from April 2017 onwards (Bingham, 2015), unless they can prove that the child was the result of rape.[2]

As we discussed in Chapter 2, gauging whether or not these policies have been a success is actually rather harder than it might seem at face value. Simply looking at the number of births or the birth rate is problematic because fluctuations in this could just be a reflection of changes in the number of women overall and their age structure. Similarly, looking for changes in the TFR is rendered more problematic by our inability to adequately separate out the potential role of the 'tempo' effect. More fundamentally, without in-depth qualitative investigation, it is also difficult to know the extent to which these policies have served to 'change anybody's mind' or whether they were going to have these children anyway.

Given this uncertainty, it is perhaps reasonable to assert that any major impact on period TFR is rather difficult to discover. As already noted, fertility across most of Eastern and Southern Europe and East Asia remains at rock bottom (with some notable exceptions such as Estonia and Russia). Demographer Paul Demeny concluded that 'The policy measures now applied to remedy this unrecognized crisis by trying to raise fertility have so far proven ineffective, and their application in heavier doses promises no better results' (2016: 111). For Pacific Asia, meanwhile, Jones, Straughan and Chan claimed that 'the general consensus [on] pronatalist policies in East Asian countries seems to be that they have failed because there is no evidence that fertility has risen as a result of their introduction' (2009: 15). So the question is: why do these policies seem not to be working?

Who's to 'blame'?

To a degree, the answer to this question could be related to how the entire issue of low fertility is framed. Low fertility is considered to be a 'problem' that, in turn, leads to other 'problems' such as population ageing and decline. All problems, to a certain degree, involve apportioning a degree of 'blame', and here much of it appears to be placed directly on the shoulders of young people. Consider again the verdict of Pope Benedict referred to earlier in this chapter, lamenting that 'it seems [Europeans] no longer want to have children'. This notion accords with recent demographic theory built around the so-called 'second demographic transition' (SDT), which posits the development of 'secular individualism, the quest for individual self-fulfilment, and a decline of the traditional "bourgeois" family', all operating at the expense of fertility (Sobotka, 2008: 27). Using Maslow's 1943 *Theory of Human Motivation*, the SDT puts this in terms of 'reaching for higher order Maslowian needs'.[3] Others, meanwhile, are not so generous. The perceived selfishness of those who either postpone childbearing until a later age or eschew it all together is very strong in the popular narrative around fertility. Indeed, this narrative runs right down from the very top. Pope Francis continued the pontifical theme of pronouncing on the apparent evils of low fertility by telling an audience in St Paul's Square that this is 'a society with a greedy generation, that doesn't want to surround itself with children', and that 'the choice not to have children is selfish'. He continued:

> It might be better, more comfortable, to have a dog, two cats, and the love goes to the two cats and the dog. Is this true or is this not? Have you seen it? Then, in the end, this marriage comes to old age in solitude, with the bitterness of loneliness ... The joy of children makes their parents hearts throb and reopens the future ... Children are not a problem of reproductive biology, or one of many ways to realize oneself in life. Let alone their parent's possession. Children are a gift. Do you understand? Children are a gift. (Quoted in Kirchgaessner, 2015)

The online magazine *Flare* put the question in a rather more down-to-earth manner: 'Are childless millennials selfish A-holes?' (Heinrichs, 2015). An article in the Canadian *National Post* led with the headline: 'Trend of couples not having children just plain selfish' (O'Connor, 2012). A recent anthology of personal essays on childlessness is entitled *Selfish, Shallow, and Self-Absorbed: Sixteen Writers on the Decision Not to Have Kids* (Daum, 2016). Jonathan Last, in his bestselling apocalyptic view of the future of demography entitled *What to Expect When No One's Expecting: America's Coming Demographic Disaster*, stated that 'Having children is difficult but important work and ... the main threat to fertility comes from a worldview that places the self at the centre' (quoted in Renzetti, 2013).

As for the consequences, what do the pundits speculate? In 2013 *Newsweek* set out to demonstrate 'why the choice to be childless is bad for America' (Siegel, 2013). Finally, in early 2016, the *Daily Mail* led an article with the headline:

'How the rise of childless women could change the face of Britain: Rampant infidelity. A struggling economy. Meltdown for the NHS. And shorter life expectancies' (Brookbanks, 2016). To respond by 'blaming' young people ties quite neatly into the narrative of the feck-less millennial being judged by their elders and betters. Returning to the *Daily Mail*: 'The wasted generation: even millennials think they are self-absorbed and lazy, claims study' (Zolfagharifard, 2015).

These casual remarks about millennials in Europe and North America are translated into much more pointed claims in some Asian societies. Consider some of the words employed, for example, in Japan. The *furītā* lifestyle is characterized by 'hopping between short-term jobs and devoting energy and time to foreign travel, hobbies or other interests' (Smith, 2010). 'Herbivores' (*soshoku-danshi*), meanwhile, is a term coined by columnist Maki Fukusaw to refer to young men who are uncompetitive and not properly committed to work. Perhaps the most offensive is the so-called 'parasite single' (*parasaito shingurui*), coined in the late 1990s by Yamada Mashiro, referring to 'people who exploit their parents by remaining unmarried and continuing to live in their parents' houses, depending on them for the basic needs of food and housing, while having independent incomes from their own occupations' (Lunsing, 2003: 261). All of these feature as part of the so-called 'social recession' in Japan, and all have the theme of selfishness running through them. Indeed, this 'selfishness' is implied in the pronatalist claims made in Russia, Turkey and Iran: that young people have somehow forgotten their 'duty'.

It is easy to envisage a world of young people too distracted by their own careers and maximizing the pleasure in their own lives to bother with children, either now or possibly forever. There is almost certainly going to be an element of truth in this. Indeed, a recent online survey about 'Why millennials don't want kids' certainly shows some anecdotal evidence about children getting in the way of reaching for these higher order Maslowian needs (DiDomizio, 2015). The following quotations represent the standard view of the 'selfish' millennial: 'My dream is to visit all 195 countries in the world (been to 23 so far) and I really don't feel like a child fits into the nomad lifestyle I want to live. With the way I want to live my life, kids would get in the way. I don't want kids because they're a fuckton [*sic!*] of work.' But some young adults are just much more practical, perhaps relating to their work and time of life: 'When I imagine my future, I just don't see any [kids] ... I love what I'm studying and I want to get the most out of my career ... whether that includes endless overtime, sleepless nights, relocating, and/or travel.' Some of the other reasons given are related to the body – 'The idea of carrying a child makes me nauseous'; or to general attitudes about children – 'Children always have irritated me to no end. The only time I enjoy children is when they are quiet, humble, intelligent beings. Obviously these conditions are unreasonable to expect of the tiny humans, so for me, the logical solution is to not have any of my own.' Other much more broad issues relating to global overpopulation or the way society functions are also given as a reason: 'Honestly our society is kind of fucked up; I don't need to send someone out into that' (all of the above quoted in DiDomizio, 2015).

These quotations indicate that it is not just pure selfishness or the abdication of childbearing which is driving lower rates of fertility. Of course, these are self-selected data from an online magazine, and taken disproportionately from the United States, which does, of course, have a rather higher rate of fertility.

Fortunately, demographers are not only concerned with counting and measuring the things that people *do* – like being born, moving, getting married, getting ill and dying. They are also very interested in examining what people *would like* to do, and also what they *intend* to do – two similar but rather distinct measures. Doing this is important for a number of reasons. Firstly, by looking at *intentions* we can get some idea about what might happen in the future. These studies are a little like making informed 'microprojections' for individuals and families. Secondly, they can tell us something about *aspirations* and *ideals*. As we mentioned earlier, many women in poor countries wish that they had had smaller families than they ended up having. This means that the gap between *ideal* and *actual* fertility represents something 'going wrong' in some way or other. Policies could help to remedy this, for example through providing proper family planning, education or empowerment. Thirdly, these ideals or intentions can also act as a kind of 'bellwether' or barometer for society's attitudes towards childbearing, acting alongside actual fertility rates. We are fortunate enough to have pretty good comparative data for Europe on fertility ideals and intentions, and some patchy data for East Asia.

In the light of all this talk about the selfish millennial losing interest in childbearing, then, it is perhaps insightful to take a look at Figure 5.4. Using data from the comparative Eurobarometer survey taken across the then twenty-seven member states of the EU in 2011, Maria Rita Testa identified that both the mean *ideal* (optimum) and *intended* family size of young people across Europe was not only a little more than two children, but that their ideals were barely any different from those at older ages (Testa, 2007). Indeed, taking data from across Europe – even in very low fertility settings such as Austria and Greece – the story of a two-child ideal is the same. This two-child norm has been investigated by Sobotka and Beaujouan (2014a) who find a remarkable consistency since 1979 in Europe. It is probable that these preferences merely reflect a cultural norm – a meme that has *currently* converged on two; but even so it is still interesting that millennials should not be stating an alternative – in aggregate they don't really want fewer children but they do find it harder to have them. Yet, the Eurobarometer also asks respondents

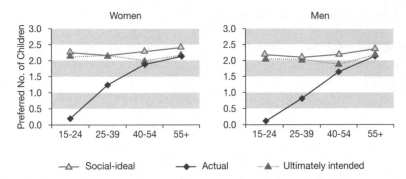

Figure 5.4 Mean social-ideal, intended and actual family sizes by gender and age, EU-27, 2011

Source: Testa, 2007.

to differentiate between their own *personal* ideal, and the *societal* or *general* ideal, which we will call the *social-ideal* family size. For young men across the Europe, the optimum is actually much *higher* than their own ideals, at around 2.5 – the highest among all the age groups. For women too, the optimum is rather higher at just under 2.5. All of this suggests that across Europe young people are not 'going off' children – at least as measured by their preferences for them. There is also much evidence from East Asia which points in the same direction, namely of the ideal number of children being around two (Sobotka and Beaujouan, 2014b).

This gap between the optimal number of children and actual fertility has been used as a strong justification, or legitimation, for policies to increase childbearing. This is because rather than being framed in the narrative of 'increasing the birth rate' it can be framed in the sense of 'meeting aspirations'. This can be seen in a 2005 European Commission's Green Paper in which the authors' note that 'there is a clear positive relationship between fertility and two other factors – an early transition from the parental home into one's own home, and a successful transition from education into secure employment without going through youth unemployment or precarious employment' (Commission of the European Communities, 2005). Similarly, in Singapore, home to one of the world's most comprehensive family policy and pronatalist programmes, the justification for pronatalism is as follows:

The Government remains committed to helping Singaporeans achieve their aspirations of getting married and having children. The 2012

Marriage and Parenthood Study showed that 83% of singles intend to get married, and 84% of those who are married intend to have two or more children. But we need to shape our whole society to foster a pro-family culture where starting and raising a family are central to our life choices and fulfilment. (Singapore Government, 2013: 20)

All of this, then, represents a puzzle. If people *want* to have two children, and states are enacting lots of policies which will directly support families to *have* more children, then why are fertility rates seemingly stubborn in non-response? We would argue that the reason for this disjoint is because if you see low fertility as the 'problem' then you will enact policies intended to 'fix' it. If, however, you look more deeply at just *why* there is such a gap between ideal and actual fertility, and understand *why* these aspirations are ultimately frustrated, you will get a better picture of why fertility is low and, therefore, of what role policies can play in supporting people to be able to meet their aspirations.

Part of the reason why young adults' fertility aspirations are not matched by their behaviour can be found in the onset of the financial crisis in 2007–08. A recent study, again using the Eurobarometer survey, found that between 2006 and 2011, fertility intentions across the EU actually stayed constant. However, a notable change occurred in the *certainty* of being able to meet those intentions; and this was closely linked to personal circumstances. In other words, as the authors conclude, 'the more negative assessment of the household's financial situation, the higher the reproductive uncertainty' (Testa and Basten, 2014: 688–9).

This is perhaps most noticeably demonstrated in the case of Greece. As Figure 5.5 shows, ideal and intended family sizes have stayed relatively constant over the period 2001–11 (Testa, 2007). However, between 2006 and 2011 a notable decline occurred in the *certainty* about whether these intentions would be realized (Testa and Basten, 2014). The decline is also especially significant for Greek men. Of course, this maps onto the deep economic and social travails of the country. Indeed, it is possible to argue that the nature of the sovereign debt crisis in Greece was such that the biggest pressure was actually felt *after* 2011; as such the data from the 2016 Eurobarometer survey would be very revealing.

Of course, if we look to the economic crisis for reasons to be uncertain about childbearing prospects, we do not need to especially stretch our imagination. Indeed, the link between that crisis and the fertility rate has already been made in this chapter and explored

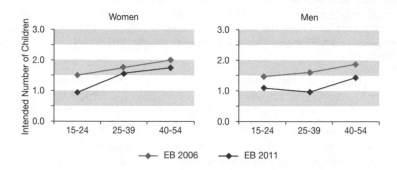

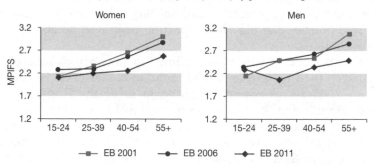

Figure 5.5 Mean intended number of children, and mean personal-ideal number of children, males and females, Greece, 2006–11

Sources: Testa, 2013; Testa and Basten, 2012, 2014.
Note: EB = Eurobarometer Survey

in depth elsewhere (Sobotka, Skirbekk and Philipov, 2011). Think about the labour market: jobs are increasingly scarce (Europe has never had so many unemployed young adults), and so many jobs are short-term or zero-hours and come with little protection (Adsera, 2005). This is linked to a growing, profound sense of frustration among young people and the realization that the 'dream' they were sold of good employment, prosperity and a happy (financially secure) family life after becoming the best-educated generation in human history is not going to become a reality.

Social welfare support systems are increasingly undergoing a process of retrenchment; while in many sectors most affected by the crisis it is a case of moving from bad to worse. This has implications not only for supporting families, but also in terms of a safety net in the case of sickness or unemployment. In some countries, especially the UK, the affordability of housing is such that getting a foot on the property ladder is nigh on impossible for very many young people, and most rents are exorbitant. In other words, young people's lives today are characterized by a very large amount of *risk* – and risk which they increasingly have to shoulder themselves (Beck, 1992). This same set of parameters could equally be applied to much of low fertility East Asia.

This debate may so far seem very intuitive, but demographers can also go beyond *measuring* ideals and intentions, and how they change under different circumstances, to explicitly studying *why* they change by going directly to the source. Qualitative inquiry is increasingly becoming a central component of demographic research. Statistical models can tell us a lot about change over time, and can even *predict* outcomes for individuals based on a host of both individual characteristics and societal circumstances, but the models do not tell us why what is happening is happening. We can link the qualitative sources to quantitative outcomes to paint a picture of, for example, contemporary childbearing and the factors that influence them, but one thing that all these models are less good at doing is identifying the *how*. How do these various drivers influence child-bearing in contemporary society? A great part of the problem is that human lives are messy and humans are not always rational creatures. They not only have children in optimal economic and social circumstances, they also often have them in non-ideal circumstances. By interviewing people we can get a much clearer, more holistic picture of how they made their decisions about what they did and what they would like to do, and how these decisions relate to the world around them.

Returning to why fertility is so low in East Asia, we might be able to identify a wide set of factors and drivers. But how do they operate together? A recent qualitative study from Taiwan sought to identify more clearly how each of these drivers act together, and in tandem with other features of society. But what the research reveals is often not a complex weighing up of economic challenges and opportunities, but a reflection of the day-to-day reality of caring for children, and how this collides with the aspirations of women. For example, as one mother-of-one put it:

> My husband pays very limited attention to our child! ... He will just provide lip-service: 'I love kids!' But, why do you spend so little time on him? ... I just feel he makes little effort on it which deters me from

having more kids ... If he is the person who is very actively involved in children, I would be looking forward to having another baby. But, he is not! Sometimes he is at home with his child [rather than at the office or his leisure activities], but he does his own business! Oh! Surfing with his mobile phone ... the child is left alone, he doesn't play with him, interact with him ... So I just feel the child is my responsibility. I have to take care of him, keep him with me. I just think, forget about it ... I don't want to have a child now. Really, I don't want to. Because I feel the pressure is all on me. If I give birth, I have to bring them up ... One is already tough, I don't want a second. It is pretty tiresome. Moreover, I love myself more! *I feel I want my own life* instead of being too much deprived. (From Gietel-Basten's interviews with Taiwanese women with one child.)

Underlying this quotation, clearly, is a whole package of issues relating to gender inequality in the home coupled with the opportunities – even *expectations* – for women to succeed in a career of their own choice. Other quotations in the same study again identify the complex set of relationships between the household and the economy, and between men and women – even with existing children, which shape childbearing decisions (see Figure 5.6).

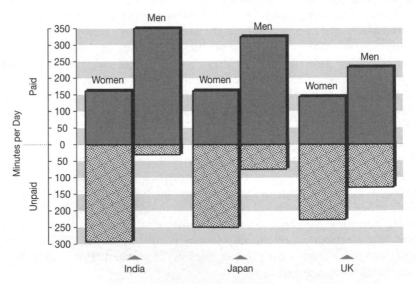

Figure 5.6 Variations in the number of paid and unpaid hours spent working a day, India, Japan and the UK, 2015

Source: Drawn by the authors using data published by the UN Human Development Report 2015, Chapter 4: Imbalances in paid and unpaid work.

Rather than being a 'problem' that requires a 'cure' through various policy interventions (carrots and sticks), might we instead see low fertility as being a 'symptom' of some of the broader issues in society; as being another measure of unrealized dreams, or aspirations not being reached? As such, instead of the selfishness of the millennials being the primary driver of low fertility, it is rather their ultimately precarious position that is driving this 'crisis'. This precariousness needs to be tackled through wide-ranging policies relating to the labour market, housing, social welfare, gender equity *and* family policy.

Returning to the policies which have been implemented to support fertility, most of them are directly linked to specific elements of childbearing and family formation. However, as Frejka, Jones and Sardon describe for East Asia, these policies have failed because 'little attention is devoted to generating broad social change supportive of children and parenting'. In particular, they note that because 'patriarchal customs and attitudes in the family, the workplace, and the political domain are deeply engrained ... changing the patriarchal social environment will require special focus on policies to increase male involvement in the household and in the upbringing of women and to change the attitudes of employers'. They conclude that 'unless current conditions are radically changed and child- and family-friendly environments are fostered, it is difficult to believe that fertility patterns will change' (2010: 603). All of this goes way beyond simply providing a few thousand dollars and some extra parental leave. It requires a truly transformational approach to society.

Conclusion

At this point it might be worth returning once again to the pontifical interventions noted above. Remember that Pope Francis said that a society which 'considers [children] above all worrisome, a weight, a risk, is a depressed society' (Kirchgaessner, 2015). The problem, of course, is that for many people society itself has become more worrisome, more risky and more depressed. To respond to this by eschewing childbearing makes some sense. But what of the earlier quotation from Pope Benedict? It was widely reported that he had claimed the people of Europe 'seem no longer to want to have children', and the whole speech was boiled down to this soundbite. But looking at what Benedict went on to say reveals a more insightful story. Firstly, he recognized the context of contemporary childbearing, the 'social and financial problems, as well as worries and struggles, day after day; the dedication required to give children access to the path towards the future'. But he also considered issues of *time*, again reflecting something that comes up in the interviews quoted above in terms of a broader sense of 'alternative' uses of time:

> A child needs loving attention. This means that we must give children some of our time, the time of our life. But precisely this 'raw material' of life – time – seems to be ever scarcer. The time we have available barely suffices for our own lives; how could we surrender it, give it to someone else?

Benedict also talked much more fundamentally about values, and the uncertainty about which values to transmit to children. At a very basic level, he suggested that:

> Contemporary man is insecure about the future. Is it permissible to send someone into this uncertain future? In short, is it a good thing to be a person? This deep lack of self assurance – plus the wish to have one's whole life for oneself – is perhaps the deepest reason why the risk of having children appears to many to be almost unsustainable. (Pope Benedict XVI, 2006)

Again we see the link to the 'selfish' motivation to eschew childbearing. But we also see this rather profound statement about self-assurance in the contemporary world. Perhaps Benedict was framing this more in a sense of 'spiritual' self-assurance and security. But the same can be said about 'economic' self-assurance, or even knowing where we stand politically and socially in a tumultuous society. It is this fragility, interlinked with high degrees of risk, which is in turn linked to (changes in) various systems and institutions, and which is possibly the key underlying driver of low fertility in different parts of the industrial world. Furthermore, this risk, or fragility, could also be a driver of the high levels of migration we are currently seeing. While migration is itself a risk – moving to a new country or city, taking on a new life, starting again – it is seen as preferable to the perceived risks of staying put. Therefore, in this universe of competing risks, of which childbearing and family formation is just one, one parameter to be altered is really the true context of fertility. In Chapter 7 we will consider how this view might also be applied to other rapidly developing countries, but for now let us recognize that today's demographic is seen as problematic everywhere, just differently in different places.

Because of demography's now ubiquitous existence and, at a basic level, because it measures things we think modern governments should know, demography matters greatly today for policy, politics, economics and the future of our societies. In Chapter 2 we made clear that accurate representation of demographic data allows a truer picture of contemporary society to be presented. In this chapter, again, we have established that basic demographic techniques are at the heart of *showing* the current state of affairs regarding fertility in industrial and post-industrial societies. The figures and charts presented here can be linked back to the discussion in Chapter 3 about projections.

However, where demography really matters, or really comes into its own, is where it works holistically, both methodologically and alongside other disciplines, to try to understand *why* a particular thing is happening. In the case of low fertility, for example, we can go beyond simply stating that 'this is the way it is' to trying to understand *why* it is so. We can do this through both quantitative and qualitative methodologies, and we can then engage with policy to try to create a better world.[4] A better world is one in which fewer people's hopes and desires are frustrated and we are able to understand each other far better than we currently do.

Ultimately, we need to try to get closer to understanding whether a demographic phenomenon is a 'problem' in itself, or whether it is in fact a consequence of other societal problems. In other words, one reason why demography matters is because it can hold a mirror up to society to allow us to better see how these 'front-end' measures relating to fertility and mortality might relate to the 'back-end' drivers and determinants which are shaping them. In an ideal world this would mean that we concentrate on the real problems driving the demographic outcomes instead of – or certainly as much as – the perceived 'problems' with the outcomes themselves.

In this chapter we have focused on the phenomenon of low fertility in Europe, North America and East Asia to show how it might be the consequence of broader societal issues, perhaps leading to an explanation as to why recent attempts to shore up fertility rates through family policy have been less successful than one might have hoped. However, we could have conducted the same kind of exercise by looking at contraceptive prevalence rates in poor countries, or sex-selective abortion, or health inequalities, or even certain patterns of migration. Each of these are demographically measurable outcomes of a much wider range of 'back-end' processes which require our focus. Demography matters, therefore, not only because our measurements and data can focus attention on these issues, but also because in understanding these processes better, we might be able to contribute to making people's lives better, through addressing their health, their well-being or their ability to meet their aspirations and reduce their suffering. In short, those who want to have children should be supported. Those who don't shouldn't be hounded to do so.

6
Population Ageing

In this chapter, we explore issues of ageing in greater depth and attempt to discern the extent to which the issue of population ageing really is the cataclysmic threat to states that the popular press presents it as. Firstly, we explore the underlying causes of population ageing, and briefly consider the demographic 'levers' which could, it is often argued, stop demographic ageing in its tracks; namely, pronatalism and/or replacement migration. Next we discuss the ways in which these underlying drivers fit into the different stages of population ageing, and describe the different ways in which population ageing is measured. While this might, at first glance, appear to be a rather dry subject, we argue that the commonest way in which population ageing is (misleadingly) measured is fundamentally linked to our entire construction (and perception) of ageing as a 'threat' and a 'problem'.

The dementia 'epidemic' is, perhaps, one of the ultimate achievements of human endeavour. More and more of us worldwide are now able to live long enough to even be able to suffer from it. This reflects the double-edged sword of population ageing – the triumph of public health and modern medicine together creating many new challenges. Our response could be either positive or negative; here, we want to try to be a little more positive. For example, the most recent evidence on dementia suggests that more recently born cohorts 'have a lower risk of prevalent dementia than those born earlier in the past century' (Matthews et al., 2013: 1405).

Help the aged?

Population ageing is often held up as one of the greatest challenges of the twenty-first century. Indeed, it is a unifying threat that is seen as a growing problem in both post-industrial countries as well as to what are termed 'emerging markets', to use the often hopeful rhetoric. The hope here usually comes from those who think that in future they will be able to sell more to those markets. But an ageing population can be harder to sell goods to, or at least goods they don't really need. When Coca-Cola flooded the world with what was largely a sugary substitute for water, the message of much of their advertising was that this was the drink for the young. A great deal of advertising is aimed at younger, more naive consumers, including children.

In some countries, overall population decline is seen as matching the perceived threat from ageing. The metaphor used for population ageing in the media is, once again, the 'time bomb', this time an 'ageing bomb'. Articles on population ageing in different settings, ranging from Greece to Guernsey, have used just this metaphor – and we are getting a little tired of reading it. The scale of the panic involved has been such that at one point, in October 2015, a major cyber-attack on the US insurance giant Anthem, which compromised the personal data of some 80 million people, was blamed on Chinese hackers seeking to 'learn how medical coverage is set up in the US as Beijing grapples with providing healthcare for an ageing population' (FT.com, 2015).

In the post-industrial countries, ageing has been presented as an existential threat to the very viability of a future welfare state and health-care system. The burden of ageing on every aspect of public expenditure is picked over and analysed in academic, popular and policy documents and discussed on a daily basis in some news story somewhere in the world. The capacity of states to provide adequate pension coverage or universal health care, in the context of ever more complex and expensive medical treatments, clearly looks threatening given what appears to be an exponential increase in the number of older people. In many poorer countries, meanwhile, the threat from population ageing is generally related more to the apparent lack of capacity to provide cheap labour to fuel economic growth, rather than to sickness, and often poverty, in old age.

To put it simply, the prevailing view of population ageing is based on an outmoded, increasingly inappropriate view of what it means to be 'old'. In this vein, we discuss some alternative ways of conceptualizing what being 'old' might mean in the twenty-first century – taking into account the huge changes in life expectancy that have occurred in recent decades. Apart from in the UK and US, with their current health and political crises (Hiam et al., 2017a), these increases as yet show little sign of abating in the majority of countries worldwide.

Building on this, we then explore some other ways of assessing the changes over recent decades, and those projected into the future, which are likely to fundamentally alter how we envisage 'old age'. We also consider how preventive medicine and preventative social policy can shape an alternative future – developing the notion, presented in Chapter 3, that projections are just one view of the future. But not everything in this chapter is good news, even given our glass-half-full approach. We conclude by looking at some of the big challenges that population ageing might bring, challenges that may not yet have been adequately explored in either the academic or popular literature.

What causes population ageing?

Demographers often describe population ageing as being driven by two complementary factors – ageing from above (due to increased life expectancy) and ageing from below (due to falling birth rates). We can consider these processes by looking at practical examples of population pyramids from three countries, represented in Figure 6.1 below. These figures, from quite different points in time, represent what might be thought of as 'classic' population pyramids. The child-bearing age populations in the pyramid were characterized by high levels of fertility, resulting in large numbers of children. However, mortality in these populations was still relatively high, with the biggest age group affected by premature death being the young. As such, the number of children who survived to old age was relatively small. Figure 6.1, therefore, represents the pyramids for various 'young' populations.

Figure 6.2, in contrast, shows what might be thought of as 'old' populations. Here, though, different pictures emerge. Figure 6.2 is made up of more bottle-shaped diagrams, and is representative of some of the European and English-speaking countries characterized by higher levels of fertility. *Ignoring migration*, the group of childbearing women might have, on average, around two children, thus roughly replacing themselves (with some cohort differences). However, mortality is very low. The chances of surviving not only to adulthood, but well into old age, are very high. The 'top' of the pyramid starts to fill out. This is what is known as 'ageing from above' – i.e. more people survive to old age, and survive for longer while *in* old age.

The current UN projections for Singapore show what is possible if population ageing continues unabated. There are, however, some profound differences *within* aged populations, in terms of

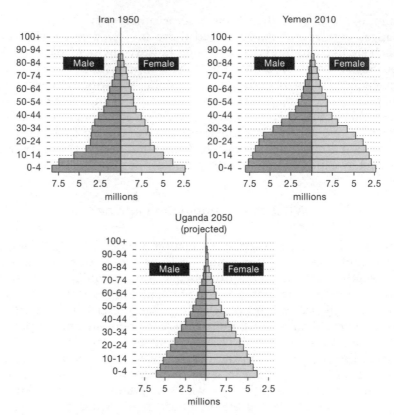

Figure 6.1 Population pyramids of 'young' populations: Iran, Yemen
and Uganda

Source: Drawn by the authors using data published by the United Nations
Population Division 2015, World Population Prospects.
Note: Population totals in millions; Uganda 2050 is as projected.

cross-national comparisons for both today and in the future. Levels
of fertility largely drive these differences – if we ignore migration.

Take the three forecasts for Taiwan for 2065 in Figure 6.3 – a territory currently characterized by one of the lowest fertility rates in the
world. If fertility were to stay at its current rate (i.e. a period TFR of
around 1.15, the middle projection of the three), then the shape of
the Taiwanese population pyramid would more resemble a 'kite' than
the bottle shape we saw in the first two pyramids in Figure 6.2. Clearly,
this looks like a much more 'extreme' vision of population ageing.
The two other pyramids in Figure 6.3, meanwhile, show how the future
population pyramid for Taiwan looks in the context of different future

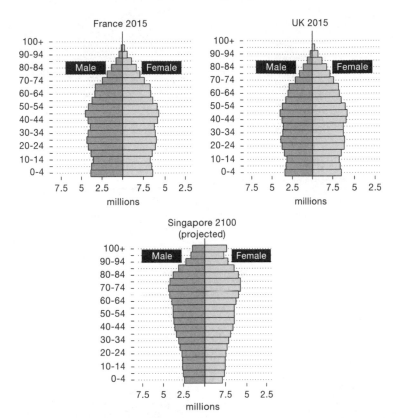

Figure 6.2 Population pyramid of some older populations: France, UK, Singapore

Source: Drawn by the authors using data published by the United Nations Population Division 2015, World Population Prospects.

Notes: Population totals in millions; Singapore 2100 is as projected.

trajectories of fertility (as we presented in the previous chapter, and will return to in the next chapter). In each case, the shape of the 'pyramid' *in the top half* is the same because these people have already been born; but the shape at the bottom is clearly very different. We will return to this theme later on when we consider how different age groups are presented as being 'dependent' on others – but for the time being it is enough to show that these are clearly more extreme outcomes of population ageing.

Clearly, the three different outcomes seen in Figure 6.3 demonstrate one of the most obvious 'demographic levers' that can be 'pulled' to change the future age structure of a population – namely, increasing fertility. Indeed, as we discussed in previous chapters

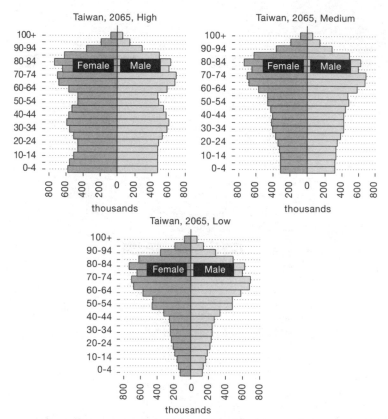

Figure 6.3   Alternative population pyramids for Taiwan by variant of fertility

Source: Drawn by the authors using data published by the United Nations Population Division 2015, World Population Prospects.

concerning low fertility, implicitly and explicitly pronatalist policies around the world have relied on a narrative of 'increasing the birth rate to offset population ageing'. In Chapter 5 we discussed the likely success of these policies, while in the next two chapters on the global economy and the politics of demography we will concern ourselves with some of the underlying reasons for them.

Before moving on from these 'demographic levers' however, it is important to briefly consider the role of migration. The idea of 'replacement migration' to 'fill out' the middle of a population pyramid is, at first glance, a simple and effective way to ameliorate population ageing. Figure 6.4 shows, in the foreground (the light and medium grey bars), the population pyramid of Beijing taking into

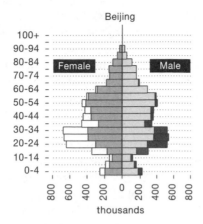

Figure 6.4   Illustrative effect of adding internal migrants
to Beijing's population

Sources: Beijing Statistical Yearbooks, 2014 and 2003.
Notes: The age distribution of migrants is only given in earlier yearbooks while the
accurate age distribution of citizens is only given in later ones! As such, the 'migrant
profile' from 2003 has been fitted onto a genuine demographic profile of citizens
from 2014. The migrant profile is shown as a shadow behind the main profile. All
figures are in thousands of people.

account only citizens with full household registration (or *hukou* status
in the city; not rural migrant workers). Thanks to thirty years of strict
implementation of a one-child limit (following rapid fertility decline
in the 1970s and improving mortality), the population pyramid is,
unsurprisingly, 'old'. However, if we also factor in those internal
migrants who travelled to work in Beijing (shown in bars in the
background of the figure), we clearly see a very different picture. Not
only is the ageing population rapidly ameliorated, but we see that the
largest group of people are those of what we might call 'prime working
age'. Similar exercises could be performed for countries that have very
high rates of immigration coupled with (relatively) low fertility, as well
as similar residency and citizenship restrictions, such as the United
Arab Emirates. So why not solve all population issues with migration?
   The challenges of replacement migration come from two distinct
fields – one policy-practical; the other demographic. The policy-
practical issue is that the migrants who make up the working-age
population will themselves age. This means that unless the state is
willing and able both to deny them support in old age, and to replen-
ish them with new working-age migrants, the solution may only be
a short-term one. Denying support means giving them status only
as guest workers, people who have to leave a country when they are

no longer employed. Guest workers often also have no right to have children, or, if they do have them, then their children have few rights, for example to education.

China is one of the few countries in the world that has been able, with varying degrees of success, to regulate the flow of migrants and their access to services through its *hukou* household registration process, although this highly discriminatory system is due to be phased out because it is so unfair to rural people (Tiezzi, 2016). All attempts at regulating internal migration have a rather mixed history. Consider, for example, the Russian state issuing passports for this reason prior to the First World War. Revolution ensued. Some of the other political and cultural challenges associated with such large-scale migration will be considered in Chapter 8.

The other main barrier towards a future of replacement migration is a simple demographic one. In order to maintain a long-term stable age structure through the medium of replacement migration, the sheer number of migrants required quickly becomes very large – especially in countries where fertility is very low. In the past, replacement migration has helped very affluent states, such as Sweden and the UK, balance out the swings of fertility. Thirty years after the lulls between baby booms (Marshall, Read and Nazroo, 2014) more migrants did arrive in both countries (as demonstrated in a series of figures shown later in Chapter 7 of this book). But this is not a mechanism that can easily be implemented widely, at least not without a great deal of luck and much tolerance of migration.

So far, we have considered the transition from a 'young' population to an 'old' population. While having a very 'young' population is said to bring its own disadvantages, clearly the 'threat' from an 'old' population is commonly perceived to be much greater. Before we examine this in more depth, however, it is worth pausing to consider what actually happens in *between* having a very young population and having an 'old' one.

The demographic dividend

In our experience, one of the most mis-answered questions in undergraduate exams on population and demography generally relates to the negative economic consequences of population ageing. Students tend to fall into the trap of assuming that populations just 'become old' and that this is economically troublesome. But the reality is that the first stages of population ageing are generally perceived to be economically *good*. Returning to our examples from earlier in the chapter, we can see that between the 'young' population (e.g. Figure 6.1) and the 'old' population (e.g. Figure 6.2) there is a quite different shape – almost like the dome of an orthodox church (or an 'onion', depending on taste), as represented for China by Beijing, when the in-migrants are ignored, in Figure 6.4. During this transitional period, fertility has clearly fallen, leading to the hollowing out of the lower part of the pyramid. This has some clear economic benefits in terms of lowering what demographers call 'dependency'. In crude economic terms, this means that the 'effort' required to sustain a population of (largely) economically inactive young people can diminish and be redistributed. In a more practical example from the Republic of South Korea, the decline in the number of children led to the closing of many primary schools and the reallocation of resources towards tertiary education.

What about ageing from above? The key to better understanding this is to recognize that improvements in mortality are not usually uniform across age groups. The first major improvements tend to be in the earliest years, then in early adulthood and only latterly in old age mortality. This means that a relatively large cohort will disproportionately survive into adulthood (becoming the 'bulge' seen around the year 1990 in Figure 6.5), while the delay in old age mortality means that the older age groups remain relatively small. In turn, the 'dependency' of the (economically inactive) younger population, as outlined above, is compounded with lower dependency levels in regard to older people. Later on in this chapter we will challenge these concepts of 'dependency', but for the time being the point holds that during this part of the transition towards population ageing, the part of the population which might be generally considered to be of 'working age' is disproportionately large. This point in the transition has been called the period of 'demographic dividend', or 'demographic bonus' (Lee and Mason, 2006), during which it is possible for firms to take advantage of their disproportionately large younger labour force, and the generally concomitant lower wages, to build up economic growth. Take some recent economic success stories as examples: as a crude measure, we might consider the point at which 20–24 year olds, as a key group in the labour force, represent the largest single age group in a country – in China, this occurred in both 1990 and 2010, while in Brazil it occurred in 2005.

Of course, the story of the demographic dividend is not quite so straightforward. Firstly, there is no guarantee that such favourable demographic circumstances will be translated into GDP growth,

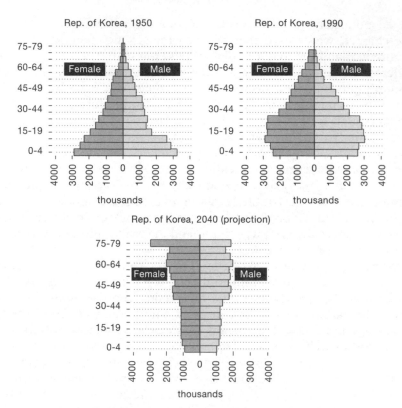

Figure 6.5 Population pyramids for the Republic of Korea: the coming
and passing of the demographic dividend

Source: Drawn by the authors using data published by the United Nations
Population Division 2015, World Population Prospects.

which requires the availability of productive work. In Brazil, which
is one of the most economically unequal countries in the world
(Dorling, 2017c), the peak year of 2005 did not result in spectacular
increases in productivity, let alone economic stability. Related to this
is the notion of the so-called 'youth bulge', which will be discussed
again in Chapter 8, alongside replacement migration. In settings
where little productive employment is available, and/or there is a lack
of civil engagement, disenchantment can set in. Some have argued
that a large group of young people can become a threat to security,
or, from another perspective, a motor for driving through societal
change. Tunisia, the cradle of the Arab Spring, would be the classic
example of this. Secondly, the transitory nature of the 'dividend'
must never be forgotten. Indeed, the population economist Naohiro

Ogawa noted how Japan quickly transitioned from a 'demographic bonus' to a 'demographic onus' (Ogawa, Kondo and Matsukura, 2005). If countries fail to make the most of these favourable demographic circumstances, they can easily find themselves ill-prepared for the inevitable onset of an 'older' population. While Japan may have flourished economically over the course of its 'ageing transition', its frightening levels of public debt and current economic travails could bode ill for future expenditure on pensions and health care. However, since most of that debt is internal, owed by the young of Japan to the old, it can also be seen as a form of control exercised by the latter over the former.

Finally, according to a recent study by Jesus Crespo Cuaresma and colleagues at the Vienna University of Economics and Business, the 'demographic dividend' is in fact an 'educational dividend', inasmuch as the economic return is primarily driven by improvements in human capital, more so than solely by the shape of the population age distribution (Crespo Cuaresma, Lutz and Sanderson, 2014). As Phil Mullan (2002) argued almost two decades ago in *The Imaginary Time Bomb*, the preoccupation with ageing at the time had little to do with an actual demographic problem, but was being used to justify a reduction of the role of government in the economy and a reduction in the size of the welfare state. If that is also extended to a reduction in educational spending on children, then the human capital dividend is never realized, or becomes far lower.

The demographic dividend is a relic of the distant past in most European and post-industrial countries; so distant that when fertility first began to fall it was still the era of widespread child labour. What's more, it was not such a huge dividend, so Europe had high levels of out-migration during these years, although the colonization of other countries did benefit European economies if not the countries that were colonized. The demographic dividend is only a dividend if used wisely, and it cannot be used as it has been in the past. It is important to remember that if the process of transition towards low fertility and low mortality continues in other parts of the world, as we expect it to do over the next century or so, more and more countries will age and in the process go through these *potentially* favourable circumstances of demographic dividend. And a skilled worker is much more likely to improve quality of life compared to a child labourer.

We can use projections from the UN to attempt to predict when the 20–24 age group might become the largest in any given country, for example Vietnam around 2015, and Bangladesh and Myanmar in the 2020s. Being able to harness these favourable circumstances is clearly a major challenge that will require careful planning on the part of these countries. However, in the context of a globalized economy often characterized by a 'race to the bottom' in regard to wages and support for workers' rights, it may well be that the timing of each demographic dividend will become a good predictor of when and where global capital might choose to invest (albeit perhaps fleetingly) over the course of the coming century.

Measuring population ageing

So far we have used just one visual means of representing the extent to which populations 'age', namely the population pyramid. While visually intuitive, relative scales on the x-axis can be misleading. As far as planning for the future is concerned it is really the actual numbers we are most interested in, not necessarily the shocking ratio changes highlighted in Figure 6.6.

The Figure shows the over-65 population growth for a sample of poorer countries[1] and other countries indexed to their level at 1950. We can clearly see why the popular narrative concerns the 'threat' of population ageing. In each case the total size of the population aged over 65 grows very rapidly over the next few decades. In some senses, the scale of the change can make it seem as if any adequate response is impossible. At the end of this chapter we will return to

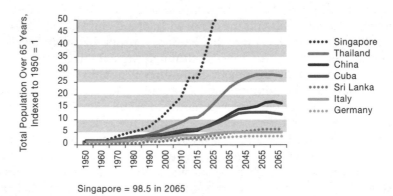

Singapore = 98.5 in 2065

Figure 6.6   Population size over age 65 (indexed, 1950 = 1), sample of countries

Source: Drawn by the authors using data from the United Nations Population Division estimates published in 2015 by the UN Department of Economic and Social Affairs.

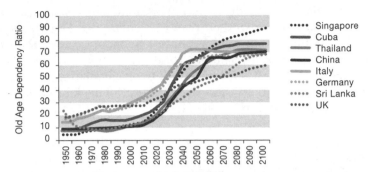

Figure 6.7   Old age dependency ratios in a sample of countries

Source: Drawn by the authors using data from the United Nations Population Division estimates, published in 2015 by the UN Department of Economic and Social Affairs.

these important numbers. In the meantime, however, we can use them to introduce one of the most widely employed measurements of population ageing.

The *old age dependency ratio* (OADR) is a very simple measurement. It is simply the total population aged 65 or above divided by the total population deemed 'of working age', variously defined as being either 15–64, 18–64 or 20–64, depending on the education and labour market characteristics of a given country as well as the defined 'age of childhood' – which goes up to 20 in Japan. By definition, those aged 65 or above are 'old' and supposedly 'dependent' upon the working-age population aged, say, 20–64.[2] The OADRs for a sample of countries are presented in Figure 6.7.

It is hard to overstate the prevalence of the OADR in the academic, policy and popular narrative on population ageing. It is the de facto measurement employed. See, for example, an article in *The Economist* (2014) that uses this measurement under the headline 'Age invaders: the big shift', or a recent World Bank report on the economic impact of ageing in Europe and Central Asia that uses the OADR to paint a grim future of ageing in numerous countries, not least Poland:

The ratio of the country's population over 65 as a percentage of the population aged 20–64 (the old-age dependency ratio) is expected to increase from 20.9% in 2010 to 58% in 2050 and 70.7% in 2060 while the share of the *working age population* (15–64) is projected to drop from 71.3% in 2010 to 53.4% by 2050. *All of these trends spell potential economic trouble for Poland.* (World Bank, 2014; emphasis added).

The OADR is implicitly included in statements such as: 'there will be *x* pensioners per worker' by a particular year. Some presentations go even further. In Paul Wallace's book, *Agequake: Riding the Demographic Rollercoaster Shaking Business, Finance and Our World*, for example, the OADR is literally built upon calculating the relationship between the 'workers' and the 'drones'.[3] This kind of language is, we would argue, not only offensive, but also clearly fundamentally inaccurate.

The notion that every 65-year-old is 'dependent' and 'old' while someone aged 64 is 'independent' is clearly ridiculous. Furthermore, the idea that 65-year-olds are uniformly *equally* as dependent as 100-year-olds doesn't make much sense. So why on earth would we use such a misleading measurement? In order to understand this we need to go back to basics to explore just what we mean by 'old'.

Though pensions can be traced back to classical times, the roots of modern pension systems lie in Bismarck's Germany and the gradual introduction of social insurance, including contributory retirement benefits in 1889. In 1916, when Germany lowered the retirement age from 70 to 65, the social theorist Isaac Rubinow declared that 'Age 65 is generally set as the threshold of old age since it is at this period of life that the rates for sickness and death begin to show a marked increase over those of the earlier years' (quoted in Graebner, 1980: 14). In the late 1930s, various US government committees were tasked with coming up with an appropriate age for railroad workers to retire and gain their pensions. The choice was determined by their observation that 'It is a commonplace fact that physical ability, mental alertness, and cooperativeness tend to fail after a man is 65' (quoted in Graebner, 1980: 160). Finally, during the period of the design of the modern welfare state in the UK, such luminaries as Beveridge, Hoffman and Ostler decided that the retirement age should be set at 65 because workers after this age 'lacked mental elasticity' and 'adaptability to technological change'. These sentiments reflected the circumstances of the time, in particular that pension systems were being designed for a population largely made up of industrial labourers. This group would be (generally) characterized by relatively low levels of both of the core elements of human capital – health and education. As well as their health being harmed by poor housing conditions and lack of access to decent medical care, the nature of industrial work and manual labour would often have had further deleterious effects on health.

People aged biologically significantly faster in the past when life was more arduous, work was physically harder, homes were often cold and damp, and many serious infectious and industry-related diseases were far more prevalent. Finally, given what were commonly very low wages, the capacity to adequately save for a period of retirement was severely limited, meaning that support from the family was required before the development of national pension systems. In short, while a little arbitrary, there were certainly reasons for assuming that many 65-year-olds at the time might justifiably have been called 'dependent' in terms of their economic and physical well-being. There were also in total far fewer people over 65 back then.

Since then, in the countries referred to above – the US, Germany and the UK – there have of course been incredible changes in all of the factors that effect retirement. Through a variety of mechanisms, the health, longevity and working patterns of these populations have changed almost beyond recognition. So much so that applying the statements above to contemporary populations is not only laughable, but would often be regarded as *ageist*. Yet, despite this, our most widely used measurement of ageing is still based upon a supposed watershed at age 65 – which amounts to at best an outdated, at worst a completely flawed, assumption.

There is, perhaps, an argument for maintaining the OADR as a core measurement of ageing. The main reason is that it provides a useful shorthand for the relationship between pensioners and non-pensioners. Indeed, in 2010 the 'normal pensionable age' of males in nineteen of the thirty OECD countries was, indeed, 65. However, even here we now encounter a few more problems than we did just a few years ago.

Firstly, 65 is not a universal pension age. This is clearly the case if we include both the *female* pension age (which is 65 in only twelve OECD states) and pension ages in other settings. In a recent overview of pension systems in twenty emerging market countries, the male pensionable age was 65 in only six countries and for females in just two (Mexico and Peru). Secondly, there is an assumption that pensionable age and common age at finishing work is the same. Of course this is not the case. In the Republic of South Korea in 2010, the male pensionable age was 60, while the average effective age of labour-market exit was 70. On the other hand, while the normal male pensionable age in Luxembourg is 65, the average effective age of labour-market exit there was just 57. At what age, then, does 'dependency' kick in? Thirdly, it may be incorrect to assume that there is some key redistributive relationship between 'workers' and 'pensioners'. It is true that in classic 'pay-as-you-go' type pension systems this is the case, but this is just one type of pension system.

Many countries around the world are characterized more by systems that rely on either individual saving (such as a mandatory provident fund) or familial support. Besides, the OADR is a poor substitute for calculating a proper pensioner-worker ratio. A proper ratio would take into account differentials in both those contributing and those receiving (Bongaarts, 2004).

A second major challenge effecting the conventional ratio concerns the issue of defining 'old'. By assuming a fixed boundary at 65, the OADR clearly does not take into account either the huge mortality reductions that have occurred over the past decades, or the very different mortality scenarios that we see around the world today. In other words, it fails to take account of either temporal change or spatial variation in life expectancy. Indeed, it is not hard to imagine how in some countries an average boundary to 'dependency' might occur *earlier* than 65.

Of course, it is possible to imagine many things being different than they are now. Many of us work too hard for too long doing things that are often counterproductive to the general good. Working in an advertising industry that persuades people to buy things they could do without is hardly helpful in a world that needs to rapidly become more environmentally sustainable. If human beings are to grow up a little, and ageing should certainly help that, there is less need for so many of us to be employed in the military worldwide. Visionaries have long argued for a basic income whereby people can choose to work less (or not at all) and still receive enough to survive – where in effect we choose our own retirement/career-break age, as well as the age at which we might choose to re-enter the labour market. But we are still a very long way from such utopic visions. For now, in demography, we need to concentrate on determining the next practical steps needed to move us on to a better understanding than we have now.

So what can be done, having established that the OADR is not really fit for purpose? The first thing we can do is dispense with ratios altogether and simply consider the raw number of people at certain ages. Of course, for pensions or other benefits with an age threshold, knowing how many people are aged x and above is important, and these are figures that can be quickly calculated. If, however, we want to build upon newer concepts of ageing and dependency, we might want to derive a new age threshold to take into account changes in life expectancy. In this vein, many scholarly, policy and popular narratives distinguish between 'young-old' and 'older-old' and calculate the increase in the number of people aged over, say, 80. This works on the assumption that those who are 'very old' are more likely to be the most 'dependent' in terms of complex health needs and least likely to be able to engage in civic society. Indeed, it is often in terms of these elderly care needs and morbidity that the 'ageing time bomb' is debated.

However, concentrating on much older ages can present almost exactly the same problems in terms of spatial differentiation and temporal change. At what age would we have set this 'older-old' boundary in the past? And how might we anticipate it changing in the future? Is 80 as old in Switzerland as it is in Swaziland? The idea of older-old is complex enough when considering just one country, but how would this 'boundary' be set in different countries across the world in order to maintain comparability?

Demographers have come up with a way around this problem. The saying '40 is the new 30' is widely known. This can be quantified by stating that a 40-year-old today would expect to live for the same number of years as a 30-year-old expected to in earlier times – for the sake of argument, let's say thirty-five years ago. In other words, a 40-year-old today and a 30-year-old then would share the same 'remaining life expectancy' (RLE). Using this simple concept we can start to rethink ageing and dependency. If we think of the kind of complex care needs discussed above as being closer to 'true' dependency, we might consider that these would be most likely to occur in the last years of life. This is certainly the case with health-care expenditure. Earlier studies suggested a 'boundary' to dependency where an individual's RLE was fifteen years (Fuchs, 1984). Although fairly arbitrary, the figure is also helpful because RLE at age 65 at the time of the formation of pension systems in the mid-twentieth century was around fifteen years (those who didn't make it to 65 being excluded from this calculation). This means that the figure bears some resemblance to what those making the earlier key statements on old age quoted above may have had in mind.

Earlier we suggested coining the term 'doterty' as the mirror for puberty, to refer to the point at which we are unlikely to contribute as much economically as before, just as we do not expect children to contribute much in affluent countries today. We may need a nicer term than dotage, or we may be able to recapture the word. Why should we not expect to enjoy our dotage as we now expect children to be able to enjoy their childhood? Not too long ago childhood was a state to be feared, in which you were often exploited and from which you tried to escape as quickly as you could. Today many fear their coming dotage.

Put simply, an arguably better way of defining a boundary to dependency is to base it not on the number of years a person has lived, which as we have seen is difficult to justify across time and space, but rather on the number of years a person is expected to live for. This way of thinking has been developed in the recent ground-breaking work of Warren Sanderson and Sergei Scherbov, with their concept of 'prospective ageing' (Scherbov et al., 2014; Scherbov, Sanderson and Gietel-Basten, 2016). Returning to the '40 is the new 30' idea, this means that the 40-year-old today and the 30-year-old in the past have the same 'prospective age'. On the assumption that 'dependency' is likely to be more concentrated at the end of life, we simply take the life expectancy over time, and subtract fifteen years from that to find the age of the 'boundary' to dependency – death minus fifteen years in other words.[4] Figure 6.8 compares the age at which the average person has an RLE of 15 years in a selection of countries.[5] Straightaway we can see two clear patterns. The first is that the RLE15 age has increased almost linearly in all sorts of settings, giving further weight to the idea that keeping 65 as a boundary to dependency misrepresents the scale of ageing. The second is that the current retirement age – and indeed the forecast changes in the future – often bear no resemblance whatever to the changes in life expectancy. If we assume that current state retirement ages were, at some point in the past, linked in some way to expectations of life, surely that link is now wholly broken.

A third key feature to note from the evidence presented in Figure 6.8 is the fact that the 'boundary to dependency' is so different in different parts of the world. In France, for example, average RLE15 was at age 65 around 1970. After 2025 it is set to exceed 75. We can say, then, that 75 will become the new 65! By maintaining the old age threshold at 65 we overestimate the degree of dependency in the population. Indeed, in the case of France, where the normal male state-pensionable age was 60 years old in 2010, the relevance of 65 as a key age is even more limited.

The argument being made here is not limited to high-income countries, those traditionally thought of as 'ageing' and the focus of most of the literature. While most attention is paid to these *macro-level* concerns about population ageing, comparatively little has been written about the growing needs and human rights of older people in populations which are not yet characterized by having an 'old' population pyramid. To anticipate future care needs and the extent to which current institutional systems might be able to cope or, indeed, be better designed in order to cope, it is again

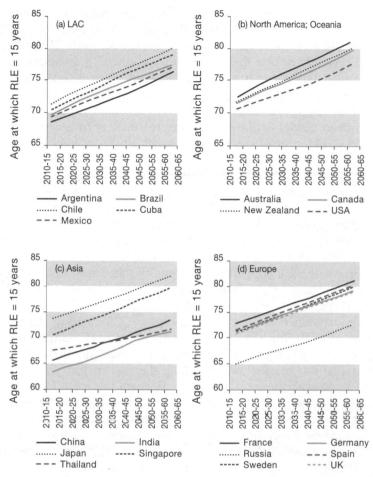

Figure 6.8   Age where remaining life expectancy is fifteen years, 2010–65 projections; twenty countries

Source: Drawn by the authors using data from the Wittgenstein Centre for Demography and Global Human Capital (WIC) Data Explorer.

important to have a better understanding of this age boundary to dependency.

There are numerous countries in the world where the current (and indeed future) age at which RLE = 15 is *lower* than 65 – most of them in Africa. In Asia, the average RLE15 was between 62 and 63 years in 2010 in India, the Philippines, Laos, Nepal, Kazakhstan and North Korea. In 1980, the respective age was often below 60.

To take a more extreme case, in Nigeria the RLE15 was just 54.7 years in 1960, rising to 57.3 by 1980, and to 57.7 by 2010. By 2025 it is forecast to be 59.2, rising further to 61.3 by 2050. While Nigeria would certainly not be the first country one would associate with an ageing population (with a current TFR of around 6.0), its rapidly developing economy means that institutional structures could be further developed to improve the lives of older people. Following a European model of limiting access to some entitlements to those aged 65 or older, however, would not include many who might in fact be characterized as being dependent.

Having rethought where the boundary to dependency might lie, we can then recalculate the number of people who might be character-ized as (elderly) 'dependent'. This can produce a very different rate to the old ratio, now comparing the dependent population to the popu-lation which is set to support it. Defining the numerator, therefore, is straightforward: the total population above the age where RLE = 15, changing over time according to mortality schedules; but what about the denominator? Calculating this as the 'working-age' population aged 20–64 clearly takes us back to square one with our assump-tion about what these ages actually mean. Calculating the number of those in full-time employment might be a useful alternative, but this would only really be relevant for those countries characterized by a formal labour market, one in which the vast majority pay tax, and where large-scale financial redistribution via the state exists. It also assumes that dependency is only an economic burden. In short, the easiest way to calculate a rate may be simply to assert that the popu-lation aged between 20 (or some other reasonable lower boundary) and the age at which RLE = 15 is the *new* 'working-age population'. This is not, of course, to say that 72-year-olds are working – nor that 72-year-olds *should* be working. But it simply recognizes that the upper age bound at which it is most likely that citizens will be net economic *contributors* (either through work, voluntary activity, looking after grandchildren, or spending and consumption) is being pushed ever higher.[6] Taking these two populations, therefore, we can proceed to calculate a figure that may be more useful: a *prospective old age dependency ratio* (POADR).

Table 6.1 compares the traditional OADR with the POADR for the same countries as in Figure 6.8. We can see three distinct pat-terns emerging. In the first block of countries, there is relatively little difference between the two measurements. This is because fertility is still generally rather high; but despite this the increases in POADR by 2050 are around 100 per cent lower than for OADR. In

Table 6.1. Comparing the old age dependency ratio with the projected old age dependency ratio, selected European Countries and emerging markets

	OADR%			%CHANGE		POADR%		
	2015	*2030*	*2050*	*2015–2050*		*2015*	*2030*	*2050*
(a) Latin American Countries								
Argentina	0.17	0.21	0.33	94	25	0.08	0.09	0.10
Brazil	0.12	0.20	0.38	217	120	0.05	0.07	0.11
Chile	0.15	0.27	0.43	187	100	0.06	0.08	0.12
Cuba	0.20	0.38	0.71	255	133	0.09	0.11	0.21
Mexico	0.11	0.18	0.32	191	100	0.05	0.06	0.10
(b) North America and Oceania								
Australia	0.23	0.32	0.40	74	43	0.07	0.09	0.10
Canada	0.23	0.37	0.43	87	33	0.09	0.11	0.12
New Zealand	0.22	0.32	0.39	77	38	0.08	0.09	0.11
US	0.22	0.32	0.37	68	33	0.09	0.11	0.12
(c) Asia								
China	0.13	0.24	0.46	254	138	0.08	0.12	0.19
India	0.08	0.12	0.22	175	67	0.06	0.07	0.10
Japan	0.43	0.54	0.79	84	31	0.13	0.17	0.17
Singapore	0.15	0.30	0.44	193	100	0.06	0.09	0.12
Thailand	0.14	0.25	0.39	179	113	0.08	0.12	0.17
(d) Europe								
France	0.30	0.40	0.49	63	30	0.10	0.12	0.13
Germany	0.33	0.49	0.62	88	36	0.14	0.15	0.19
Russia	0.19	0.29	0.39	105	25	0.12	0.16	0.15
Spain	0.27	0.37	0.67	148	45	0.11	0.11	0.16
Sweden	0.31	0.37	0.41	32	0	0.12	0.12	0.12
UK	0.28	0.36	0.44	57	18	0.11	0.12	0.13

Source: Drawn up by the authors with data from the Wittgenstein Centre for Demography and Global Human Capital (WIC) Data Explorer.

the second block of countries, ageing has been *underestimated* in the past – and in some cases (possibly) in the future – because of higher than expected recent mortality rates. The third block represents some examples of settings that are characterized as being 'ageing populations' by virtue of having a rapidly growing OADR – even if some are not necessarily countries which might be thought of as 'ageing' in the popular view. Here, though, comparing the OADR to the POADR yields a very significant difference. As an extreme example, take Singapore – home to people who now have one of the lowest fertility rates in the world. In Singapore the OADR in 2050 is forecast to be around 0.44 while the POADR is around 0.12.

Compared to 2015 this implies a doubling of older age requirements in future rather than the measure of them being multiplied by almost three (193 per cent). The fourth block shows just how little ageing of great importance there may be in countries that already have older age structures.

The POADR is certainly open to a number of criticisms – not least regarding the setting (and keeping) of RLE = 15 as a 'boundary' to dependency as well as for its oversimplified view of the denominator population. But it offers an alternative view of ageing which better takes into account past and forecast changes in life expectancy to provide a more realistic view of the *demographic* nature of the challenges ahead. However, it is crucial to emphasize that the POADR only examines *numbers* of people, and does not explore potential changes in their specific care needs, how they will be paid for, and who will do the caring. We would argue that it is these issues, rather than the raw rates presented in the apocalyptic graphs above, that represent the real core of the challenge of the ageing population. In particular, if an increasing number of very frail, dependent people survive into great old age then we will have to better plan for that, but we have only very recently seen evidence that this may be occurring (Marshall et al., 2015).

The problem of ageing is organizational and distributional, rather than one that is impossible to meet. It is a political decision to present these challenges as insurmountable, or as necessitating both cutting back on services and making people work longer. In almost all the countries that have grown wealthy enough for people to be able to live longer there are sufficient resources to meet the challenges of population ageing. One suggestion is that retirement age should be based on years spent in the labour market. Those who enter the labour market later, because they spend longer in education, should on average leave it later too. This makes added sense when you take into account that their jobs are less likely to be physically arduous and that their individual life expectancies tend to be longer.

Beyond numbers: the real challenges of the ageing population

There is no doubt that many countries (and companies) are currently undergoing a crisis in terms of the future provision of pensions. This is especially the case for countries with pay-as-you-go pension systems. These are systems where current taxpayers are paying the pensions of current pensioners. However, pension systems that rely on individual savings and investment now also face a series of crises as interest rates have been so low for so long and because most people on low incomes are not included in such schemes.

The pension crisis has been largely brought about for precisely the same reason that OADR is still the de facto measurement of ageing – namely because changes in life expectancy have not been adequately built into past changes in pension entitlement and retirement age. Previous forecasts of life expectancy did not foresee the linear increase, which had been observed for decades, continuing (Oeppen and Vaupel, 2002) – it is currently continuing unabated in Japan (Tokudome, Hashimoto and Igata, 2016), although in the US and UK the linear increase has recently stalled (Hiam et al., 2017a).

At face value, the pensions crisis is a relatively simple problem to solve through a series of parametric reforms. In short, you can force people to pay more, raise the pension age, decrease the size of the pension either absolutely or by shifting it from defined benefit to defined contribution, or from final salary to career average, or a combination of the three. Through these and other mechanisms, citizens might choose (or in effect be forced) to take more personal responsibility (and risk) for their pensions through the market, thus further relieving pressure on the state (and, in theory, generating capital for investment). However, when investment markets fail, as share prices can at times follow roller-coaster trends, such an approach might not be seen as being that far-sighted.

The solutions just presented are described as 'easy' because it is simply a case of 'cutting'. But the reality is that implementing such policies is extremely difficult for a number of reasons. While improvements in life expectancy are almost certainly known to the entire population, they are not explicitly applied to the individual experience of work and retirement. Indeed, it sometimes feels as though a longer period receiving (often generous) pensions should be an entitlement; a reward for human ingenuity in improving health and mortality. This is also partly related to the fact that death is arguably the last taboo. A 2014 UK government plan proposed to inform citizens of their likely life expectancy in order to help them decide whether or not to purchase an annuity to unlock savings in their pension plans; it deliberately tried hard to avoid being 'crass and insensitive' (Dominiczak, 2014). But for any individual these average predictions of life expectancy make little sense after the age of 65 or 70. They could die at 75 or live beyond 95, and much of what happens to them will, on an individual level, be extremely unpredictable.

The relationship between population ageing and voting behaviour also presents a significant hurdle for the implementation of these reforms – at least in the short term. In countries where voting is non-compulsory, there is nowadays increasingly often a linear relationship between age and likelihood to vote (Dorling, Stuart and Stubbs, 2016). Given that the population itself is also ageing, policies that 'squeeze' the elderly are generally vote losers. This is especially the case among those in their 50s or early 60s, for example, who are likely to be most affected by a change in pension entitlement. In other words, no generation wants to be the one to be 'hit' by the reform – and no politician wants to be the one to make that call. In this context, Pieter Vanhuysse's (2014) recent work on constructing an index that shows the extent to which a given state's social spending is skewed towards the elderly could be very useful.

Of course there are many different ways to implement possible parametric reforms in order to minimize resistance to our adapting to growing older. In 2010, when President Sarkozy sought to increase the French retirement age from 60 to 62 and the full state pension age from 65 to 67, the result was a two-month long general strike which spilled over into riots (BBC News, 2010). On the other hand, countries such as the UK have sought to link rises in pension age to annual increases in life expectancy (DWP, 2013). Neither country has yet tried to ensure that mundane work is not something to be feared by many citizens who still often see retirement as an escape.

Dealing with pensions is just one element of the future challenges presented by an ageing population. Think about the number of complex chronic diseases we are likely to see, the forecast increases in neurodegenerative diseases and so on; then translate these into future demands for social care. Many remain largely challenges for the future, not least because the vast majority of actual ageing is yet to happen.

These changes to come can, and will, pose quite different challenges in different parts of the world. In post-industrial nations characterized by comprehensive health-care systems, based either on management by the state or through private insurance, the costs related to the development of adequate facilities to manage these co-morbidities are likely to be extremely high. In other areas of the world, or where health-care systems begin to fail, ageing may be slowed down as few people survive into very old age due to inadequate care.

Meanwhile, although many emerging markets do have universal health-care systems, these are primarily geared towards the delivery of primary care services, with only very weak long-term or social care provision. If a sizeable part of the labour force in the majority of these settings remains informal, the capacity to build the necessary infrastructure will clearly be limited as a consequence of low tax receipts. This poses a challenge not only in terms of the institutional capability to serve these needs, but also in terms of the capacity of the family, and especially children, to take care of their elderly parents. This latter feature is, we feel, likely to be an aspect of one of the greatest challenges brought on by population ageing in what are so often called 'emerging markets' worldwide.

In the absence of adequate systems to support older people either financially or physically, in many poorer and not so poor countries it is still generally expected that their children will be the main source of support for elderly parents. This is usually implied as the de facto choice – but, in some cases, it is in fact the de jure future. However, this is now a key area where demography matters. Because of rapid changes in fertility, discussed in Chapter 5, the number of children available to support their parents has decreased significantly. Furthermore, we need to add in to this the remarkable changes in migratory patterns around the world, as discussed in Chapter 8, as well as changing patterns of urbanization. Many adult children now live many hundreds of miles away from their ageing parents, possibly in another country. This means that just as older people will be living for longer, eventually often requiring care,[7] the likelihood that there will be an adequate pool of local relatives to provide this support is likely to decrease year on year.

An extreme outcome of the impact of the transition towards (very) low fertility upon ageing at the individual level is the case of the so-called *shidu fumu*, or 'deprived parents', in China (Wei, Jiang and Gietel-Basten, 2015). Currently, more than 1 million of those many millions of couples who were allowed to have only one child under the family planning restrictions have seen their only child die – and they are now beyond reproductive age. Given that most of these parents have invested in their children at the expense of saving for their own old age, and in the absence of any adequate state provided care, these people now find themselves in an extremely vulnerable position. As well as being in a difficult pecuniary situation, these *shidu fumu* are also frequently ostracized and stigmatized. These combined factors lead to very low levels of both physical and psychological well-being for this growing component of the elderly population in China. Forecasts suggest that the number of such *shidu fumu* in China could rise to as many as 11 million by 2050 (Jiang, Li and Sánchez-Barricarte, 2013).

One might suggest that the *shidu fumu* are simply a very particular result of China's family planning policies and not of relevance elsewhere. However, as we describe in the chapter on low fertility, the current locations of low and very low fertility around the world are increasingly in poorer countries that are still characterized by significant high mortality rates. As we described in Chapter 5, the preference for having just one child can be found in many relatively poor settings, especially in South and South-East Asia. In this context, adults out-surviving their children – their primary source of support in older age – could become an increasingly important consequence of the transition towards low fertility.

Finally, it should be noted that these possible futures take into account only the demographic variables. The assumption that filial obligation (however defined) will still be a characteristic feature in many emerging markets is taken for granted – but is this necessarily the case? Partially driven by demographic changes, the inevitable modernization of the family unit may well have fundamental implications for the willingness of children to care for their parents.

Conclusion: challenges and opportunities

There is no doubt that the issue of population ageing will be one of the defining demographic narratives of the twenty-first century. While it is currently almost invariably presented as a 'ticking time bomb', conjuring up images of a cataclysmic future, we have argued that this is not a practical or helpful metaphor for a number of reasons. Firstly, many of the challenges associated with population ageing are with us as we speak – so the 'bomb' must have finished ticking. And indeed life expectancy in some affluent countries has even stopped rising, although hopefully only temporarily (Hiam et al., 2017b). Whether the challenge is that of managing overburdened pension systems or of fewer 'workers' producing the high levels of wage inflation we see in China, population ageing is with us right now. Secondly, the 'bomb' metaphor suggests something universally bad, destructive and uncontrolled. But because of the way in which we traditionally measure population ageing, the phenomenon has been artificially exaggerated. This is not to say that challenges don't remain – they absolutely do. But they need to be more carefully addressed and thoughtfully tackled, rather than shouting 'Panic, panic'. Furthermore, the positive aspects of population ageing need to be represented as well as the challenges – harnessing the potential economic power of the first demographic dividend, for example. Lee and Mason have even identified the potential for a second demographic dividend whereby healthy, well-educated older people with high levels of savings and assets make a significant economic net contribution. The burgeoning literature on the so-called 'silver-hair market' – developing goods and services explicitly designed for older people – is a case in point (Coulmas, 2007). A 2014 report by the China National Working Commission on Ageing estimated the value of China's silver-hair market at $652 billion – rising to $17 *trillion* by 2050 (Roberts, 2014)! Furthermore, an older, wiser labour force might want to work on more socially useful projects and may be less manipulatable by those seeking simply to profit than the young have been.

In one way, perhaps, the time-bomb metaphor is partially valid: most bombs can be defused. By investing in human capital – health and education, not least through lifelong learning – and other means to ensure well-being, it is more likely that the levels of 'dependency' we might anticipate may not come to pass. Changes to the labour market to allow for more flexible working practices that are more sensitive to age (including making it easier for younger people to take career breaks to look after elderly relatives, something which could be very cost effective) may also serve to lessen the economic burden while not denying work to younger generations. There are multiple ways in which the potential challenges of population ageing can be mitigated. If we consume less and throw away less in future, then we will not need to make as much and hence work as much. If we make clothes that last longer and wear them until they wear out; if we waste less food; if we make fewer journeys, commute less and have more sensible holidays; if we buy our children fewer toys and play with them more (both our children and the toys); if we rely less on cars and more on public transport – if, in short, we were to grow up and be a bit more responsible, then we could adapt as a species to ageing in a way that we won't be able to if we try to carry on with business as usual. Who does many of these things already? Often it is the elderly (and the poor). In many ways old people are not expensive, but young people are. If we fail to adapt there are clearly huge challenges ahead and uncomfortable decisions to be taken by politicians, families and older people themselves.

That population ageing is seen as a huge societal problem is symptomatic of how human processes have been shoehorned into economic concerns, how they have been monetized. We have become so myopic that we have lost sight of the bigger picture. Ageing is a triumph of humanity, achieved through improved mortality and lowering fertility. More importantly, though, every policy brief or news report that sees older people as 'dependents' – as 'millstones' around the neck of the rest of us – dehumanizes and diminishes us all. Indeed, those who bemoan the old as a burden in this way would do well to remember that they – like the rest of us – get older by the day, becoming the burden to the next generation.

One of the authors of this book lived for a decade in Sheffield, but didn't go out to listen to music often enough. The other author grew up in Nottingham, and the first big music event he went to see was Pulp at the Sheffield Arena – in the band's hometown. As such, it seems appropriate to end this chapter by mentioning one of their songs: 'Help the Aged'. If you have access to the internet then now would be a good time to listen to it, for what it says about ageing and about you. Unfortunately we cannot reproduce the lyrics here for copyright reasons – but they are better listened to than read!

7

Population and the Global Economy

This chapter concerns the story of population and the changing global economy. The economy sometimes seems very impersonal, but it is all about people. People are the ultimate consumers of economic goods. If there are fewer people there is less demand. People are also the producers of goods. We have used tools to produce goods for as long as we have been fully human. Today we are often concerned that those tools will replace many of us and that robots will do what we now do. Such concerns are not new and can be traced back at least to when we first used machines to help us plough more effectively and to spin cloth instead of spinning by hand. However, there is no need for millions to face misery just because we can now produce what we need so much more efficiently than in the past. Often the concern about 'too many people' is a concern about 'too much consumption', and that in turn is a concern about just how easy it is to produce so much nowadays – so many plastics, cars, greenhouse gases; but again, there is no need for more people to mean more pollution and over-consumption. What is actually needed to live a good life is far less than what is used by those who currently consume the most. And often those who consume the most in the world are not especially happy.

'Too many there, too few here'

Reading this book so far, it is easy to imagine that we live in something of a disjointed world. Indeed, this is often how global demographic trends are presented in the media. Half of the world is experiencing tremendous population growth with relatively high fertility (Chapter 4); meanwhile the other half, as a consequence of very low fertility, is tracking a general course towards rapid ageing (Chapter 6) and, ultimately, population decline or 'civilizational collapse' – depending on your rhetorical preferences (see Chapter 5).

The politics of migration and demography will be discussed in greater depth in Chapter 8, but here we want to touch briefly upon how migration can play a mediating role in this high/low fertility world. One of the things which people often say when reading about this supposed 'twin-track' world is: 'well, if there's *too many* people there, and *too few* people here, why don't they just move?' Indeed, the recent narrative around the so-called 'refugee crisis' in Europe has periodically referred to the 'need' for Europe to receive more migrants, or at least seen the 'crisis' as an 'opportunity'. This has been especially argued in relation to Germany, an industrial powerhouse with one of the lowest fertility rates in the world.

The double-edged-sword view of the current 'crisis' is exemplified by the title of a research report from the Pew Research Center: 'Aging Europe, Youthful Refugees: Crisis, Opportunity, or Both?' As Christian Bodewig of the World Bank argued in a Brookings article:

> The real policy question for the countries of Central Europe and the Baltics today is therefore not whether to accept migrants or not but, rather, how to turn the challenge of today's refugee crisis into an opportunity ... [Many migrants] have the potential to not just alleviate declining numbers of workers but also to boost innovation through bringing fresh ideas and perspectives. (Bodewig, 2015).

Others, of course, take a less optimistic view, as in the right-wing online magazine *Breitbart*'s headline: 'Experts conclude Merkel's migrant madness wouldn't have helped German economy anyway'. 'Experts' here referred to an anonymous article from the pressure group Migration Watch UK criticizing an article in the *Financial Times* that suggested the opposite (Jones, 2016).

Of course, not everything is clear-cut. One person's refugee, in need of sanctuary, is another person's 'economic migrant', travelling in their own economic interest and not someone who, as defined by the Oxford English Dictionary, 'has been forced to leave their country in order to escape war, persecution, or natural disaster'. We will return to these issues in Chapter 8. Migration flows can be disruptive to overall population trends, as well as highly productive. Think about the Spanish colonists in the Americas for an extreme example of the disruptive effect of the arrival of just a few European migrants, and their germs.

Many centuries later, within Europe, migration does indeed play an important role in shoring up population growth in some low fertility but rich countries like Germany and re-charging (or super-charging depending on your viewpoint) population growth in higher fertility countries such as the UK. Yet, outmigration *exacerbates* low fertility in the home countries of emigrants, such as Bulgaria and Spain. Often the countries that are net losers of young adults do not fare well as a consequence, just as cities such as Glasgow and Liverpool fared so badly between the 1970s and recent years, when so many of their young left the city and were replaced by far fewer in-migrants. By the time the UK's 2011 census was released it was evident that only migration from Eastern Europe had pre-vented both cities shrinking further and having to demolish yet more housing. Coincidently, a majority of voters in both these cities voted Remain on 23 June 2016.

We will get into the rights and wrong of EU policies on refugees in the next chapter. The current 'refugee crisis' in Europe is presented as indicative of a two-track demographic world – where one half is characterized by uncontrolled population growth, few or no eco-nomic opportunities, and occasional war and chaos. Already from Syria alone, about a million of the 11 million who have had to leave their homes since 2011 have 'invaded' fortress Europe. 'Invading a fortress' is actually a rather poor metaphor for what is happening in this part of the global economy. But, given that the metaphor exists, and that migration is being represented in this way, it is worth think-ing briefly about whether that is actually what is really occurring.

As we have seen, various reports and policy documents have identified the migrants coming to Europe – or, indeed, to any other low fertility setting around the world – as being demographically advantageous. Yet, to what end? Is it just about maintaining the current total population size? If so, has anyone taken a step back to ask what, precisely, is the benefit of maintaining this particular population size, reached at only one particular point in history? Why would an even larger population be a problem? Admittedly, in classical economics and the calculation of GDP, total population size is important. But is that the be-all-and-end-all of what matters most? A shrinking population need not always be a population that is becoming poorer.

In many political debates centring on demographics it is argued that it is not total population *size* that counts, but rather the 'working-age' population, which needs to be 'shored up' in order to ameliorate the effects of the ageing population. In the previous chapter we argued that the so-called 'ageing crisis' – so many 'crises'! – has to a certain degree been exaggerated, and that policies other than those simply aimed at supplying more babies or workers might be better 'solutions'. These include not stopping older but fit people from working if they wish to work, and starting to introduce a universal basic income so that not everyone has to work if they are prepared to subsist on a low (but survivable) income – perhaps to do something really useful like their own childcare. Being unable to give adequate childcare because one 'has to work' is a common reason given for not having children. People might value looking after elderly relatives, but could only do so if in receipt of a basic income; or they might just want to do what they really, passionately, want to do – rather than taking a job they see as pointless.

Furthermore, the argument about shoring up the working population requires those making it to assume that Europe is currently in a situation of full employment and has a great industrial capacity that needs to be filled by more workers. In the second quarter of 2013, total job vacancies in Europe stood at 72 per cent of those in the first quarter of 2008 (European Commission, 2015). Despite a global economic recession there were still many vacancies to be filled, but they are not necessarily for jobs that those out of work can do, or would wish to do given how arduous and lowly paid some of these jobs are. Most readers of this book will not need to be reminded of the current unemployment rates in Southern and Eastern Europe, which are much higher for the young than for older workers (Eurostat, 2017).

The demand for labour

While there is certainly a demand for labour in Europe, this tends to be polarized somewhat between highly paid niche sectors and often undervalued low-paid occupations (rarely called professions), including elderly care. According to the 2014 European Vacancy Monitor report, published by the European Commission, the then top five *growth* occupations in Europe in terms of hiring were: refuse workers; heavy truck and bus drivers; agricultural, forestry and fishery labourers; personal care workers in health services; and cooks. Between 2008 and 2013, the sharpest *relative* falls in hiring across the EU were in the category of 'legislators, senior officials, and managers' – this was a reflection of austerity measures, the rolling back of the state, and possibly even a recognition that we need fewer people in these expensive 'senior' jobs.

Given that the better-paid professions make up only a tiny sector of the labour market, it is especially significant that the second and third sharpest falls in European job vacancies after 2008 were in 'craft and related trades workers' (down 30 per cent) and 'plant and machine operators and assemblers' (down 27 per cent). All this, argues the European Vacancy Monitor report, comes as 'a direct result of the difficulties in sectors such as manufacturing and construction caused by the [economic] crisis' (European Commission, 2015). Reflecting more broadly on this, however, we might suggest that the economic crisis is merely an exaggerating factor in the long-term migration of industrial prowess to other parts of the world through the processes of globalization.

This global economic reorientation will be the main focus of this chapter. Firstly, however, it is important to 'put to bed' the notion that migration can be the catch-all answer to the supposed demographic travails of certain countries, or at least a solution that comes at no cost to other countries. Again, we have to think about what we want migration to do. Is migration good because it helps to maintain current total population levels in the right places (migrants tend to have fewer children than the people in their home countries); because it helps to maintain the current ratio between those of so-called 'working age' and those over 65 years (the so-called 'dependency ratio' – a concept used regularly, but debunked in the previous chapter); or because it helps to move a 'surplus' population away from where it is less needed and towards where there is far greater need for it?

All these issues will begin to matter greatly a few years from now. Population decline is around the corner (if not already present) for a number of European countries. On current projections, in order to maintain their 2002 population size, by mid-century some 3.5 million people would need to move to Bulgaria, 4.7 million to Germany, 6.6 million to Poland, 1.2 million to Hungary and no less than 8.8 million to Romania. However, if we think that the real concern is about population ageing being a threat to economies and societies, rather than a modest decline of the total population per se, then we might have to think about the numbers needed to maintain various support ratios (of 'workers' to 'pensioners'), and develop a more sophisticated version of any support ratio we wish to argue over. Maintaining any current support ratio – in the context of (sometimes very) low fertility, unfavourable age structures, improvements in mortality, and, of course, the ageing of migrants themselves – would involve incredibly high future potential in-flows of replacement populations.

For instance, in order for Poland, which in 2002 had a population of 38 million people, to maintain its current support ratio by mid-century, some 108 *million* migrants would be required between 2002 and 2052 if fertility levels remained low and the current ratio was to be maintained into the distant future. In Germany this figure would be more than 130 million. For the EU27 (with the UK included) to maintain its support ratio to mid-century as a whole, some 828 million people will be required to migrate to those twenty-seven countries over the period 2002–52 (Bijak, Kupiszewska and Kupiszewski, 2008). Similar figures can be seen in other parts of the world that are now already ageing. Indeed, one demographer with a particular interest in migration noted that, 'in the extreme case, preserving the [2000 support ratio] in [South] Korea would require the entire [2000] population of the world to go to live there by 2050' (Coleman, 2002: 587). By this standard, the 524 million people required for Japan to maintain its 2000-level support ratio appears modest (suggested in UNPD, 2001). The figure for Korea is so extraordinary because of the very rapid decline of fertility in the country; but the point still holds – that maintaining previous support ratios into the far future is demographically unrealistic, and often impossible. However, the migration of some young adults from areas where there are more young adults to areas where there are fewer clearly does have a positive effect on these ratios, but one which is not sustained in future by the children those migrants have, if and when they have fewer children themselves.

The foregoing discussion, as we have presented it, is a very economic, or demographically deterministic, way of looking at migration. Of course, the political and cultural implications of migration are huge, and will be covered in the next chapter. But in this chapter we wanted to dispel the notion that swapping 'too many' people here for 'too few' people there (or, more accurately, too many old people relative to young people) can be a simple long-term solution to ageing. All countries are going to have to better understand and deal with ageing, either now or very soon, because fertility is falling everywhere. Of course migration can reinvigorate certain industries, fill skill gaps or labour shortages, and fulfil all sorts of extremely valuable economic, social and cultural functions – and, above all else, it is an expression of human freedom. It can even present a short-term amelioration of certain demographic concerns. Whether it is a long-term solution, however, is very much open to question. This, we think, is again a key example of why demography matters and why understanding demography a little more matters.

Rural to urban migration

Migration is a short- to medium-term solution to economic imbalances. It was through internal rural to urban migration that cities grew to the sizes they now are. In fact, in the past, someone could have produced statistics about internal rural to urban migration as apparently fanciful as some of those quoted above relating to replacement migration – but in many parts of the world such large-scale migration away from the land did come to pass. In other places it now appears to have stopped. So there are many cities about to shrink, but also still many bursting at the seams.

The maps in Figure 7.1, showing the growth of the city of Oxford, are quite a good illustration of how the population in more affluent countries began to grow more rapidly with the advent of the industrial revolution, but then settled down and stopped growing at all, at least in Europe and Japan. Oxford itself keeps growing in terms of population, but not as fast as it grew in the past and hardly at all in terms of new residential buildings; as such it is an example of a high population pressure area within a relatively stable demographic regime. The pressure now is caused mainly by a refusal to allow more building due to the imposition of a very tight green belt around the city. Other cities in Germany and even China are now experiencing actual population declines, but this is not generally the case in the UK, as yet.

Oxford is a city that is getting younger, not older. It is a city with more jobs than people and so tens of thousands commute in every day. It is also a city that could expand geographically and still be relatively small in size. Those who are involved in these debates, over cities like Oxford as well as whole countries, need to think again about the bigger picture. Thinking demographically allows us to go beyond the short-termist political cycle and to think much more conceptually about population, economies, society and the environment. In the short-term, migration can indeed offset some concerns about the apparent demographic malaise of Europe. However, by focusing on this as a solution, we run the risk of not properly addressing the underlying *reasons* for low fertility that in turn underpin the concerns regarding ageing and decline. It is not

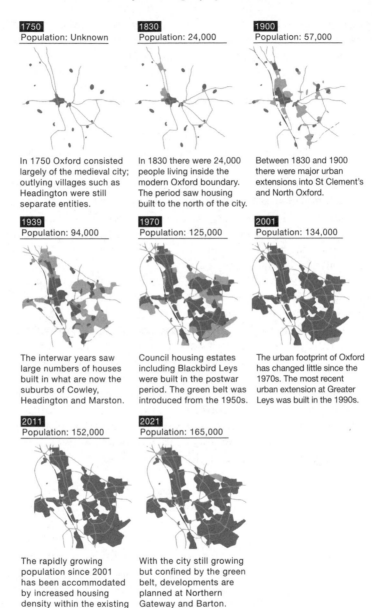

1750
Population: Unknown

In 1750 Oxford consisted largely of the medieval city; outlying villages such as Headington were still separate entities.

1830
Population: 24,000

In 1830 there were 24,000 people living inside the modern Oxford boundary. The period saw housing built to the north of the city.

1900
Population: 57,000

Between 1830 and 1900 there were major urban extensions into St Clement's and North Oxford.

1939
Population: 94,000

The interwar years saw large numbers of houses built in what are now the suburbs of Cowley, Headington and Marston.

1970
Population: 125,000

Council housing estates including Blackbird Leys were built in the postwar period. The green belt was introduced from the 1950s.

2001
Population: 134,000

The urban footprint of Oxford has changed little since the 1970s. The most recent urban extension at Greater Leys was built in the 1990s.

2011
Population: 152,000

The rapidly growing population since 2001 has been accommodated by increased housing density within the existing urban footprint.

2021
Population: 165,000

With the city still growing but confined by the green belt, developments are planned at Northern Gateway and Barton.

Figure 7.1   The growth of the city of Oxford, 1750–2021, population and physical extent

Source: Mark Fransham for Oxford City Council (2015), reproduced with permission.

about being anti- or pro-immigration. *Rather, migration is about human choice and freedom, and is neither, necessarily, a solution nor a problem in itself.*

Migration is easy to blame. It can offer an easy get-out, allowing policymakers and businesses to shirk big and difficult questions about jobs, rights, children, families. The migration solution also assumes that it only has a one-way effect, and ignores the consequences of 'brain drain' or 'human capital flight', which does not always balance out. Therefore, as well as the unfair arguments about 'selfish' millennials refusing to have children, migrants of a similar age are either unfairly saddled with the blame for the current travails of Europe, or are seen as the solution to Europe's demographic problems. This is all completely wrong.

Emerging markets, fading markets

Living in Europe, one could be forgiven for thinking that the global demographic issues revolve around the problem set out above: 'too many' people in one place – often associated with pictures from sub-Saharan Africa or refugee camps in the Middle East – and 'too few' people, or 'too many old people', closer to home. Of course, this betrays an extremely partial view of the world. For the remainder of this chapter we will concentrate on the countries 'in the middle'. These are the countries which, so it is said, are currently the prime drivers of the global economy, or will be over the next century or so. They are grouped together under a range of names. BRICS (Brazil, Russia, India, China and South Africa) is the most familiar acronym, along with MINT (Mexico, Indonesia, Nigeria, Turkey). But there is also the so-called 'Next Eleven' of South Korea, Indonesia (again), Iran, Mexico, Philippines, Turkey, Bangladesh, Egypt, Nigeria, Pakistan and Vietnam (Lawson, Heacock and Stupnytska, 2007). They are all members of a more amorphous group labelled 'emerging markets', although precisely which countries are included in this group will vary according to the particular criteria of individual analysts. While events of recent years have seen the 'stars' of these groups somewhat tarnished by economic and political difficulties, the perception of them as critical to the future of the global economy is still very strong because the traditionally richest countries have all had faltering economies since at least 2007. In future decades it is likely that new acronyms will be coined as new groupings of countries begin to behave in similar, 'emerging', ways.

The claim of many of these emerging markets to being economic powerhouses is primarily based upon their natural resources and mineral wealth. Within just the BRICS and MINTs, Russia and Nigeria (and to a lesser degree South Africa) would fall under this category. More broadly, we could also put Venezuela, the UAE and Qatar squarely in this group. With the exception of infrastructure development (most notably in the Gulf States), the 'power of people' is less important in these economies because a great deal of money making is driven primarily by extractive industries. It is also worth noting that they often rely on migrant labour to carry out much of the extraction. From the first 'gold rushes', through the mass migration to the Welsh coalfields, to today's mobile oil workers, extraction has usually involved migrants – often but not always, temporary.

For other countries in the lists above, a strong manufacturing base lies at the heart of their economic status, complemented to a greater or lesser extent by flourishing primary (agriculture, mining etc.) and tertiary (service) sectors. If you think we are being rather vague, we can prove this is the case very easily: Please take off your trousers. Look inside at the label. (If you're squeamish about doing this, or sat in a library, or not wearing trousers for whatever reason, pick another item of clothing). Even if you're wearing the finest Harris Tweed, or handmade dirndls, there is still a very reasonable chance that you will be wearing *something* that was made in an emerging market. In fact, the chances that the label will have the name of China, India, Bangladesh, Vietnam, the Philippines, Indonesia, Turkey or Pakistan printed on it are very strong. If you are sat at a desk, or on your sofa at home, or, if you are fortunate to still have one in your area, in a library, look around you. There will undoubtedly be more than one thing which was made in one of the countries listed above. There is a very good reason for this: cheap labour.

The era of cheap labour – at least *that* cheap, apart from zero-hour contracts and the like – in Europe and North America has long gone. As the global economy has developed over the past century, and Europe sits at the end of a long supply chain which now wraps around the world, the loci of industrial production have undoubtedly moved and are still moving. The cost of labour is, and has increasingly been, a critical driver of the location and characteristics of industry. As global markets expand and supply chains become slicker, the cost of accessing labour in different parts of the world, and of transporting its products elsewhere, has diminished rapidly, effectively pricing out Japan, Europe and North America in many sectors.

But cheap labour is not only available in the kind of emerging markets we have talked about already. Labour is also cheap – very cheap – in plenty of other places, especially in parts of sub-Saharan Africa, central Asia and the Middle East. So why is 'stuff' made in China and not in Tajikistan? Because, of course, raw labour is just one input. Other factors include existing infrastructure and the capacity for it to be developed; access to water and constant supplies of cheap energy for production; easy access to both raw materials and local supply chain services; the ability to export, usually via a sea route; and political issues related to stability, governance, corruption and labour laws (all of which can work in various directions).

Taking a longer term view, susceptibility to natural disasters and escaping the effects of imperialism are other important factors – think of the 'Great Divergence' between China and Europe and the differing pathways of industrial growth, which may in future be exacerbated by climate change (Pomeranz, 2001). Think of how the Chinese economy was repeatedly decimated when, under the watch of imperial gunboats, the British insisted that they had a right to sell opium grown in their Indian colony to the Chinese (Dorling and Lee, 2016).

In terms of people, it is not solely a question of the number of hands within one territorial unit able to provide the labour. From the first glimmers of industrial development in England centuries ago through to today, the movement of 'excess' rural labour into concentrated areas – towns, cities, factories – has been at the heart of industrial development, and has been driven by both push and pull factors. This can be seen in developments in agricultural management and technology, freeing up labour to be relocated. Together with changes in the broader economy to accommodate that labour in either the secondary (manufacturing and construction) or tertiary (service) sectors, the changing world economy helps drive migration. Related to this is the skill-set of the population, and the capacity to develop a functioning industrial base. From another political viewpoint, peasants were forced off the land when it was enclosed, and became a cheap migrant labour force just at the time others were opening up mines and building mills that needed that labour. What occurs is as much about coercion, trickery and dominance (politics), as supply and demand (economics).

Just as there are many different ways of looking at the recent past, so too are there many economic forecasts for the future. Neither of us (nor anyone else) is qualified to pronounce on the future of each of the myriad, interlinked components of the global economy. But we can concentrate on just the demographic 'bit' – recognizing that demographic change and the global economy are fundamentally linked together in a two-way process, involving people both as producers and as consumers. Steve Emmott's (2013) book focuses on an apocalyptic vision of the future in which 10 billion people are consuming the entirety of an ever-growing basket of cheap goods. But in the remainder of this chapter we want to focus a little more on people as *producers* in the global economy; on what the implications for future demographic change might be if people were to begin producing different things in different ways; and on what happens if they have fewer children, and have them later in life, as a result of the extra education they require to become such service producers. Emmott's view of our future – namely that we are 'fucked' – assumes that we will carry on producing the same kind of goods as before, goods that wear out quickly and that require a huge amount of energy to produce along with the unsustainable depletion of natural resources. But what if we were to produce more goods that weighed less[1] – more *ideas* and fewer plastic toys; more *digital music* and fewer vinyl records; more appreciation of *local areas* to visit and fewer exotic overseas holidays? What if there were going to be fewer workers in future in those places that currently specialize in manufacturing, and more in those countries where the service sector already dominates, but fewer than is currently thought most likely?

The mysterious vanishing act of the global labour pool

In Chapter 5 we examined the increasing trend towards low and extremely low fertility around the world. We also mentioned that rising fertility was now being seen in a few places where one might not expect it, but still below the replacement rate of just over two children per woman. Would you be surprised to learn that fertility in Thailand is now lower than it is in Japan and the same as in Italy, Germany and Spain? Similarly, would you be surprised that the fertility rate in Vietnam is lower than it is the Netherlands (see Figures 7.2 and 5.3)? In Bangladesh, where the GDP per capita is just US$957 per year, fertility stands at 2.2, just 0.1 above New Zealand, where GDP per capita is US$41,555.[2] Take all this into account and then consider what on earth is being suggested in Figure 7.2 for the years 2050 and 2100. Is that uniformity really likely, especially around the 2.0 child level?

At the sub-national level, the divergence in fertility rates becomes even more striking. In Ho Chi Minh City, Vietnam's largest city,

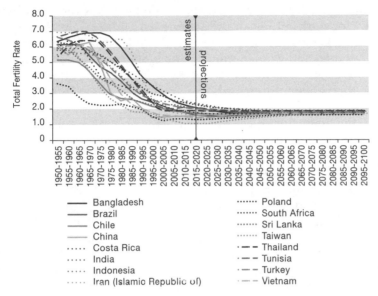

Figure 7.2   Recent trends and the 'medium variant' assumptions
for fertility in selected emerging markets

the fertility rate today is just 1.4 (Knoema.com, 2016). We have
already noted that in some provinces in India fertility rates have
fallen to around 1.6 or 1.7, and the 2011 Indian census suggests
that fertility in the megacity of Kolkata (formerly Calcutta) has
plunged to just 1.2 (Livemint, 2014; Sen, 2012). In China, fertility
has fallen to very low levels especially, but not only, in big cities;
and the evidence suggests that this is not merely an effect of the
country's historic family planning policies, but it is mainly due to a
new and mostly voluntary choice to limit childbearing (Basten and
Jiang, 2014). Finally, and perhaps most striking of all, in Nepal,
one of the poorest countries in all of Asia, the TFR in parts of the
Kathmandu Valley – Nepal's most urbanized and developed zone –
could now be as low as 1.3.[3]

   In light of our discussion in Chapter 2 about how fertility is calculated, these figures should not be taken absolutely at face value. The
projections in Figure 7.2 are suspicious. Does the UNPD believe that
there is some biological/natural-justice principle to cause *all* those
countries to converge on a TFR of around 2? Really? In the same way
that patterns of migration can skew national fertility rates in Europe,
so, of course, they can in emerging markets. The very low fertility

rates in Nepal, for example, may be related to many men leaving the country for work in India or the Middle East; conversely, the very low rates in Kolkata and other large cities, not least in China, could be linked to men and women moving (possibly together, possibly separately) to those cities for work and either postponing childbearing or having their children in their home areas, possibly to be cared for by grandparents.

But, the point still holds. Low fertility is no longer a 'rich' country phenomenon. Comparing Figure 7.2 to Figure 5.3 in Chapter 5 showing fertility rates in the rich countries, it is clear that the fertility trends in these two groups are often increasingly similar. But they may be similar at lower levels than currently projected, at 1.8 or 1.6 children per woman for a few decades into the future, rather than 2.0. We will return to the implications of these changes for the future labour force in terms of the importance of overall population size shortly. Suffice to say, though, *it matters*.

Figure 7.3 below presents possible consequences of the UN's 'medium variant' assumptions for future fertility rates in this selection of important emerging markets, as well as the low fertility projections. Before going any further it is also worth pointing out that the term 'emerging markets' does unfortunately assume a somewhat linear view of history where countries that have been poorer in the past, often due to the actions of rich countries, are expected to become like those richer countries in future. This is unfortunate because it is never how history actually develops. That is not to say that poor countries will always be poor, but rather that if (and as) they become better off, they will not become better off in the same way as richer countries in the past did – not least because they won't be in a position to exploit a set of even poorer countries beneath them in the way that the richer countries imposed unfair terms of trade in the past. They will also not have the population growth that countries such as the UK, the US and Switzerland experienced when they were becoming rich, because their fertility has already fallen so fast. Therefore the pressure to export local populations to 'new colonies' will be far less – which is very fortunate, although it is far from certain how it may all play out in the near future.

As noted in our discussion of projections in Chapter 3, it is worth remembering that the UN's 'authoritative' forecasts represent only one particular scenario, largely based upon societies following a broadly European pattern. But this has already been put into question by recent trends suggesting that fertility is now often falling faster in emerging markets than it did in Europe in the past. Again, we are suggesting that there are many reasons why fertility in future may be lower than the UNPD projects, because they assume a very sharp break in current falls, a break for which there is as yet scant evidence.

The possibly highly flawed current predictions are of a future stabilization at rates that are relatively close to replacement levels. What we have already seen, however, is that not all countries are following this particular pattern. Take for example Taiwan, where cohort fertility appears to now be moving with some determination to very low levels (Myrskylä, Goldstein and Cheng, 2013). We also need to think more conceptually about the similarities and differences between European societies and the emerging markets. Thinking about the reasons for the transition to low fertility in these latter countries, some will be related to family planning programmes, some to improvements in mortality, some to education, some to urbanization and so on. But, there has also been a demand-side revolution in terms of economic opportunities and the ability of an ever-greater proportion of the population to engage – however meagrely – with the industrial economy. There is also a growing array of choices on issues ranging from how to live, through to what contraception to use, if any. In contrast to rural living, urbanization and industrialization have brought about a *liberation* from some traditional norms, together with changes in patterns of fertility, and in the role of children within families and households (Cleland and Wilson, 1987). Fundamentally, this 'transition' is not so dissimilar to that in historical Europe and other industrialized countries – it has just occurred far more quickly, progressed further, and benefited some groups more than others in each country. Such slight differences will, however, have profound effects if they are more widespread. If the expansion of choices is spread more quickly to more people than is currently expected then much lower overall fertility than is currently projected could be the global result.

There are also a number of important dissimilarities with previously affluent countries that could impact upon the future of fertility in emerging markets. Unlike many industrialized countries, the majority of emerging markets, as identified in Figure 7.2, did not – or haven't yet – developed adequate or more than absolutely minimal social security systems. If we think of childbearing as a 'risk' that competes with other risks, opportunities and concerns in life, which welfare systems – or at least some degree of risk-pooling with family, employer or the state – can ameliorate, is it possible that this could be a check on further fertility falls (see, for example, Chan, 2009)? In other words, in traditional Europe, 'risk' in the past would have been pooled with the family. With the onset of industrial development, it would be pooled with both the family, the employer and, eventually, the state. Increasingly today, with the retrenchment of welfare systems, the demise of the 'job for life', powerful trade unions and/or the paternalistic employer, plus the atomization of family structures, risk is being transferred to the individual. It is quite possible that this is *the major reason* for young people in Europe currently being so reluctant to have children. It is also possible that in many emerging markets we are seeing a supercharged version of this transition, but one that has some characteristics akin to leaping straight from the first to the last stage of previous demographic models in one dramatic bound. In other words, the mismatch between the opportunities currently available in terms of 'riding the wave' of the global economy and the direct costs of having children, coupled with the lack of support 'if things go wrong', could easily translate into a lower fertility future than is expected.

A further feature which could drive fertility lower relates to social welfare, especially for when people cannot work. Most emerging markets have only limited elder-care provision, whether in terms of financial support through pensions or adequate medical care. This is also the case with long-term social care for those suffering from chronic illness (see Hinton and Chen, 2016 for Asia, for example). As the so-called 'mortality transition' spreads through these countries, the main causes of death change from infectious diseases to often more longer-term and chronic diseases characterized by the possibility of more specialist medical support and the need for structural care (Byass et al., 2013). This will likely become an ever more important responsibility not only for individuals themselves, but for their children. Remember that in most emerging markets, the primary responsibility for caring for older (and sick) parents rests with children (see Ikels, 2004 for Asia). While not only culturally mandated, in some settings this is even enshrined in law.

Recently in China, many reports have emerged of how this law has been strengthened (Coonan, 2013), with show-trials in some places for errant 'children', as well as a remarkable story from Shanghai according to which children who do not visit their parents may have their credit scores altered (Iyengar, 2016). These clampdowns stem from the decisions of policymakers and employers to negate their responsibility for providing adequate support for the elderly. Where this burden of responsibility – a further 'risk' – rests on the shoulders of working-age parents, and more particularly *women*, the idea of adding further to that burden by having children (or having more children) is often seen as unrealistic.

All these issues are, again, especially important in China where a generation of many millions of only-child families has created a widespread so-called '4–2–1' family structure, where '2' parents are responsible for the financial, emotional and general well-being of not only their '1' child, but also, in the absence of brothers and sisters, both sets of grandparents: the '4' (Jiang and Sanchez-Barricarte, 2011; Wang and Fong, 2009). Of course, grandparents can also *relieve* the burden of childrearing and not all will require intensive support. But, these factors have been cited as an important reason for why changing the '1' to '2' is not necessarily an attractive prospect for many Chinese parents. Finally, while China is something of an extreme case in terms of its one-child policy history, it is a general principle that under circumstances of prolonged low fertility, more chronic illnesses and increased life expectancy, family structures everywhere tend to 'narrow', leading to fewer people having to take responsibility for more older people for longer at the household level. This, as discussed in Chapter 6, is one of the greatest challenges of population ageing, and one which can also have a negative feedback effect on population by itself reducing fertility further. However, if this were to occur for the next few decades it might not be negative in overall effect. As world population stabilizes, what happens over those decades could very well determine the level at which it stabilizes, and hence the total global human population for many decades to come. That all relies on many factors, which is why this is a book and not an academic paper!

Consider the notion of care in older age. Currently working-age adults are going to be thinking about making provision for their own future. Here there is something of a paradox: research seems to suggest that while there is a growing sentiment that children will or should play less of a role in taking care of parents in the future, many parents do not appear to have a 'plan B', because adequate state or private provision rarely exists (Basten, Muttarak and Pothisiri, 2014). This feeds into the notion of a so-called 'quantity-quality' trade-off in terms of children, which is not a new phenomenon in demography (Becker and Lewis, 1973), nor constrained only to the study of humans.

In the case of the very low fertility that is now occurring in Kolkata, for example, Saswata Ghosh of the IDSK (Institute of Development Studies, Kolkata) suggests that such a trade-off is in place there, where couples would 'much rather have one child and give him or her the best education and facilities they can afford, rather than spread resources thinly between two children or more' (quoted in Livemint, 2014). Indeed, this kind of attitude can be seen in many different settings, both elsewhere in India (Basu and Desai, 2012), and in our qualitative research in China and Taiwan, and likely in many other countries worldwide. Of course, part of this can also be a market-driven effect, where free public education is undermined by more expensive private education that drains family resources. But back in the 1970s and 1980s in the UK it was commonplace to hear that a working-class family trying to climb quickly into the middle class would have a single child and pour all their resources into that one basket.

Again, however, it is important to remember that most parents do not act purely or even at all on the basis of economic models, or as a result of the careful application of decision-tree algorithms. Investing more in children as a kind of personal plan might be some-where in the mix, but may not be the primary motivator. Rather, each generation has often come to want the next one to have a better set of opportunities or life chances – or, in the case of rich countries (especially given the global recession today), at least 'as good a set as they had'. For a generation that has seen many more economic (and social) opportunities than the generation before – and in the context of both a rapidly changing world and lower childhood mortality – investing in education, despite limited resources, appears to be the optimal means of assuring that the next generation can succeed, or at least that the 'risks' that life may throw at them are minimized.

It seems apparent that if people, and especially the elite, in such emerging markets are truly worried about low fertility and want to do something about it, then investing in decent free public educa-tion, adequate provision for the elderly and some rudimentary social/labour protection systems would be a better approach, rather than pushing through either crude pronatalist policies or narrowly defined family policies.

A final piece of new evidence that we need to consider before drawing this chapter to a conclusion concerns fertility preferences. If you recall, in Chapter 5 we presented evidence that young people across Europe – like their older peers – stated a strong preference for a two-child family. This was seen as a sign that fertility could rise if some of the factors that currently discourage people from achieving this aspiration could be altered. In many emerging markets, however, there is growing evidence that a one-child family is becoming increasingly idealized. Recent research has shown this to be the case for growing proportions of the population in India (Pradhan and Sekher, 2012), Thailand, Nepal and China – even after the switch to a two-child policy (Basten and Jiang, 2014). Furthermore, in some places, a preference for boys plays a role in wanting two children; but there is also the risk that where only one child is desired, and that one child (in at least one parent's mind) *has to* be a boy, further increases in sex-selective abortion could occur. Indeed, in China in recent years we have seen an increase in the sex ratio at birth among first-borns – a relatively new phenomenon of many more boys born than girls – but still nowhere near the much higher chances of a second child being a boy (which is only possible through selective abortion). It has been argued that this practise will decrease – from a rather economically deterministic and harsh perspective – because the shortage of women has 'increased their value', especially on the marriage market. Other reasons include the fact that women are more likely to be reliable caregivers in one's old age (for more on the sex ratio transition, see Guilmoto, 2009).

Family planning and peak working-age population

In this chapter we have presented a vision of a lower fertility future for some of the very large so-called emerging markets. Of course, we may be – and probably are – in some way wrong, and much will not play out as we think it might. But what is important is that the reasons for family size are complex, and cannot be reduced to a single factor causing an inevitable trend. There are reasons why fertility could go back up: a return to traditional cultures and values; seeing that there is no fantastic return to modest investment in private education and switching back to 'quantity over quality' (or not 'putting all your eggs in one basket'); effective policy interventions to support families allowing 'quantity *and* quality'; restrictions to family planning or just general shifts in attitudes to the role of children. You never know, more people might even find out that children are fun. What follows, then, is highly speculative, but shows that very different futures to those most often currently imagined are possible.

Translating the alternative trajectories for fertility into labour force projections is surprisingly difficult, but can be done (see, for example, Bijak et al., 2007). Doing so requires all sorts of intervening assumptions about *who works*, by age, by gender, by region, and how this changes over time. Here, though, we are going to present some very simple projections with some pretty heavy caveats. Figure 7.3 shows

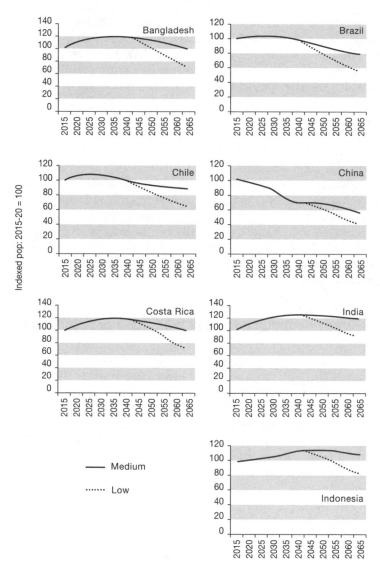

Figure 7.3 Relative size of total population aged 25–45 to 2065–70 according to medium and low variant of fertility, selected emerging markets, indexed to 2015–20

Source: Drawn by the authors with data published by the United Nations Population Division 2016, World Population Prospects.

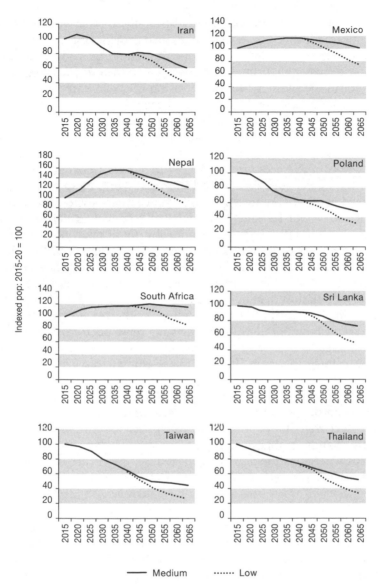

— Medium   ⋯⋯⋯ Low

Figure 7.3 Continued

the total population aged 25–45 in a sample of emerging markets under two conditions of fertility over the next fifty years: the 'medium variant' of the UN projections (i.e. reflecting those TFRs shown in Figure 7.2 above), and the 'low variant' which is simply a TFR of 0.5 lower than that of the medium variant. The caveats include the fact that labour participation rates (especially among women) could change dramatically. These age ranges also provide only a snapshot of the total working population, but one that could be said to represent what some might call 'prime' working ages. In the previous chapter we talked about the synthetic nature of using 65 as an entry point to old age so we have explicitly avoided that here. However, we are realistic enough to suggest that global capital is unlikely to turn to older rather than younger workers. Finally – and this is the case throughout this whole discussion of the global economy – we have not considered different *sectors* of the economy and how they might change, especially differentiating between formal and informal work. Note also that the variants diverge markedly after twenty-five years, when the fertility rates of today will be felt. This delayed response is called 'demographic momentum' – but, as we note shortly, it takes no account of either emigration or immigration altering these figures in the meantime and beyond. Despite all of these caveats the figures are striking.

Remember that these figures are presented as a concern not just in terms of population decline and the relative size of the labour force, but also in terms of population ageing. In the previous chapter we talked about how population ageing may have been misrepresented as a challenge to these and other societies. But surely the changes in the labour force shown in Figure 7.3 are going to have a tremendous effect?

The 'demographic destiny' view stalks both the popular and policy literature relating to many emerging markets, disregarding the fact that it overlooks the prospects for employment – for example, Saudi Arabia and Egypt are very young, growing countries, but where are the *jobs?* Compare how the future demographic and economic futures of China and India are presented, not least in the pages of *The Economist*. The *Independent*'s 2014 headline 'India will soon be the new China. It's the demography, stupid' is fairly typical of this simplistic view (McRae, 2014). As we point out throughout this book – especially in Chapter 4 with respect to the use of resources and Chapter 5 with respect to the future of economies – the raw number of people is not the only resource. Comparing the variant demographic futures of India and China, for example, the RAND Corporation noted that: 'how much these demographic changes affect economic growth will depend on several other factors, including the infrastructure, education system, and health care systems in each country and how well each country integrates women into its workforce' (DaVanzo and Dogo, 2011). Very true; but again to a certain degree this view still 'plays by the old rules' of country-by-country analysis, and obscures the true nature of global capital and its need for ever new sources of profit. Looking around the world today, we can see a number of different ways in which both governments and global capital (acting in different ways) respond to profound changes in labour force needs, frequently to increases in labour costs. These 'needs' could be in factories, or in services. In brief, the responses are:

- *Move the 'need' to where labour is cheaper.* This largely explains the demise of much of the industrial sector in older, richer countries; but consider the more recent changes to the industrial sector in settings such as Hong Kong or Taiwan, where production has been relocated to mainland China and elsewhere. This is why we see a growth in moves to ever more 'exotic' locations such as Mauritius, Sri Lanka and so on. We suspect that this explains the significant degree of interest in the political future of Myanmar, a country with a large pool of relatively skilled young people, a growing infra-structure, ample resources and a good geographical location for transport purposes. However, this is likely to be a merely transient benefit.
- *Move the people to where the 'need' is.* Or, at least *allow* them to move there. Again, this has been a feature of internal migration for centu-ries. While net international immigration within China is very low, its 'floating population' of internal 'migrants' accounts for some 250 million people (Goodkind and West, 2002). Ground-breaking new work reconstructing migration flows shows just how many people are 'on the move', especially *between* emerging markets. The huge flows into the Middle East for construction and infrastruc-ture development are well known, as perhaps are more niche exam-ples such as the 300,000 domestic helpers in Hong Kong, largely from South-East Asia, who make up around 5 per cent of the total population (Cheng, 1996). But perhaps more hidden are the large numbers of Nepalese workers in India, Burmese in Thailand and Indonesians in Malaysia.

Alternatively, systems of production can themselves change:

- Countries can 'move up the value chain of innovation' and switch, in an extreme representation, from producing yo-yos to producing semiconductors. Again, this has happened in the past and is hap-pening today. Until recently, what remained of steel production in the UK was largely geared towards producing high-precision parts because mass production was not competitive. Korea, Taiwan and Japan all led the way towards turning out high-return technological goods for export.

- Furthermore, as well as up-scaling the *output* – which will inevitably be linked to improvements in education, as the RAND report cited earlier rightly suggests – we can also foresee an up-scaling of the mechanisms of *input*. As well as investments in human capital (e.g. health and education), investments in *fixed* capital can offset rises in labour costs and other shortages. Again, this has been seen throughout history with the increased mechanization of work. Studies have suggested that the potential of further technological innovation to make jobs redundant (and hence to offset these demographic changes) is very great. The World Bank, for example, estimates that automation could replace 85 per cent of jobs in Ethiopia, 77 per cent in China, 72 per cent in Thailand, 69 per cent in India and 67 per cent in South Africa (Citi GPS and Oxford Martin School, 2016). Even in the UK, it is estimated that 35 per cent of jobs are 'at risk'. Of course, 'automation' can cover everything from a machine to screw on a bottle top right through to the most advanced Artificial Intelligence imaginable, but much in the above estimates is based on what is already happening elsewhere.

It is crucial to remember that these responses are not an either/or, especially in the context of a system of global capital which shows ever less respect for operating within national borders. On the other hand, it is instructive to note the plans of China. As stated elsewhere in this book (perhaps *ad nauseam*), the country is facing a rapid decline in its working-age population and – in the classical view – a 'threat' from rapid population ageing. The response of its elites to this is, in some ways, relatively orthodox: up-scaling and increasing domestic productivity. However, its confusingly named 'One Belt, One Road' initiative – intended to dramatically increase trading routes and cooperation – explicitly seeks to take advantage of the favourable demographic characteristics of Central and South-East Asia, the Middle East and East Africa, developing their infrastructure in order to allow these economies to take off – with China as patron (Fallon, 2015).

Each of these different possible responses to demographic changes *have* happened to a degree, and each *will likely happen* in the future. Of course there are limits to how far each can go, both in terms of why things are made in China and not Tajikistan, but also because the world only needs so many semiconductors (do you really need your belt buckle to be able to access the internet?). Indeed, there is even an argument that the current era may be unique in human history, where the 'stars have aligned' in terms of cheap labour and cheap resources all being 'in the right place', allowing for a global economic boom (prior to 2008) and, if you will, the proliferation of a multitude of goods and services that may have been undervalued. For instance, we have recently undervalued clothes and the real cost of the energy and cheap labour input required to produce them. Much the same can be said of many other manufactured goods, hence the throwaway society. Conversely, we may well have overvalued lawyers and their advice, accountants and their requirements, and advertisers and all that they produce!

Here is where we feel that demography really matters. We tend to think of 'demography as destiny' because it gives us an easy way to conceptualize the future. It means we don't have to think about just how complicated the recent history of the global economy has been, and just how complex, unpredictable and different it is likely to be in the future. Using demography, we can boil it down to a soundbite. China = ageing = declining = screwed; India = younger = bigger = better. And this can be repeated and insinuated for many other countries in the world. Yet of course demography is just one part of this extraordinarily complex machine, made up of what at times can feel like an infinite number of moving parts. And, of course, the demographic component is not even fixed! We have already seen that past demographic trends have been profoundly affected by changes in the global economy, therefore we must assume that they will continue to be in the future. In other words, the two-way relationship between demography and 'everything else' merely serves to add another layer of complexity.

Alternative projections

Since we are adding complexity in this book, why not go a little further as we bring this chapter to an end? Every couple of years the UNPD – the UN body that produces the global estimates taken so seriously by so many – updates its estimates by pooling information and by making a series of assumptions. Figure 7.4 shows the UN projections of 'change in change' published in 2011 and 2015. This is also called the second derivative of change, but it is easier to think of it as the rate of acceleration or deceleration in population growth. It may sound complex but it is not. What is tells us, however, is complex.

The 2011 UNPD estimates suggested that in some years in the 1960s the annual global increase in population had *itself* increased by up to nearly 4 million people a year. In 1966 the global population was estimated to have reached 3,400,800,000 people, having risen by 68 million people in a year. It had risen by 64 million people the year before and thus the change in change was about 4 million (3.7 million to be precise). The 2011-based estimates suggested deceleration had occurred briefly in the 1950s, for a few years in the 1970s, for longer recently, and that it will be 'the new normal' in future. Deceleration means that the increase in global population is not increasing as fast as it was before. One reason why deceleration might have occurred at these times is that the population of childbearing age worldwide was a little low in the 1950s due to fewer births in the 1920s and '30s, was low again in the 1970s due to fewer births in the '50s, and so on and on. And all the time that this is occurring there is the overall reduction in fertility worldwide to consider, causing the overall trend in both graphs in Figure 7.4 to be downwards.

The second graph in Figure 7.4 shows not just what they now think will happen in future, but also the change in just four years in what they think has happened over the past sixty years! The differences may appear small in a world context, the odd million in a world population of billions, but they have an extremely large impact on projections. If we don't know that there has been any 'change in change' then we will assume that things will continue to change as

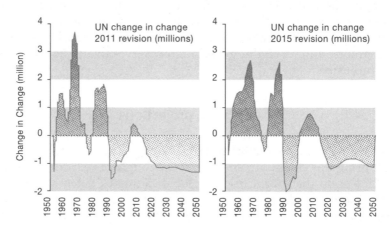

Figure 7.4   Acceleration and deceleration of global population, 1950–2050, UN estimates made in 2011 and 2015

Source: Original analysis by the authors using data derived from the United Nations Population Division 2011 and 2015, World Population Prospects.

they always have done. These figures reveal whether the accelerator or the brake is being pressed on global population growth. The immediate effect is fairly slight, which is why it has been so hard to measure this effect. However, the long-term effects can be huge. Reduced fertility suggests that world population will peak earlier than previously thought. The acceleration and deceleration figures imply this directly – because of the overall downward trend they reveal. They tell us that global population will likely soon peak and they can be used to estimate when that will happen. Using both the 2011 and 2015 UN best-estimates of the past and the future, the trends can be seen sloping downwards in Figure 7.4. What matters most is whether they are sloping downwards fast enough to properly reflect what has actually happened in the last sixty or seventy years.

Anyone can work out the numbers shown in Figure 7.4. You simply take the world population estimates published by the UNPD for each year, subtract one year from the next year to calculate change (in millions), then subtract that change from the change the next year to calculate 'change in change' (again in millions), to calculate the past estimated and future predicted rates of population acceleration and deceleration and how those estimates and projections changed between the years 2011 and 2015. To put it another way: the change in population between any two years is the later year's population less the earlier years' population. If the change is worked out for the next pair of years then the 'change in change' is the later change less the earlier change.

In less than five years, because of the slight alterations shown in Figure 7.4, the UN revised its projection of the world population for the year 2050 to 9.73bn, up from the 9.31bn it had predicted in 2011. However, Figure 7.4 shows that plotting the change in change in its estimates suggested that the drop between the most recent peaks of population growth acceleration, 1986 and 2007, had been steeper than was realized in 2011. New information had come to light between 2011 and 2015 to suggest that the deceleration in population growth, a deceleration that reached its maximum in 1991, was by 2015 *even greater* than was realized in 2011. But that needs to happen again, by the years 2020 to 2022, by a deceleration of –2 million a year (not –1), if we are to be on track for population stability this century. This would be a relatively tiny change and one that is very hard to measure even retrospectively. And, of course, these changes are all about revisions to the UNPD's middle, central, estimate.

Figure 7.5 shows the effects of the revisions on the change in population taking into account the deceleration now expected each year.

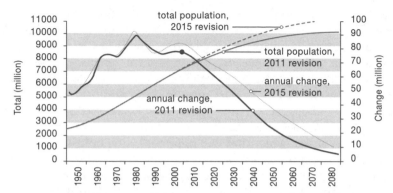

Figure 7.5 UN-predicted annual change in global population
projections, 1950–2090, UN estimates made in 2011 and 2015

Source: Original analysis by the authors using data derived from the United Nations
Population Division 2016, World Population Prospects.

These annual changes are shown by thick and dotted lines measured
by the right-hand scale of the graph in millions – they are simply the
size of the global rise in population thought to have occurred each
year in the past and thought to be most likely to occur each year in
the future up to 2090. The overall global population estimates produced by both the 2011 and 2015 revisions are shown by solid and
dashed lines and follow the left-hand scale of the graph, also showing
the count in millions, with 10,000 million being 10 billion.

   The new 2015 UN medium projection is for 11.2bn people by the
year 2100, up 1.1bn from its 2011 projection. It was revised upwards
because the global human population was thought to be rising by
around 8 million more a year by 2014 than had been projected in
2011. But what if the UN central projections made in 2011 and 2015
are both wrong? They may have missed a key trend that should be
projected forward but is not being taken into account – baby booms.
Figure 7.6 shows the UN data up to 2011 and 2015 and then an
alternative projection produced especially for this book. The new UN
figures, revised backwards as well as forwards by the UNPD, suggest
a slightly slower decline with peaks now in 1966, 1986 and 2007. So
what if the next peak is in 2032, twenty-five years on from the last
one? That is a sensible period of time to expect because it is roughly
the length of a modern human generation.

   Figure 7.6 was drawn by taking the actual change-in-change
estimates worked out from the published UN data up until 2011
and 2015 respectively and projecting those actual changes forward.

These are shown in the Figure and can be seen to differ slightly from each other. They are exactly the same trends as shown in Figure 7.4 above, up until those respective dates. After those dates the trends for previous years have been use to project forward in a different way: to project a series of rises and falls in the acceleration and deceleration of population change as if *the past was to be repeated into the future.*

If we are seeing a series of baby booms and busts working their way forwards in time then these projections would be more realistic than the current UN projections, which assume that each country in the world will head towards a two children per woman norm. The future will probably not work out as either of our alternative projections, or as the UN projections, suggest; it may not even be somewhere in between. But it is useful to look at a wider range of projections than those currently most widely discussed. What we show is what will happen if the UN demographers have missed a trick and not seen the pattern of global baby booms for what it really is. In other words it is what happens if fertility falls faster than is currently generally assumed likely.

If the low fertility seen in many cities in Asia today becomes more widespread, then our alternative projections of change in change shown in Figure 7.6 will be nearer the mark. We will also be able to tell which projections are better in the decade ahead of us to 2027, as our alternative suggestions suggest a rapid divergence from what

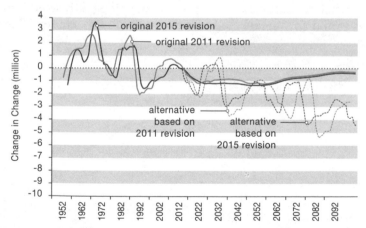

Figure 7.6 Alternative predictions of change in change, 1950–2100, based on UN estimates made in 2011 and 2015

Source: United Nations Population Division 2011 and 2015, World Population Prospects; Dorling, 2013a; and calculations by the authors.

the UN currently predicts for those years. The two 'alternative' lines drawn in Figure 7.6 are what we consider to be plausible alternatives to the 2011 and 2015 (current) UNPD median projection for annual change in change in global population growth. The UN lines move towards 0 change in change because the UN projects future stability and a move towards a two-child norm. Our lines show the alternatives if the past up-and-down patterns are simply repeated in future. What we are suggesting is that deceleration may carry on for a little longer than the UN demographers envisage.

Finally, in presenting these alternative scenarios, Figure 7.7 shows what the annual change in global population would be under the two alternative projections for the 2011 and 2015 change-in-change scenarios. Under the 2011 scenario global population peaks at just over 9 billion in the 2060s and then falls. This scenario was first published by one of the authors in his *Population 10 Billion* (Dorling, 2013a). The second alternative scenario uses exactly the same methodology of projecting change in change forward, but is derived from the latest 2015 UN best projections. Global population would then peak a little higher, but still not quite reach 10 billion, and could be as low as 8 billion by 2100. That is only just over eighty years away from today.

If something closer to the new alternative scenarios happens then world population will peak at 9.72 billion in 2066 rather than 9.27 billion. Very slight increases in births now have large effects, as now do very small reductions. Further increases in longevity would matter also, as would any unexpected falls in future life expectancy. The one

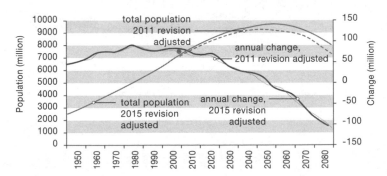

Figure 7.7 UN-predicted annual change in global population projections, 1950–2100, UN estimates made in 2011 and 2015

Source: United Nations Population Division 2011 and 2015, World Population Prospects; Dorling, 2013a; and calculations by the authors.

thing we don't have to worry too much about when making global projections is migration. It is very unlikely that many people will leave planet earth in the next eight decades and even more unlikely that humans from elsewhere will arrive! But other than that – the future is in our hands, and it could be very different from what is so often prophesized.

Conclusion: no such thing as destiny

To return to the quote from Casanova that appeared at the very start of this book, this, then, is where we see that demography matters. By examining more deeply the dynamics *behind* demographic change, we can move towards a much more holistic, two-way understanding of what people do in relation to the ever-changing world they inhabit. Again, this can help us to hold a mirror up to society to see how different elements of the world in which we live, work, fall in love, learn, vote, protest, hate all serve to shape who we are and what we do. In doing so, we can think more effectively about whether this is a world we like. Are we really meeting our aspirations? In short, demographic thinking can turn our focus to a 'human-centred' world rather than one governed by macroeconomic models, distant capitalists and trade bodies. In this way, we believe, it can give us the best chance of determining our own destiny, rather than surrendering it to someone, something or everything else.

To conclude, consider Figure 7.8. If such change in human development is possible in just twenty-five years, why do we not believe that change just as remarkable as this is not possible in the next fifty or 100 years? Whatever does happen will not be down to chance. There could be 'just' 8 or 9 billion of us in less than a century's time, not 10 or 11 billion – or far more or far less. There is no one today on the planet who knows with any certainty what will transpire in the lifetimes of many babies born this year. That can be both frightening and exhilarating. Our future is in our hands.

Demographically and economically the world has never changed as quickly as it is changing now. Figure 7.8 shows that in 1990, the year of peak births in human history, the majority of the planet's 5 billion people lived in countries of extreme poverty – labelled as 'low human development' by UNPD. Just ten years later, as the millennium turned, the by then 6 billion people on the planet mostly lived in countries of medium or higher 'development' – because very poor countries had become less poor. This is one key reason *why* fertility

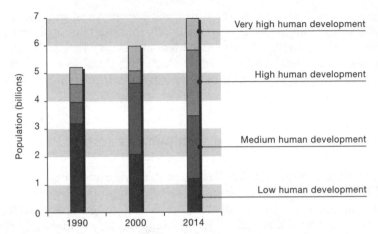

Figure 7.8 The population of the world by human development,
1990–2014 (billions)

Source: Human Development Report 2015, © United Nations 2015, reprinted
with the permission of the United Nations.

has dropped so rapidly. By 2014 more people were living in countries of high and very high 'development' – in other words, average income, average education and average health were much better. A large part of that population growth, the increase in people, was due to ageing, not a great increase in births. Look again at Figure 7.8 to see *how quickly* the proportion of people living in very poor countries is shrinking – as there are fewer and fewer such countries, and as fewer babies are born in those countries than were born just twenty-four years earlier. Then try to imagine what all this might mean for the kind of global economy we will have in the near future. It has to be very different to what we see as normal today.

8

Population and Politics

In 2016 demography was on the political frontline. Donald Trump became the Republican nominee in the US presidential election and promised to build a wall across the Mexican border. Once elected Trump insisted he would keep that promise, and that the Mexicans would pay for it; the Mexican president refused to meet him. In the UK the 'Brexit' referendum campaign resulted in a 52:48 majority (among the 72 per cent of registered voters who voted) for leaving the European Union. The main issue in the referendum was immigration. After Trump was elected in the US, the UK prime minister Theresa May intimated that she was going for a 'hard Brexit' that would allow as little in-migration as possible. In China the already weakened one-child policy was relaxed further, as China's political leaders began to look into their demographic future with growing concern. Across Europe mortality rates were no longer improving as quickly as they had been, perhaps due to the Great Recession that began in 2008, but perhaps also because the falls in previous decades had been partly due to factors that mostly improved life chances at very young and intermediate ages, but much less so in old age. However, the greatest setback in mortality in Europe was in the UK (2020 Delivery, 2017). Politicians worried even more about the cost of pensions and duly raised pension ages across the continent, despite the slowdown in mortality improvements. Meanwhile, across much of Africa and Asia, fertility declines accelerated, and in Latin America rates of economic inequality fell dramatically as a new politics swept the continent. But that new politics stalled abruptly in 2016 in the most populous country, Brazil, in which fertility had already fallen earlier. Across the world uncertainty about the immediate future was the common theme. Having fewer young people in future might well require a very different politics, as well as a new economics. The era of population slowdown may also be one of more controlled economic growth and more careful inspection of how power is distributed. Not least because it is also the era in which we will learn what the repercussions of enhanced human-induced global warming will be.

Politics, demography and history

As we explained in Chapter 4, the world changed demographically after 1492, when the Old World met the New. The population of the New World encountered new diseases and then colonization. The South of the Old World also suffered. Africa was depopulated through slavery and the ravages that accompanied it. Europe began to grow relatively much richer from the plunder of silver. First it was Spain and Portugal, then the trading city of Venice, and later Amsterdam where money concentrated and people flocked. What is now the Netherlands experienced a 58 per cent population increase in the sixteenth century and had become the richest country on earth by the seventeenth century. The UK population experienced a 57 per cent rise in the sixteenth century, and England, Wales and Scotland (much less so Ireland) went on to become the richest set of countries on the planet. Due to the previous demographic disaster in the Americas, and the subsequent overspill from Europe, what became the US increased in population in the eighteenth century by almost 900 per cent, following two centuries of population decline! The overthrow of the Ming dynasty in China in the seventeenth century, and the slow growth of Japan – these are just two of the many complex stories that lie behind the bare figures shown in Table 8.1.

Politics and demography are not separable. Politics concerns the gaining and exercising of power, altering what other people can do. Issues of political concern have featured in every chapter of this book so far, but here we will focus on them directly. The brief introduction above hints at just how big a topic this is. With historical hindsight it is possible to go into greater depth and, when talking about events that occurred many centuries ago, appear to be far more impartial. But in truth, there are still many different ways in which those events can be interpreted. Few historians dwell sufficiently on the demographic changes that accompanied the sweeping political changes the world has seen since 1492. Population did not grow everywhere, and declined in many areas, especially where slavery grew; it tended to

Table 8.1. World population summary, 1500–1820

	Population (millions)		Population change in century (%)	Population change in century (%)
	1500	1820	16th	17th
Netherlands	1	2	58%	27%
United Kingdom	4	21	57%	39%
China	103	381	55%	−14%
Total Asia	284	710	33%	6%
Total Western Europe	57	133	29%	10%
India	110	209	23%	22%
Japan	15	31	20%	46%
Total Africa	47	74	19%	10%
United States	2	10	−25%	−33%
Total Latin America	18	22	−51%	40%
Mexico	8	7	−67%	80%
Peru	4	1	−68%	0%
Total everywhere else	31	92	23%	20%
Total World Population	438	1042	27%	9%

Source: Data from Angus Maddison's estimates, available on www.worldmapper.org.

grow fastest either where it had previously fallen the most or where the most political power was concentrated.

The word 'statistics' has its origin in the word 'state' because it was the state that first required demographic accounting. The first statistics were not too concerned with people, at least not with the people who didn't count. The Domesday Book did a better job of counting ploughs than peasants. The record made of England in 1086 was for the purpose of taxation, so it recorded the land area of estates, details of the nobles that lived there, and the arable land being farmed. There was very little industry back then. The Book was compiled twenty years after William the Conquer invaded England. He suspected the landowners of tax evasion (some things don't change!). Recent archaeological findings have suggested that the population of the UK was, in fact, far higher than that supposedly recorded in the Domesday Book (Wright, 2017).

The first modern population census was not completed until 1703. The king of Denmark wanted to know the name, age and social status of all the inhabitants of Iceland (UNESCO, 2017). Again the reasons for collecting the demographic statistics were political. The same is true of the first American census of 1790, which counted the number of 'Free White males of 16 years and upward [to assess the country's industrial and military potential]; Free White males under 16 years; Free White females; All other free persons; [and] Slaves' (USCB, 2017). Again the reason was political. The War of Independence ended in 1782 and the new country did not know what it was actually capable of, either militarily or proto-industrially.

The first UK census was taken in 1801 in the wake of fears following the publication of Malthus's *Essay on the Principle of Population*, first published in 1798. The 1801 census included the numbers of inhabited and uninhabited houses, of baptisms and burials, and the population in each parish:

> The first census of England and Wales revealed a total population for England and Wales of 8.87 million, which, together with a count of just under half a million military personnel, seamen and convicts who were not included in figures for the census itself, gave an estimate of 9.4 million ... close to the previous year's estimate of 9.2 million. (National Archives, 2017)

We could carry on and discuss the first French census (1772), or how the censuses that were held in Germany in the 1930s were used to determine the proportion of the population who were Jewish, and even the areas from which Jewish people would be rounded up in the Holocaust. We could go back to that census in the Roman province of Judea referred to in the New Testament (over the timing of which, admittedly, there is some confusion[1]). People were being counted because they had to render unto Caesar what Caesar decided they owed. The parallels with population enumeration and registration in the Middle East today can easily be made.

The politics of democracy can be traced back to the very first empires and states, with their concerns over whether the people are paying their taxes or are producing enough men of fighting age or enough women to give birth to enough men (and women!) – or too many, and to how the slave population is surviving and reproducing, or not. Much political incorrectness can be found in demographic data: so many of our past prejudices are recorded there, from the labelling of people as imbeciles and cripples (in UK censuses of the past) through to not recognizing gay partnerships until very recently. And someone, almost certainly, will criticize this book – written by two middle-class white men based all their working lives in elite universities – for perpetuating the binary division of humanity into male and female. At this point maybe a cartoon helps, one drawn by our

Figure 8.1   Basic biology
Source: Ella Furness, when aged 14.

friend Ella Furness when she was aged 14 and was bored at school. It explains why demographers still use the 'binary' of male and female even if in our social lives it frequently should not matter, but regrettably often does. Thankfully we have finally stopped telling the joke about being 'broken down by age and sex'...

Ella was bored because she had to be at school and her school that day was boring. She had to be at school because the state decreed it. The state decrees much more than that. The state and the organized religions that predated states have claimed political ownership of people for millennia. People could be subjects of a monarch. Suicide is a crime against the state as you are the property of the state. Abortion is a crime or a sin depending on the rules of the time and place you are in – dictating if the foetus is, or is not, yours. Contraception can or cannot be used due to similar slowly changing rules; and, of course, it was not so easily available as it is now to most people. Nor were they taught about sex, often for political reasons. And voluntary euthanasia is still a crime in most countries.

Politics and sex often mix – who can have sex, when they can have it, with whom; who can become a parent, and who can/must have an abortion. Singapore has been mentioned earlier in relation

to its policies intended to encourage some people rather than others
to have children. It is a country with one of the *lowest* rates of early
neonatal deaths in the world (Dorling, 2013b). Superficially this suggests that people in Singapore enjoyed the lowest rate of such suffering in the world. And Singapore certainly has a first-rate health-care
system. But before celebrating this 'fact' please consider the denominator. Demographers are always worrying about the denominator.
Who were the 'people' being measured?

Japan and Singapore were jointly ranked first among 200 countries as having the lowest recorded early neonatal mortality rate

Table 8.2. Countries with the lowest and highest early neonatal mortality in
the world in the year 2000

Rank	Territory	Value
1	Mauritania	52
2	Liberia	48
3	Iraq	46
4	Afghanistan	45
5	Cote d'Ivoire	44
6	Sierra Leone	42
7	Nigeria	40
7	Mali	40
7	Angola	40
10	Pakistan	38
...		
185	France	2
185	Germany	2
185	Republic of Korea	2
185	Italy	2
185	Spain	2
185	Belgium	2
185	Sweden	2
185	Czech Republic	2
199	Singapore	1
199	Japan	1

Source: Data from the World Health Organization's 2005 World Health Report.
Note: An early neonatal death is when a child dies during the first week of his or her
life. Fourteen territories reported two early neonatal deaths per 1,000 live births
(Austria, Norway, Finland, Iceland, Monaco and San Marino are not shown); four
reported thirty-eight deaths per 1,000 births (Ethiopia, Guinea and the Central
African Republic are not shown). Those where the most births happened are shown.
See: http://www.worldmapper.org/posters/worldmapper_map260_ver5.pdf for
further information.

in the world in the year 2000. While this is not surprising in the case of Japan, given what else is known about that country, it is odd that in Singapore, a country with very high income and wealth inequality, infant health should appear to be so very good. In 2009, for every 1,000 infants born alive in Singapore, only two died before their first birthday. Table 8.2 shows that just one in 1,000 died in the year 2000 in their very first week of life. Singapore reported the lowest rate of infant mortality in the world at that time and it still does today. To begin to discover why it appears to do so well you have to delve beneath the headline statistics. The key is to look at the denominator, which is what the rate is calculated out of. Here that denominator is 'live births'. If a birth never occurs then it is not included in the statistics, but not all the women living in Singapore are 'free' to give birth. Many of the poorest women in the country are the maids who work for around one in five of all middle-class households as personal cleaners, shoppers and childcarers. Most of them are 'guest-workers', who are not citizens but come from abroad. As guest-workers they have no right to remain in the country. Every three months the maids must take a pregnancy test. If they are found to be pregnant, they are deported (see Text Box). And as of 2015 it was still illegal for maids to become pregnant: 'Pregnancy and childbirth are prohibited under a domestic worker's work pass. Under the law, employers are technically required to report pregnancies to the Ministry of Manpower, leading to cancellation of the work permit and the worker's deportation' (Sian, 2015).

In total, migrant workers make up about a quarter of the population of Singapore and are mainly at the bottom of the income range, where you'd expect infant mortality to be highest. This section of the population is effectively removed from the picture by deportation and the threat of it. Coercing poorer women into not becoming pregnant, and removing them from a country when they do, are ways in which infant mortality can be reduced. Babies who might have died are never actually born, are secretly aborted, or are born abroad and count as a death abroad if they die. This is the reason infant mortality rates in Singapore are so very low.

Things do very slowly get better, but not yet as regards the rights of maids in Singapore to become mothers. In March 2012 a plan was announced to try to at least allow the 200,000 domestic workers of Singapore a few hours off work a week. In 2012, 88 per cent of the maids worked seven days a week (Hodal, 2012). Their pay currently ranges from between 20c and 60c an hour in a country where average (mean) GDP per capita was over $40,000 by 2010. The mean

Maid Employer's nightmare – Asia One News, Tuesday, 23 December 2008, verbatim:

Under Singapore law, if a maid gets pregnant, she will get repatriated immediately or employers stand to lose their $5,000 security deposit.

However, for Madam W L Lim's maid (Nina), regular medical tests failed to indicate her pregnancy and eventually she gave birth to a premature baby boy.

In the local newspaper report, Madam Lim was shocked when she was rang up by the police who told her Nina just gave birth. It did not occur to her that this is possible given that the doctor cleared her tests just two months ago. But nothing prepared her for the size of the hospital bill.

The sizeable bill of $5,500 for her maid's Caesarean delivery on Dec 11, ballooned to $67,000 for the hospitalisation of Nina's 27-week-old premature baby boy, now warded at the KK Women's and Children's Hospital (KKH) Intensive Care Unit.

It was like a maid employer's nightmare come true. According to Dr Juliana Abu-Wong, a gynaecologist and obstetrician with more than 10 years' experience, the pregnancy tests currently administered comprise a urine check and an abdominal examination which are 90 to 95 per cent accurate. 'So how is it that the doctor failed to detect my maid was four months pregnant?' Madam Lim questioned.

A blood test for pregnancy would have been more accurate. Blood testing is not made mandatory to keep costs down for employers. But to Madam Lim, this added cost is a small price to pay to avert the 'stress' now brought about by Nina's birth.

In Madam Lim's defense, lawyer Mr Mark Goh said that the undertaking was signed by Nina's friend Ms Shushma, a maid. 'Though the rules require the employer to bear the full cost of the maid's medical care, nowhere does it say the employer should bear the medical cost of her kin,' said Mr Goh.

The hospital's stance is clear as it will not pursue Ms Shushma for payment.

Said Mr Johnny Quah, KKH's chief financial officer, 'Part of the admission process includes financial counselling. As the staff was unable to contact Nina's employer, she explained the estimated charges to Nina's friend and the signature obtained was more as an indication that she understood the charges and would convey it to Nina's employer.'

Source: Asia One News, 2008.

average income tells us very little in a very unequal country, just as does the apparently extremely low infant mortality rate.

You can't take statistics such as national averages at face value; you need to examine them a little first. You should be especially suspicious when issues of politics might be involved. Looking out for oddities such as these is very often revealing as it is not always due to error (Palen, 1986). Often there are clues. In the now widely publicized graph shown in Figure 8.2, all the significant outliers have their own specific reasons for being where they are.

Behind the issue of fertility control lies the murky world of eugenics. We have not mentioned eugenics yet in this book. We thought it better to leave it to the end. Aldous Huxley's *Brave New World* was written as a criticism of eugenics and made the phrase 'Alpha, Beta and Gamma children' well known as a criticism of the idea that children are born with greatly varying abilities and that these abilities are closely related to the supposed abilities of their parents. Eugenics is part of the miserable history of demography that is often hidden today. It is hidden because it is still too recent a memory. Eugenic ideas came to the fore after the publication of Darwin's *Origin of Species*, when a few people became inclined to look for supposedly inherited biological justifications for why the lower social orders were lower. 'Survival of the fittest' was given as an explanation for the survival of the British class structure. People supposedly rose to the top in 'civilized' human society because they and their offspring were fitter, more able, more suited to lead. Others were seen as more

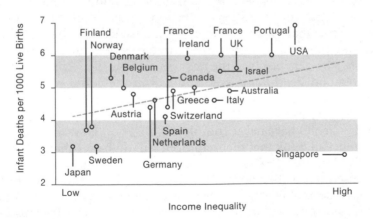

Figure 8.2   Infant mortality rates versus income inequality in affluent countries

Source: Wilkinson and Pickett, 2009.

feeble and destined to be led, and at the extreme as people who should be exterminated for the collective future good of the race. Sterilization of people thought of as feeble-minded was common in Scandinavian countries through to the 1970s, and of black people in institutions in the Southern US states up until around the same time.

All of this, of course, was greatly at odds with the actual theory of natural selection. That theory is about entire species, not about individuals. A species mixes and its members become remarkably similar to each other because of that mixing. Occasionally there is an adaptation in a species due to genetic mutation. If the adaptation is advantageous it is likely to soon spread throughout the species, which is why almost all humans have a fully opposable thumb.[2] If it is not advantageous then those members with the adaptation are less likely to survive and the quirk peters out. The most recent frequently cited possible human adaptation due to natural selection concerned the increased tendency of African-Americans to hypertension. This was attributed to genes that made their forebears, forcibly taken by slave ship to the Americas, more likely to survive the passage. However, even the veracity of this idea has been doubted for at least ten years (Kaufman, 2006).

Eugenics can be traced back at least as far as Plato, who suggested selective mating to produce a guardian class, and talked of children as having souls of gold, silver, bronze or iron kinds. Much later, boosted by Francis Galton (a half-cousin of Darwin) in the nineteenth century, theories of eugenics became widespread, with even progressive politicians believing in it until the middle of the twentieth century. Today the opposite is true, and no self-respecting academic would argue that there are marked differences in the population separating the weak from the strong in terms of mental ability which are passed on genetically to the next generation. The American biologist Raymond Pearl hammered the nail in the coffin of that theory in 1927 when he wrote about Shakespeare, Lincoln and Pasteur and their parents (Pearl, 1927a, 1927b). However, the assumptions behind eugenics have never completely died out. How many successful people still think that their children will do better than other people's children due to their inherited genetic advantages, rather than admitting that, if they do well, it is due to all the other advantages they have been able to give them, or often just a case of sheer luck? Even if some quirks of mental ability are inherited, we now know that

> a myriad of Mendelian influences of individually tiny effect contribute to the heritability of intelligence ... [the] shuffling of such

tiny Mendelian effects could, Pearl said, 'be relied on, I think, to produce in the future, as it has in the past, Shakespeares, Lincolns, and Pasteurs, from socially and economically humble origins'. (Davey Smith, 2012: 238)[3]

The eugenicists were unable to see that the economic element was the most significant factor holding back the vast majority of potential future writers, politicians and inventors.

At this point we could talk about the bell curve theory of ability, and the social attitudes that prevailed at and before its inception.[4] We could discuss why racial prejudice led the British to allow famine to become deeper and deeper in Ireland and often in India, which suffered regularly from famine under British rule, or the extent to which US society is still divided along racial grounds due to racism. But we suspect you, the reader, would be sympathetic to all this already, so let us move on to more recent issues: first the events of 2016, and then the demographic politics of schooling in rich countries and what might actually most affect 'ability' today.

The danger of demography

If this book achieves anything, it will be to have illustrated that the implications of making political capital out of population projections can be dangerous and that their misuse to create fear is often far from a harmless political tactic. This was made evident most dramatically by the result of the 2016 EU referendum in the UK. For decades some UK politicians had been warning that immigration was too high, without ever explaining why this was so and what would happen were rates of immigration to fall or rates of emigration to rise. Social problems that had nothing to do with immigration and a great deal to do with high and rising economic inequality and a lack of investment in infrastructure were blamed on the migrants, and so when it came to the vote, 52 per cent of those who voted effectively voted to curtail immigration. It was the most salient issue of the referendum (Clarke, Goodwin and Whitely, 2017).

As Figure 8.3 illustrates, most of those in the UK who voted to leave the EU lived in the South of England, although a slightly higher proportion in the less populous North of England voted that way. The vote in Wales was almost identical to the UK average, while Northern Ireland, Scotland and London were home to a majority of

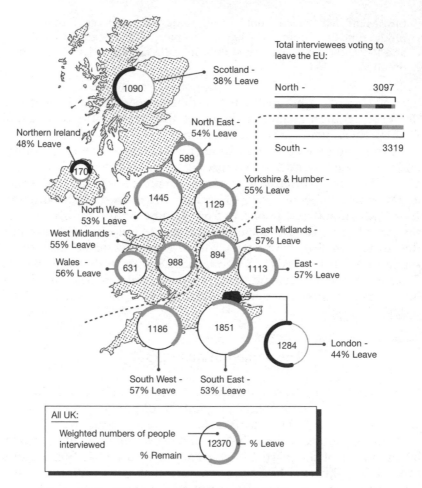

Figure 8.3 The geography of the UK 2016 referendum vote

Source: Lord Ashcroft and calculations by the authors.

Note: 12,370 people polled on referendum day after voting and weighted
for sample bias.

Remain voters. Figure 8.3 highlights the denominator (number of
voters) as well as the numerator in the voting equation by the sizes of
the circles. The first step in thinking more carefully demographically
is often to consider how many people are involved in any trend, not
just where that trend is most common.

The message the British people gave, when so many voted Leave,
was that they so disliked migration into the UK that they were prepared to leave the EU and all the benefits of membership to bring

that rate of immigration down. All the forecasts and warnings of rising population in this 'crowded island' had the effect of making people vote in a way that will very likely alter the future population size of the UK, although that might not come about for the reasons those who voted Leave were led to believe.

The UK suddenly became a much less attractive place to migrate to for those who had a wide choice over where in Europe they might live and work. So we should expect fewer 'highly skilled' migrants (including well-qualified doctors and teachers) to arrive in a place that is clearly so unwelcoming to them. More citizens of other European countries who were living in the UK in 2016 are expected to leave the UK than normally do because they now feel so unwelcome. Again, it will be those who have the most choices in the European labour market who are most likely to make such a choice not to live in the UK, and this long before any change to immigration policy is actually enacted.

The vote may also trigger other migration effects, often not forecast during the referendum debate. When during the 1960s the rights of British citizens living in most of the former British colonies to enter the UK were revoked this resulted in a great influx of people seeking to get in before the movement bans came into effect, including the elderly relatives of many people already living in the country. Mortality rates in the UK rose abruptly as a result. This time elderly British citizens living elsewhere in Europe may also be more likely to return to the UK in the months after the vote, fearing that their eligibility for free health care in other countries will soon be lost. It would not be rash to forecast that, in the near future, the UK will be home to fewer young, hard-working migrants, while also having a higher and frailer elderly population than would have otherwise been the case.

The most important drivers of immigration are almost always economic. If there are fewer economic opportunities in the UK in future, more people (who can) will emigrate and fewer will arrive or stay long if they do arrive. By projecting ever continuing high future immigration and then triggering a referendum over concerns about this, those who were making such claims may well alter the course of future demographic trends but not see the social and economic benefits that they imagined and promised would come with less in-migration. Be careful when you play with projections.

The former UK Chancellor, George Osborne, warned in private against holding a referendum. Given that he lost his job due to the result, he was right in that forecast not just for the overall effect of the vote on the economy (the pound lost a fifth of its value within days of the vote) but also for his personal economic fortune. This may also include his personal wealth, depending on how the housing market reacts and how sales fare in his family company that sells expensive wallpaper to affluent people. However, in the short term he secured a job with the American financial firm Blackrock and recorded an income of near to a million pounds in the year after being sacked as Chancellor. Clearly he thought he might well need the extra money in future. If the affluent become a little less affluent and their homes fall in value as a result of the vote, then they may have to make do with somewhat cheaper wallpaper in future. They may have little choice.

George Osborne, however, was himself not immune from meddling in population policy prior to the fateful vote. In November 2015, numerous faith leaders, led mainly by Christian churches, denounced Osborne's new policy of limiting welfare benefits to the first two children in any family as being 'fundamentally anti-family' (Bingham, 2015). Pro- or anti-family, the idea that certain, mainly homegrown, children should be defined as less deserving from birth flew in the face of natural justice. Osborne's policy was not addressed to the issue of migration to Britain but designed to encourage a particular group of people to have fewer children by threatening them with worsening poverty should they have a third or fourth child (Stone, 2016). Was he worried that there would be too many children in the UK in future, or just too many children among poorer families?[5]

At the same time, death and illness rates in the UK were rising rapidly. The graphs in Figure 8.4 show just how abruptly self-reported illness rose in the UK while Osborne was Chancellor, and those rates rose even more quickly during his final years in the job (not shown). Between two of the years shown, the method of collecting the data changed slightly from paper-based survey to computer-collected data, but that does not account for the overall decline in self-reported health. The year 2015 saw the largest absolute rise in deaths and rise in the death rate in the UK for any year since 1940. Ironically, all that became evident only when official figures were released – coincidentally on the EU referendum day, 23 June 2016 (Dorling, 2016b). Few people commented at the time, this bad news being buried by even worse news.

This recent story of the UK shows how political policies affecting fertility, mortality and migration are all interlinked and can all have a toxic political effect if combined in a particular way. It was mainly the elderly who suffered the worsening health that accompanied

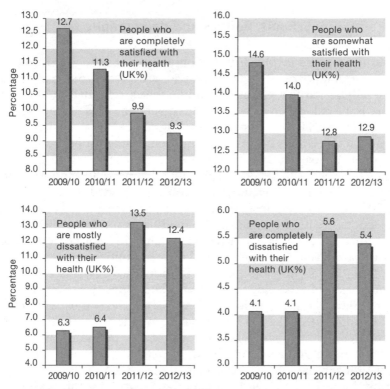

Figure 8.4 Trends in self-reported health used by ONS in annual well-being reporting, 2009–13

Source: ONS, derived from Understanding Society Survey.

Osborne's years in financial office. It was mainly the elderly who voted to Leave when told that so much would get better if they did. It was mainly the young who were subject to austerity and welfare cuts, but the elderly still relied on the young to look after them when they were ill, including many European migrants who worked in care homes and hospitals. Many care workers were overworked and stressed, on very low pay and, affected by cuts, sometimes having to take a second job to make ends meet. When the young are hit, those affected are not just the young. Care for the elderly when they need it most also suffers. Perhaps the elderly who were still fit enough to get to the polling stations in the May 2015 general election that returned a Conservative government thought that somehow all this wouldn't affect them personally, but 52,000 more elderly people in the UK died in the twelve months to July 2015 as compared to the twelve months before that.

Schools, politics and demography

Often the politics involved in demography is easy to see. If population projections are not carried out or are carried out badly, then there will be too few places in schools that are funded by the state. There is a small group of people who dislike the idea of state schools and think that all worthwhile schooling should be provided by the private sector. Others believe that children should simply be schooled at home; this particularly, in some countries, applying to girls. For those holding such beliefs, projecting the need for future school places on the basis of births and migration records is bad. It encourages the state to plan, instead of having parents plan for themselves. Projections are hard to make in the medium term, but projecting the need for school places just a few years ahead is not rocket science. When considering the connections between politics and demography we often jump from grand pictures to individual cases. For centuries the provision of schooling was not an issue, since there was none for most children, but in the last dozen or so decades most children in rich countries like the UK have been provided with school places up to later and later ages, and for most of that period the main issue was that more and more places were needed each year. From the early 1990s in the UK, that problem abated due to falling birth rates during the 1970s and 1980s. It is perhaps partly for this reason that the concern about simply providing enough places shifted towards a concern about what kind of education was being provided.

In the UK recently there has been a move to try to ensure that all *new* schools will be what are deceptively called 'free schools'. These are schools that are set up by groups of parents when they decide that there will not be enough provision for their children where they live, or where they dislike what is already on offer. The state will then fund the school, but will not *plan* for the school. If local parents do not have the wherewithal to take up these opportunities, and their children have to go to inadequate schools, then that will be the fault of the parents for not setting up a 'free school'. Of course, in areas of high population turnover this is very likely to happen, but then – so the political argument goes – a clever parent would avoid living in such an area by the time their children reach school age. It cannot be overstated how callous such an approach is, but it is one which very many parents in the UK have felt forced to take. Research in 2012 confirmed the long-suspected link between schools and house prices, and in 2016 headlines reported 'Top schools add up to 25% to house prices' and 'Living near a primary school rated "outstanding" by Ofsted adds almost £44k to house prices.'

If you believe that the state should not be taking on the role of planning for future school places then you may also believe that it is a huge waste of money if the state also continues to collect the kind of data it needs to accurately forecast the changing need for those places. You may even believe that such demographic work encourages a culture of complacency in which parents do not take on the responsibilities they should for their children's futures. In the UK and a handful of other affluent countries that have had a thriving private school sector, the elite has for generations taken on the responsibility of finding a school for their children. The market mechanism has been used to determine whether these schools open or shut and succeed or fail. A new school opens if someone is entrepreneurial enough to open one and it shuts if enough parents choose to no longer send their children there. There is no need for any state planning, since the market is said to produce excellence; but because most people do not have enough disposable income to pay for this 'excellence', those in the rest of society have to be helped in some way (Kirby, 2016).

In the 1950s the (then obscure) economist Milton Friedman argued that a system of school vouchers should be introduced so that parents who did not have enough money to use the private sector could behave as if they did, albeit with much smaller sums of money to play with. Money would follow the child to a school. School 'choice' should be opened up. Successful schools would be able to set a bar and only take children who appeared to be of sufficient academic ability. Unsuccessful schools would be found to be such because parents would choose not to send their children to them. There would have to be more school places than children for this market to work, but that would be a price worth paying for the overall increase in efficiency that would result as the 'survival of the fittest' mechanism came into play.

Sixty years later in the UK there are now more places than pupils in the school system. Most state-funded secondary schools will soon be what are called academy schools, and they have the power to turn away local children at age 16 if the school does not think they have achieved well enough, including children who have been at the school from age 11. Those children will then have to find a place in another school, but the money will follow them there. In this system, projections of the future demand for school places are seen as a distraction: the market will provide, not planners and demographers.

There are, however, many criticisms of this approach, and these have successfully prevented the majority of affluent countries from following Friedman's advice. One key problem is that parents and children are not informed consumers of education, and cannot be. Parents generally have only their own unique experience of schooling a whole generation ago to go on, and have very little personal knowledge of what other schools are like. Children, by definition, have no experience to draw on concerning what school might be like next year or the year after. Schooling is not like buying clothes; you do not get to learn from your mistakes. It is far better to try to ensure that every school is a good school and to minimize the distance children need to travel to school each day – particularly if this means that they walk or cycle to school rather than having to be driven.

Because of these critiques, the proponents of free schools and free choice of schools try to ensure that a huge amount of information on schools becomes available to inform consumers and the parents (or guardians) of the consumers. The same thing happens with university education. League tables become more common, and even surveys of pupil and student 'satisfaction' begin to be taken. Examination results become more and more important for the school.[6] The stress that this puts on children (and their teachers) is seen as immaterial.[7] Difficult children are excluded in order to improve a school's results. Ironically, despite pushing out demography from school planning, the number of statistics (much of which can be presented misleadingly) about schools multiplies greatly. But does this market produce better schools?

The two graphs in Figure 8.5 show the average performance at mathematics of children in affluent countries when tested around age 15/16 and again later at up to age 24. Each country is shown as a circle drawn in proportion to its population. The higher up on the graph a county is placed, the better its children and young adults perform at mathematics when taking a standardized international test. Almost exactly the same results are found when ability in problem-solving and literacy is measured (Stotesbury and Dorling, 2015). Have a look at the graphs and consider what they might be showing about the trends in education in recent decades in different countries. The further to the right a country is placed, the greater is the economic inequality in that country.

Children in the UK and US perform a little worse at maths at age 15/16, but as young adults they perform far worse and the relationship with inequality becomes far clearer. It is the more economically unequal countries such as the UK and US that have the most private

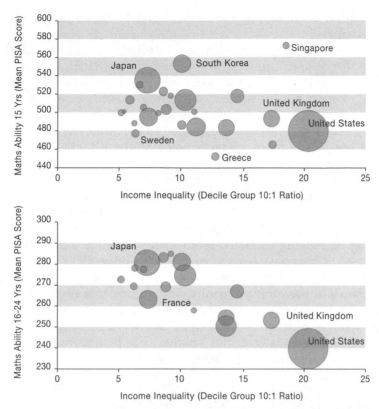

Figure 8.5 Ability in mathematics as measured in the most affluent
countries of the world in 2012, at ages 15 and then 16–24

Source: Stotesbury and Dorling, 2015.

schools and that have moved the furthest towards 'school choice' in
recent decades.

Demography affects education and the politics of education. The
numbers of students available to study at universities depends on the
birth rate eighteen years earlier. Increasing overseas recruitment can
compensate, in a more internationalized education 'market', for a
declining supply of students from a home country. However, it is far
easier to increase the proportion of home-country young adults who
can go to university. When university education is moved into the
private market then young adults become commodities and demography matters greatly to that market. Universities lobby for special
rules – student visas – that will allow them to profit from overseas
students' fees (or at least not make a loss overall). Thus the politics

of education alters immigration policy and international migration demography.

In the US, university fees influence migration patterns as they are less for in-state students whose other costs (such as housing) are often also lower than for those who cross state boundaries. In the UK, were it not for students migrating to study from the rest of Europe, then university student numbers in England would have fallen in recent years (they are expected to fall in the next few years). Part of the reason more students come to the UK than travel out to study is because UK universities advertise themselves so widely. Another reason is the EU free-movement-of-study regulations, which give everyone in the EU the right to come to the UK and take out a student loan (at least for as long as the UK remains a member of the EU or negotiates some new agreement). Student loan repayments can only be forcibly extracted from adults working within the UK. Thus the UK may have been attractive to overseas EU students who think that they might never have to pay the loan back.

Migration is the most politically contentious area of demography because it involves ideas of what is fair and unfair in relation to people who are often considered to be undeserving strangers. We will return to this issue later in this chapter, but political influences on fertility and mortality affect demography just as much.

Cultural identity, nationalism and population decline

The map in Figure 8.6 shows those countries that were experiencing natural population decline in 2002 with the area of each country drawn in proportion to the size of that decline. Russia is huge as it had so few births and so many deaths in that year. Eastern Europe is large and Western Europe is smaller with many countries, such as the UK, experiencing natural population growth then (and still today).

Detailed population statistics of the kind used to produce Figure 8.6 are a relatively recent invention because the political imperative to produce them has only recently been established, along with the resources needed to collect them. Collecting migration data, however, has historically been even more difficult. It began with a British statistician, William Farr, who worked in the Registrar General's Office for England and Wales from 1838 to 1879, and was responsible for the collection of official medical statistics. He established the first system for routinely recording causes of death alongside occupation, and was a Commissioner for the 1871 census.

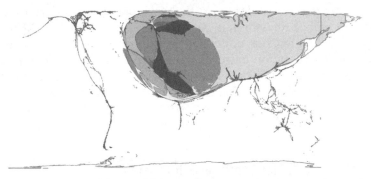

Figure 8.6   Areas of the world drawn in proportion to natural population
decline in the year 2002

Source: Worldmapper: http://www.worldmapper.org/display_extra.
php?selected=370.
Notes: This map shows only natural population decreases – places where there are
currently more deaths than births. Changes to population sizes due to migration
are not shown here. Populations in Western Europe are generally supported by
immigration. That has not been the case in Eastern Europe and Russia.

His observation that migration appeared to occur almost without
any definite law probably related to the apparently random fluctuations in the trend of annual net migration: calculated as the misfit
between counts of births, deaths and actual population changes in an
area over time, it does not involve knowing the separate in- and out-
migration data. Bearing in mind that Farr would have only observed
the first few decades of the 160-year time series shown in Figure 8.7
(below), his observation was remarkably astute.

Farr was President of the Royal Statistical Society from 1871
to 1873, and his remarks motivated Ernst Georg Ravenstein, an
employee of the Royal Geographical Society, to formulate his 'Laws
of Migration', published in the *Journal of the Royal Statistical Society*
in 1885 and 1889 (outlined by Grigg, 1977a, 1977b). While none
of Ravenstein's laws (e.g. that people will move from where things
are bad to where they are better) have been refuted, none of them
explain the apparently random fluctuations shown in net migration
trends to which Farr was most probably referring. This is unsurpris-
ing, as neither Farr nor Ravenstein had access to the data needed to
understand net migration balances, in particular a time series of good
quality data extending over at least 150 years (as presented in the
remaining figures in this chapter).

To end this chapter with a very current population dilemma, we
present a method for estimating migration over a birth cohort rather

than a time period. Building on the work one of us undertook a few years ago with Professor Jan Rigby (Dorling and Rigby, 2007), we suggest that in a few rich countries over the course of the last two centuries (or so) migration patterns have been roughly predictable given previous birth rates for these cohorts over the course of their lifetimes. With Jan's help we found that the apparent random fluctuations in net migration trends are due to short-term events and that their aggregate influence, over the lifetime of a cohort, tends to cancel out.

Net lifetime cohort migration

Existing work on cohort migration tends to emphasize the health or social circumstances of particular groups of migrants (Harding, 2004). Wider structural issues have been identified in an important body of work by Hatton and Williamson, who later observed cohort influences on migration in many countries with their proposition that 'The birthrate lagged 20 years stands as a proxy for the young adult cohort size. Its effect is positive, and it is large – suggesting that up to half of additional births ultimately spilled over into emigration' (Hatton and Williamson, 2002: 11).

Just over a decade ago, the issue of whether increased immigration may substitute for lower birth rates in affluent nations was raised (Rauhut, 2004; UNPD, 2001). On the general issue of cohort trends, Easterlin (1980) is credited with popularizing our knowledge of the importance of the specific year a person is born on their life chances,[8] but the importance of that year for general migration trends has not been widely recognized. Affluent countries have tended to replace low fertility with immigration – but that cannot continue for long due to worldwide population slowdown.

When net cohort migration is considered, the impact of changing birth cohort size on migratory volume and direction becomes very clear, at least for some of the most affluent countries in the world at a time of growing global populations. Net emigration, as shown in Figure 8.7, is the excess of emigrants over immigrants. Scaled by the second axis of the figure, this trend is far less amenable to simple description, occasionally extending beyond the bounds of the graph as it apparently fluctuates wildly. Had Farr lived beyond 1883 he might have detected an upwards trend in the nineteenth-century pattern, with emigration peaking in the years 1850, 1852, 1856, 1860, 1865, 1873, 1877, 1882, 1885, 1889 and 1897. Net emigration from England and Wales often very quickly became negative

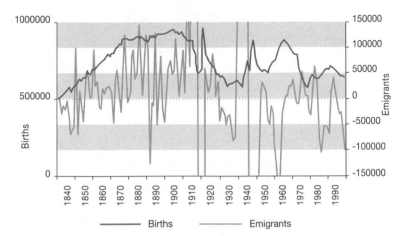

Figure 8.7   Annual births and net emigration, England and Wales,
1840–2000

Source: Dorling and Rigby, 2007.

Notes: Left axis: Total annual births. Right axis: Annual net emigration =
births – deaths – population change. Shown as positive when out-migration is higher
than in-migration to aid comparison with the trend in births.

between these dates as more people entered the country than left
it. The dates themselves are somewhat arbitrary as this trend of net
migration has a fractal quality whereby, on closer inspection, lesser
spikes appear between each major upward and downward spike
(Mandelbrot, 1982). In only one year in peacetime in the twentieth
century are the flows as large, and then of an influx of only 202,000
people in 1961. However, this record was exceeded with a figure of
223,000 for 2004 (Chappell, 2005) and then again several times in
the decade following that observation. Note that the most recent
peaks in net *emigration*, in 1974, 1981 and 1992, coincided with
periods of economic recession.

Figure 8.8 is similar to Figure 8.7, but here net migration, labelled
on the figure as 'emigrants', has not been measured over the course
of a single year *but over the lifetimes of the people born in each year*. Net
cohort migration records whether fewer or more people born in a particular year die in a place as compared to how many were born there
in the same year. Net cohort migration is most simply calculated by
subtracting from all births occurring in an area in a year the number
of deaths recorded in that area of people born in that particular year
over the subsequent century. It is the count of emigration less immigration over the lifetime of a birth cohort. For estimates of net cohort

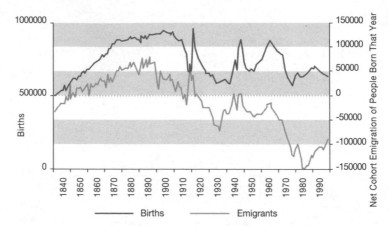

Figure 8.8   Annual births and net cohort emigration, England and Wales,
1840–2000

Source: Dorling and Rigby, 2007.
Note: Left axis: total annual births. Right axis: net cohort emigration =
births – subsequent deaths of people born in that same year.

migration after 1900 we rely to an increasing extent on official predictions of the population. Figure 8.8 can be read in the same way as
for Figure 8.7, but with cohort replacing net period migration (here
'emigrants' are net cohort emigrants, i.e. emigrants-immigrants).

Looking in more detail at the period since 1850 and the corre-
spondence between the trend in births and net cohort emigration,
we can see that emigration first peaks at over 50,000 people net
leaving per year (born in a given year) for the birth year when the
birth increase first stalls: 1876. This coincides with the raising of
public awareness of birth control connected with the Bradlaugh-
Besant trial (involving prosecution for the publication of a leaflet on
family planning). This causes the break in the slope of the process
that Chappell observes, 'whereas previously, delayed marriage and
non-marriage were the only factors reducing the number of children
borne by each woman, by the late 19th and early 20th centuries the
use of traditional methods of birth control (abstinence and with-
drawal) within marriage had become more widespread' (Chappell,
2005: 5). Births rise only a little in absolute numbers in some later
years. This is despite the number of potential mothers having risen
greatly. Absolute numbers of births per year then fall, apart from
directly after the First and Second World Wars and in the 1960s, the
decade which saw an echo of an earlier baby boom.

Like births, net emigration rates then slowly undulate, but reach a maximum of 70,000 of those born in 1898 dying elsewhere. From the last Victorian birth cohorts of the turn of the century, net emigration falls quickly away. The trend mirrors that of births a few years later. For those cohorts there is less impetus to leave as they are replacing the deaths due to the First World War and with fewer people a few years younger than them competing for space (at work and at home). England and Wales thus became net importers of people. With 'Windrush' immigration from the Caribbean, a local peak of 70,000 more people born in 1935 died in the UK than were born there. Estimates after 1965 are more problematic as they are based on actual events for only the first thirty-five years of life and official predictions from ages 35 to just over age 60, with zero net migration assumed after age 60.

Figure 8.9 looks complicated, but bear with us. It just re-projects the information shown in Figure 8.8. The former left-hand axis, total number of births, becomes the x-axis, and the right-hand axis, net cohort emigration, becomes the y-axis. Figure 8.9 suggests that when there are more births a higher number of people emigrate and net emigration is more likely than net immigration. It is possible to discern distinct periods within this overall relationship.

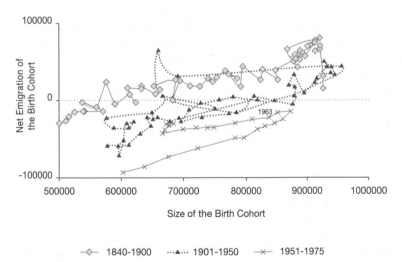

Figure 8.9   Births in, by net-cohort-emigration from, England and Wales, 1840–1975

Source: Dorling and Rigby, 2007.
Note: The lines link consecutive year data points.

The first period shown is 1840 to 1900. The left-most diamond in Figure 8.9 represents the year 1840 when just over half a million babies were born (x-axis) and a net additional 32,000 people born in that year entered and died in these countries (y-axis). The years 1841, 1842, 1843 and so on are the diamonds progressively to the right of that initial point, connected consecutively by a line. In general, more babies were born each year and fewer people entered these countries with progressively more emigrating, until around 1898. The last two diamonds in the series represent births in 1899 and 1900. The trend abruptly ends in 1899 because boys born in 1899 were, in general, too young to 'migrate' to France in 1914, from which many did not return (Brittain, 1933).

The second period, shown in the graph as solid triangles, is of those children born between 1901 and 1950. There are more atypical years in this period (due partly to peaks in births a year after surviving men return from war in 1919 and 1947), but, in general, the solid triangles of births from 1901 to 1950 lie on a line some 50,000 emigrants below the 1840–1900 trend. Hence it would be possible to create two simple equations: one which roughly predicted lifetime emigrants from births for the period 1840–98, and the other for a new era from 1899 to 1950.

The third period is from 1951 to 1975. The year 1963 is marked lower down and to the right in Figure 8.9. Readers might remember the start of Philip Larkin's poem, 'Annus Mirabilis': 'Sexual intercourse began in 1963 (which was rather late for me)'. Since 1953 the number of births each year had gradually and persistently increased. After 1963 with the mass availability of the pill, it was much easier to have sex without producing babies and each year after that the number of births declined. The babies born in 1963 would have been aged 27 in 1990, the sort of age at which young adults decide to emigrate. But the demand for 27-year-olds increased in 1991 and 1992 and onwards. Fewer people emigrated and immigrants were more welcome – there were jobs for them to do.

The crosses in Figure 8.9 that show the period from 1951 to 1975 are the most telling part of the entire diagram. As births rose from 1955 to 1965, net lifetime immigration decreased each year and then, as the number of births fell successively each year from 1963, it increased. The most recent trend moves down the y-axis to suggest net immigration (over the course of their lifetimes) of almost 100,000 people born in 1975; however this trend becomes heavily dependent upon actuarial estimates of future population numbers and deaths.

There are very few countries of the world that have very good quality long time series demographic data, a large population,

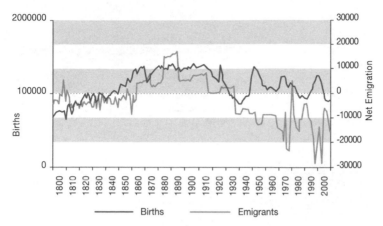

Figure 8.10 Annual births and net emigration, Sweden, 1800–2000

Source: Drawn by the authors using data form the World Mortality Database
and methods detailed in Dorling, 2009.

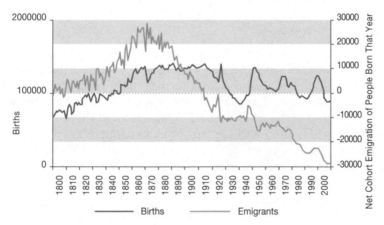

Figure 8.11 Annual births and net cohort emigration, Sweden,
1800–2000

Source: Drawn by the authors using data form the World Mortality Database
and methods detailed in Dorling, 2009.

and detailed future population forecasts to replicate this analysis.
However, Sweden does fit these criteria in having better registration data than England and Wales, and the replication of trends
there is evident (as demonstrated by Figures 8.10, 8.11 and 8.12,
which are the Swedish equivalents of Figures 8.7, 8.8 and 8.9
shown above).

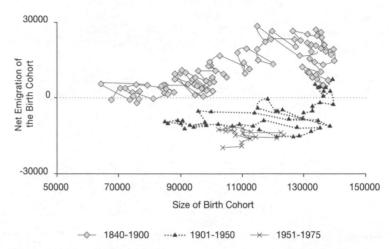

Figure 8.12   Annual births versus net cohort emigration, Sweden, 1800–1975

Source: Drawn by the authors using data form the World Mortality Database and methods detailed in Dorling, 2009.

The extent to which this work is predictive can only be ascertained in the future, and unfortunately it is going to take a long time to tell – but we know that in the long term fertility-replacement migration cannot continue. The last cohort we are at all comfortable about including is that of those born in 1975, as shown in Figure 8.9, simply to illustrate where the trend appears to be heading. Nevertheless, that first recent high estimate of net immigration of 223,000 in 2004, mentioned above, is coincident with the trough in births in 1976 (i.e. twenty-eight years earlier, with 28 being a viable representation of the mean age at which many people migrate) and is supportive of this work. It is important to remember that here we are talking of net cohort numbers.

In aggregate terms, people's behaviour appears to be relatively predictable over the course of their lifetimes as a group – if there is space for them, if they are welcomed and in demand, they will come. If they leave they are more likely to return, and so on, such that the size of their birth cohort very closely predicts their net migratory behaviour until death. This process is remarkably consistent given that it has occurred over a very long time frame of huge economic growth and dramatic change.

From these results it is possible to speculate that the premium and cost of empire (that England and Wales had from 1840 until the birth cohort of 1898 came of age) was the net export and non-return of roughly 50,000 additional people per year per birth cohort. This includes emigration to Canada, Australia, New Zealand and (though not part of the Empire) the United States.

Speculation over the 1898 turning point can occur with the great statistical advantage that this date was so long ago that the data are virtually complete (i.e. estimates are based on real deaths and not future estimates). These results also add another dimension to the possibility that current official population projections are incorrect because they assume rates of net immigration lower than those needed to replace shrinking cohorts; however, this again can only be assessed well into the future (Morris, 2004). However, in the ten years since Jan Rigby and Danny first suggested these ideas, net migration has indeed been very high, and, politically, few people connected that to sex (with much better contraception) beginning in 1963!

Human beings are not like other animals, or at least not like most animals, and only one other mammal is even slightly like us when it comes to sociability: the naked mole rat, which is a eusocial[9] mammal (it has a family structure similar to that of bees and ants). Mole rats subordinate their individual interests only to their colony. But we are capable of subordinating ours even to those of total strangers: sending money to charities, taking in refugees, volunteering as human shields (Monbiot, 2015).

It takes humans a few years to learn to love their new neighbours when migration occurs. Within a generation people talk of those whose parents were born elsewhere as being 'just like them', they marry and mix. When people talk about being nationalistic they are talking about identifying with a group of others whom they call 'us' but to whom they are often not particularly genetically related. And people can easily be led to think of other groups, who may be very like them genetically, as definitely 'not us'. The dehumanizing language of 'The Hun' was used extensively during the First World War to encourage British soldiers to shoot German soldiers. Kaiser Wilhelm II of Germany and King George V of England were actually first cousins. The DNA genetic variation between human populations can be used to identify patterns of shared ancestry and hence possible patterns of migration. Some 30 per cent of this genetic variation in White British people has German ancestry (Devlin, 2015).

In some ways we appear to have learnt very little in the last 100 years. A century ago, in 1917, America was joining the First World War, convinced by the 'Zimmerman Telegram' that Mexico was about to side with Germany. Today the American president talks of building a wall along the Mexican border and British Brexiteers again talk disparagingly of Germany, but both Germany and Mexico appear more sanguine. But then, in March 2017, people in the Netherlands, in the first significant European vote since Brexit, strongly rejected xenophobic politics, and the pro-immigration Green Party quadrupled their seats in the Dutch parliament. Such an event would have been unimaginable 100 years ago. The June 2017 general election result in the UK was even more dramatic. Mainly due to new support from the young, the Labour Party saw its popularity increase by three times more in May 2017 than had ever before happened in a month of polling. The swing in the actual votes was only surpassed by the vote swing in the 1945 general election, and a hung parliament was the final result. Both our understanding of demography, and the politics of it, are constantly changing.

9
Conclusion: Understanding Ourselves, Understanding Each Other

Anyone who tells you that they know what the demographic future looks like is a fantasist – or simply young and naive rather than old and disillusioned from having seen forecast after forecast go awry. We humans only live for a short amount of time. We place great store on how much of that time we have lived – our 'chronological age' – and may well overestimate how wise we can become in such a short time. We come into the world with our brains still growing in size, open to being forged to fit into the environment we happen to find ourselves having to cope with. To achieve this, we are made highly impressionable, often believing people when they tell us that they can foresee the future. Economists and astrologers rely on our optimism and our belief in their powers to see through the mists ahead. Demographers are the more boring (and only slightly more reliable) cousins of both professions.

We like to fit in and we tend to believe what we are told because, in the past, that has generally been a good strategy. Throughout most of human history almost all babies have been born into relatively stable social systems. In the past, those of us who did what we were told were more likely to survive and have more surviving children of our own, and so we evolved to be like this. However, because we can be born anywhere on the planet and into widely different types of society, we have also evolved to be extremely adaptable, and do not come into the world with a fixed view of how things should be. People usually accepted the religion of their parents (most demographers still assume that children can be counted as having the religion, or the atheist or agnostic beliefs, of their parents), and we take for granted most of the rules and norms of our society. Some of us rebel, but often briefly and most only modestly, keeping within the norms of the wider society. Some are more adventurous than others; others conform a little more than is usual. We all still reproduce in much the same way as each other, although increasing access to IVF may mark the beginning of a change in that.

Today, unlike just a few decades ago, we have life-spans of increasingly similar duration worldwide, and no humans have yet been cryogenically regenerated, nor has anyone lived for 150 years.[1] Technology is changing, but what is most different now compared with most of our evolutionary past is that *none* of our societies today are demographically stable; some are shrinking, others are still rapidly expanding. With these demographic changes, social norms are also changing *everywhere*, and both religious and moral beliefs are shifting rapidly. Collectively, we now need a better picture of how we fit in, because what we have to fit into is very different. We now have to understand ourselves within a global context. We cannot ignore the extraordinary diversity – good and bad – within that world, and we have to make some sense of it, and of our place in it. We are part of a far larger tribe than any previous generation could have imagined – because our tribe is now global.

Some projections can be helpful, but they need to be seen in context and the knock-on effects of one change on another need to be considered. Globally, population projections help us to realize that policies that make people's lives safer also indirectly result in them having on average fewer children than in the past. Knowing how people tend to behave when they migrate from an area of high fertility to one of low fertility is also very informative. In general, migrants have fewer children than do people of the same age from the same area who do not migrate, but they have a few more in the first generation than the population into which they mix. Thus the aggregate effect of global migration from high to low fertility areas is to accelerate declines in fertility worldwide. If we want a smaller overall total global population we would do well not to curtail people's freedom of movement.

There are many excuses that can be made for our failing to understand ourselves well, or failing to comprehend our demography. Many did not anticipate how the rapidly increased access to modern contraception, brought about by political action, would result in increased uptake worldwide, mostly from personal choice. Infanticide has been practised on every continent and by people at every level of cultural complexity, from hunter-gatherers to advanced civilizations. It took centuries for us to move from infanticide not infrequently being used as a means of population control, via Casanova's innovative if not especially effective use of lemon juice to kill sperm (don't try that at home!), to modern contraceptive methods and legal abortion. There is a long and often amusing (but sometimes depressing) history about the spread of the condom, which was followed by the much faster global adoption of the contraceptive pill and the many other methods available today.

But it was not just this increase in the availability of contraceptives that caused fertility rates to decline worldwide. Only very recently have we begun to understand the importance of the potential power of women in relationships and in society in general to reducing fertility. Men tend to want slightly more children than women, and still tend a little too often to not see why a woman with children should want a decent job, a career and a little less childrearing. The rise in access to education among girls has been one of the great correlates of the fall in fertility in country after country. Access to university education for young women has had a greater effect again. In general, increasing rights and social security reduces family size. Statistical proof of much of this has only become available recently. In sharp contrast, there is no evidence that further impoverishing already poor families is likely to reduce fertility rates.

Speed of change is one thing that characterizes demography today and makes it such an exciting science. This includes the speed of change in our understanding. Mortality rates usually fall first due to improvements in sanitation in our towns and cities, and later thanks to better medical knowledge and access to medical care. They can fall further due to safer working environments and then because of better care and respect in old age. The recent mortality spike in the UK shows how complex all this can be. The elderly have been protected by a so-called 'triple-lock' on their pensions, but this did nothing to prevent the reduction in funding for social care, creating crises that then overburdened the also underfunded NHS. The huge rises in mortality that occurred in 2012 and 2013 were even greater in 2015, as shown in Figure 9.1.

The only adult age group to see mortality rates *fall* in the UK in 2015 was that of people aged 25 to 29. This was the commonest age group for immigration that year, and migrants tend to be healthy. However, even that influx of young able people, often working in the caring professions, was not enough to prevent the rapid rises in deaths of those over age 75. Regardless of the size and stability of your pension, when your health deteriorates or you become isolated in old age, what matters to you is what is available around you. If the friendly meals-on-wheels service has been cut, if the adult

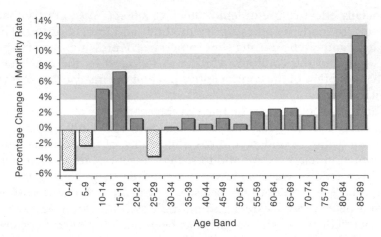

Figure 9.1   Change in age-specific mortality rates in the UK,
2014 to 2015

Source: calculated by the authors from ONS mid-year estimates of 23 June 2016.

social worker, health visitor or doctor very rarely visits, if the on-site warden in your retirement block is no longer on site, if no one notices that you are not well until it is too late, you can and do die earlier. No person is an island, and no individual can be protected when a society begins to disintegrate. The young are encouraged to compete more, and consequently struggle. Burdened by their own problems – housing, job security, money and time – they will care less.

Higher rates of migration have not just been driven by the greater demand for young labour. Cheap air travel (a smaller world) and being able to call back home for free on the internet, including by video link, makes emigrating a bit less daunting. Greater access to education worldwide opens up people's eyes to wider possibilities. The globalization of trade peaked just before the First World War and then again before the great financial crash of 2008, but the movement of people generally rises over time despite these fluctuations, just as it rose greatly following the 1929 economic crash. People seek to move to where they are most needed and where there is the greatest demand for their labour. Curtailing their ability to do that does not tend to improve the lives of the people whom they might otherwise join. All this can be very hard to understand because everything is changing so rapidly right now.

Transitions are both difficult, and difficult to understand. There are countries in the world today that appear to be skipping 'modernity' and moving rapidly to a truncated 'post-modernity'. There is very little industry in Nigeria; as fewer people in the country farm, more work in services. Not all countries follow the same 'development model'. In fact, we should expect those countries that become more affluent earlier to be the exceptions, not pathfinders for others. The slow industrial revolution in England was slow because there was so little early competition. Billions of people need not work in industry in future because far fewer people are now needed to make most of what we need. Robots make far better industrial workers than humans. However, what we may well come to *most* desire in future may not be physical objects – more clothes, more cars, more trinkets. We may move to desire more experiences, more fun, more music, more to read, to watch and to listen to – more entertainment, more knowledge and more activities – and not more bread, bicycles, or boxes of goods. If we better shared out what we had, wasted less[2] and ate less meat, then we would not have to produce that much more food, even to adequately feed the greater number of people who will soon be sharing the planet.

Our demographic measurements were mostly established during the current transition from a global population of 1 billion around 1820 to a projection of around 10 billion (or maybe less as we explained at the end of Chapter 7). Before that great transition there was little need to repeatedly measure rates of fertility and mortality worldwide. Most of the time they were stable. Migration was usually not much of an issue save for following the age-old religious adage of being welcoming and hospitable to strangers. People lived in stable social structures and individualism was generally frowned upon, as was profiting from usury and the inequalities between rich and poor.

Numerous social theories have been developed to try to explain what was, and is, happening with this great transition; often making sense at the time they were usually quickly superseded by events and changes that rendered them out-dated. The history of sociology is the history of one theory competing with another on a demographic playing field that was itself changing so fast that no single theory could ever survive long. Social norms became looser, bimodal distributions became commonplace, and the sacrosanct normal (bell-shaped) distribution ceased to be a law of nature – the middle classes had their children later and the working class earlier. None of that is sustainable, neither those distributions nor the social classes themselves. The rise of such classes was itself a feature of the great demographic transition.

For many people the planet we live on is a strange place made up of strange countries from which strangers come. Trying to understand what is happening within the city you live in can often be hard enough. Not understanding the class structures of the society you live in can be infuriating, let alone not understanding why families are changing in size and structure as fast as they are in your own country. Just understanding why your children are not doing what you did can be challenging. On top of that, the people arriving from the rest of the world bring with them somewhat different norms and values. For many, the world they are presented with is so confusing that they might as well be looking at Figure 9.2. To get a crude idea of what the world currently actually looks like, and how different it can be from what you sometimes think, we recommend a website one of us with the help of many colleagues made a few years ago, which now contains over 1,000 maps of the population of the world: www.worldmapper.org.

Change is confusing. Our lives no longer have standard trajectories, and we have moved from limited choice to uncertainty. We mostly no longer have children shortly after puberty. The nature of what constitutes a family is rapidly changing along with the notions of the 'breadwinner' and the dependent 'other-half'. Our attitudes to the roles of women and men have changed alongside how strictly we adhere to religious norms and cultural expectations. It becomes more difficult to measure specific groups, to say who constitutes a particular group, and then to make policy interventions that solely affect that one group. If you raise the school leaving age to 18 then you need

Figure 9.2   The strange and unknown unreal world that so many fear

Source: A fictional planet earth of weird coastlines, countries and borders. Drawn by the authors.

more teachers; to employ them you need to tax more effectively, and then you need to ensure that there are more jobs appropriate to a more educated workforce. Everything is connected.

Whether the issue is family policy, tax, benefits or leave entitlement, every group has a different idea of what is fair – and those ideas will change as social changes happen. Often people talk about what other people should do rather than what they themselves should do, or about what should be done in other countries rather than concentrating on what could be better done where they are. We are learning that there are no development paths set in stone. No models that, if followed carefully by the population planners of particular countries, will result in predictable outcomes. But we are also learning that there is a general convergence towards longer lives, more education provision, fewer children and more inter-dependence outside of nuclear families. Today we construct microsimulation models that try to predict the behaviour of individuals and are then shocked when they don't produce effective aggregate predictions. Populists then shout: 'You can never trust experts' – conveniently generalized to dismiss what anyone says about anything if you do not like what they say. Our predictions don't work because we don't fully understand why what is happening is happening. That is because what we are studying is very complex – it is ourselves collectively that we are studying.

There is a gap in our disciplinary understanding in anthropology, in politics and in new social theories of which there will be more in future. Until and unless the current demographic slowdown itself settles down, we will not be able to say what the future is most likely to hold, but we should not believe that we will never be able to do this. There was stability in the distant past and there may well be stability again within the space of a few generations. See Figure 4.5 in Chapter 4 and Figure 7.7 in Chapter 7 for the slowdown's current progress and just one projection of its outcome. There are already some regularities we can point to; for one we can be confident of change – and also that if we get our predictions wrong then it is likely that something fundamental will have happened.

Demographic literacy in the UK and US is poor – just as numeracy in our societies is poor – and this makes media abuse possible. Data is patchy – especially where we need it the most (in the poorest areas worldwide) – and improving that will require more than money. In demography migration is becoming the new obsession of the day, just as rising fertility obsessed demographers back in the 1960s.

Rapid change is still possible even when you think you have stability. Fertility uplift could occur for reasons we cannot yet predict.

Figure 9.3   People at a 2015 country fair in the UK, worrying about migration

Source: Photograph courtesy of a friend (who has now left the UK).

Plague, pandemic, famine, war and natural disasters are all still spectres that haunt us. We know how to prevent or ameliorate most of them, but we don't know if we are able to get on with each other well enough to do so in the event of possible future catastrophes. However, if we can become a little bit less prescriptive and a little more open, a little less fearful and a little more hopeful, then we may well be better able to cope in future with whatever chance throws at us. We would also be far better placed to deal with what we can already predict (see Figure 9.3).

A warmer future world, one in which deserts expand and the rains are less predictable, will be a far less frightening world if we can cooperate better both within and across national borders. Those borders themselves often now cause us problems that were never anticipated when they were drawn. Figure 9.4 shows the proportion of people living in each region of Europe who were not born in the country in which they are now living – and hence termed 'foreigners'. But in many cases they will not see themselves as such and their neighbours may also not see them as foreign.

Ask again why it is a problem if women have 1.2 children on average in Germany and 7.0 in Niger. If this was what people said that they wanted, it could be fine. Put these two countries together and there is little overall population change, just a slowdown in the

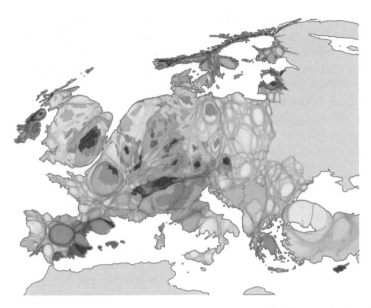

Figure 9.4   The regional geography of foreigners in Europe in 2014
(% population)

Source: Eurostat database, mapped by Benjamin Hennig.

Notes: Local regions are resized in proportion to their total population. In the
darkest areas, more than 20 per cent of the population were born in another
country; in the lightest, less than 5 per cent. The EU average is under 7 per cent.

more densely populated place and an acceleration in the poorer
much less populous country. We now know that the next generation
may make very different choices from their parents if they are in a
position to do so. We know that fertility can rise from 1.2 to 1.8 and
fall from 7.0 to 2.0 in the space of just a single generation. Perhaps it
is time we worried more about why we *do not* do more to help people
achieve what they personally desire rather than be so concerned
about the possible consequences to society 'if everyone did it'? We
now know that the consequences often differ from what was imagined in the past. Telling others what they should do or want, and
curtailing their freedom to choose, are usually much less effective
(as well as creating misery and distress) than helping people live the
lives they would most like to live when those desires do not directly
harm others.

We worry too much about the extremes, despite extremes usually
being uncommon and in any case often adding to the rich tapestry
of life. We don't worry enough about the middle, about what is

currently accepted as 'normal'. We rarely ask how many people in a country wished they could have had more children, or wish that they had had fewer. We make sweeping generalizations about people not having children because they are too selfish, or having 'too many' because they are irresponsible.

Table 9.1 lists a number of countries that have been described elsewhere as having fertility rates which are 'too high' or 'too low'. (This, of course, is nonsense because it implies that there is some 'correct' fertility rate, but never mind that for now). The table compares the overall total fertility rates to the 'ideal number of children' that young women say they would like to have. Throughout this book we have talked a lot about 'preferences' – especially relating to fertility. These have often been written off as too woolly by more serious minded and mathematically inclined demographers, who argue that they tell us very little about real life intentions, being merely about either vague personal ideas or social norms. Looking at column (b), it is tempting to say that this is, indeed, just a social norm – more precisely a 'two-child norm'. Yet, to write this off as a 'social construction' rather than an actual aspiration assumes a tremendous arrogance on the part of the social scientist. If these young people say they would like to have two children, why not assume that they *mean* it, and support them to try to do just that? Similarly, though, remember that this is an *average* figure and many will have stated that they want to have no children, while others will have said they wanted three or more. And, you know, that's fine too.

Table 9.1. Comparing total fertility rates with ideal family size (number of children) for young people

	Country (Year)	(a) TFR	(b) IFS 15–24	(c) IFS 15–19
Fertility 'too low'	Austria (2011)	1.4	2.0	
	Germany (2011)	1.4	2.1	
	Hungary (2011)	1.2	2.1	
	Poland (2011)	1.3	2.2	
	Spain (2011)	1.3	2.1	
Fertility 'too high'	Benin (2011–12)	4.9		3.9
	Ethiopia (2011)	4.8		3.3
	Lesotho (2014)	3.3		2.1
	Malawi (2010)	5.7		3.2
	Mozambique (2011)	5.9		3.8
	Uganda (2011)	6.2		4.1

Sources: Data from Eurostat 2017; MACRO International, 2017.
Notes: TFR – Total Fertility Rate. IFS – Ideal Family Size. Ages of respondents.

But the really interesting comparison in Table 9.1 comes when looking at columns (b) and (c). While we can say that there *might currently* be a two-child norm in Europe, it is impossible to identify any kind of norm for African countries in terms of either TFR or ideal family size, not least because of the rapidity of change. What we can see, however, is a general trend among teenage girls in these countries to want to have fewer children than their older sisters, their mothers and their grandmothers. But the temptation is always to focus on column (a), that is, on the population 'explosion' – despite this inevitably being an explosion *in the past*. If we focus on column (c), and unpack what this aspiration actually *means* – fewer children, better education, better rights, more economic freedom, better security – then we actually have something that can be worked towards, rather than just surrendering to an apocalyptic future. Best of all, it is an aspiration that is stated as a preference by the women themselves, rather than – as is too often the case – a target set by governments, or, more often in both the past and the present, by white men and women on the other side of the world.

In other words, the job of institutions (governments, NGOs, corporations even) should be to help people *achieve what they want*, not to be prescriptive. Part of demography's role is to help us discover such needs, and it should not be used as a threat to justify draconian measures. We should not use demographic statistics to 'play God', but to plan to help people, rather than restrict them. The evidence seems to suggest that people are pretty good judges of their own best trajectories. And the really funny thing, the hopeful thing, is that if we lived in a society where people's aspirations were more likely to be met, our economic and demographic models, when judged by 'classical standards', would actually look a lot more rosy.

We worry too much about migration and too little about opportunity. We worry too much about prolonging life and too little about its quality. We worry too much about ageing, too much about early retirement, and too little about premature redundancy. And we worry far too much about there being too many people, just as we might worry about there being too much traffic when we are sat in a traffic jam: we rarely realize that we are the traffic and the problem is one of organization – how we have chosen to get around, often stupidly sitting in cars – not the volume of potential travellers.

Figure 9.5 shows an old map of the British Empire. That empire ceased to exist a long time ago and yet it still exists in the imaginations of many people in the UK who look back to a time

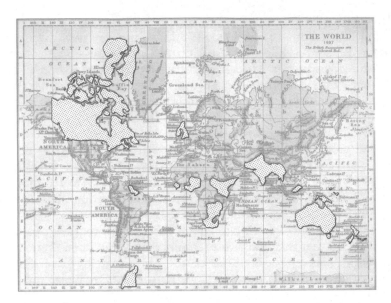

Figure 9.5　The spoils of empire – extent of the British Empire in 1897
Source: Drawn by the authors based on www.britishempire.co.uk/maproom/
pinkbits1897.htm.

when Britain was at the centre of that empire and are told that the demographic balance was better then. In fact, of course, the British were an emigrant nation. What the map actually shows is the places they mostly emigrated to and became immigrants in, almost always making up just a small minority of the population. And it was from those places that Britain drew much of its wealth over a century ago. Subsequently, British Commonwealth citizens enjoyed extensive rights to migrate to the UK. However the Commonwealth Immigrants Act of 1962 changed the rules to make it much harder for them to do so. The Labour leader of the opposition in that year described it as 'cruel and brutal anti-colour legislation'.

Population polices invariably try to force people into models that don't map onto what they want to do. Births and deaths are not just things to be counted, to be observed. They are the beginnings and ends of human lives, lives which change the world. People who move from one place to another are not just components of targets or ratios, or to be considered as fodder for the labour market. They are human beings striving to make their lives better. Population ageing is not a nuisance, a threat to our systems. It is a triumph of humanity which we should embrace.

Figure 9.6 One boy, a migrant, on an island in the Mediterranean in 2016

Source: Photograph taken in March 2016 by a geography student on a field trip from the University of Sheffield who had taken super-hero capes to the camp.

Notes: Moira refugee camp on Lesbos in the Aegean Sea. The boy was happy with his cape and his face-paint. His name is Mohammed. Shortly after this picture was taken the camp became an open-air prison, with the aim of deporting all its inhabitants to Turkey.

Demography will always be statistical but it need not be so impersonal (see Figure 9.6). The subject can become a lot less cold-hearted and a great deal less careless about the objects it studies – us. It needs to recognize when people – driven by fear, suspicion and hatred – hijack the subject for their own malevolent purposes. Demography is about us, not about them, not about strange people in strange places who are a threat because they do or don't have children, because they do or don't move, because they happen to be 'old', or too young, or too skilled, or not skilled enough, or 'too many'. It is about all of us, and we are just coming to realize that us means everyone. We are everyone, everyone in the world.

To butcher a famous line from the 1996 UK film *Brassed Off*: 'I thought that demography matters. But does it? Bollocks. Not compared to how people matter.'

Notes

Chapter 2   Measuring Populations

1   The phrase 'Are you thinking what we're thinking' became infamous in
    UK politics after 2005 as a way of talking about immigration while not
    admitting to being racist: 'Co-opted from a popular children's television
    show in Australia and adopted by a political spin doctor for a successful
    campaign by a right-wing Australian party, the slogan was appearing in
    British Tory posters underneath such provocative lines as: "Violent crime
    soars but Labour puts a spin on it," and most provocative of all, 'It is not
    racist to impose limits on immigration' (see Wiwa, 2005).
2   From World Population Prospects. The 2015 Revision. WPP2015_
    Volume-II-Demographic-Profiles.pdf: 580.
3   This is the group of smaller 'emerging' economies, compared with
    the BRIC (Brazil, Russia, India and China) countries. Both groupings
    may soon go out of fashion as not being very useful for generalization
    purposes.
4   'If current trends continue' is a caveat that has to be added to almost
    all projections. It is not uncommon for a projection to show that it
    is extremely unlikely, sometimes impossible, for current trends to
    continue.
5   The official UN definition of the TFR is: the average number of children a
    hypothetical cohort of women would have at the end of their reproductive
    period if they were subject during their whole lives to the fertility rates of
    a given period and if they were not subject to mortality. It is expressed as
    children per woman.
6   We are grateful to one of the anonymous referees of an earlier draft of this
    book for pointing this out using the example of the districts of Yorkshire
    which almost all saw TFR rise by around 0.2 over this period, regardless
    of whether this was in Bradford (with the highest initial fertility rising to
    2.4) or York (with the lowest ending at 1.5).

Chapter 4 Population 'Explosion'

1 Perhaps the best-known writer to trace the change back to 1492 was Karl Marx.
2 See https://esa.un.org/unpd/wup/General/DefinitionIssues.aspx.
3 See https://en.wikipedia.org/wiki/List_of_cities_proper_by_population.
4 Seehttp://www.npr.org/sections/thetwo-way/2011/11/03/141946751/along-with-humans-who-else-is-in-the-7-billion-club.
5 See http://www.cdc.gov/malaria/about/biology/mosquitoes.
6 See http://www.rollbackmalaria.org/news-events/latest-news/2015/un-ma rks-achievement-in-global-malaria-reduction.
7 See http://www.un.org/apps/news/story.asp?NewsID=52601#.WQBY2o WcFrQ.
8 Seehttp://www.ipsnews.net/2015/11/un-marks-achievement-in-global-mal aria-reduction.

Chapter 5 Why No Children?

1 Only the current generation has seen fertility rates as low as they are now. Mitochondrial Eve lived around 200,000 years ago: http://www.mhrc.net/ mitochondrialEve.htm.
2 See http://www.independent.co.uk/news/uk/home-news/government-bury -rape-clause-child-tax-credit-donald-trump-inauguration-victim-sexual-abuse-evidence-a7540351.html.
3 Maslow's hierarchy of needs placed the 'physiological' at the bottom, then 'safety', 'belongingness and love', 'esteem', 'self-actualization', and at the very top 'self-transcendence'. He placed sex and having an adequate birth rate at the lowest level.
4 It is worth noting, however, that this is a relatively new departure for demographers. As Paul Demeny writes, their 'role, as is the case for social scientists at large, is to describe and examine phenomena within their dis-cipline and leave formulation of policy proposals to others' (2016: 121). However, for Demeny, his concern about the extent and consequences of the European 'demographic crises' of low fertility and migration 'calls for an exception' (2016: 121).

Chapter 6 Population Ageing

1 Later in this book we will call these 'emerging markets', as they are not the poorest of poor countries.
2 Given that this chapter largely concentrates upon settings character-ized by developed (or rapidly developing) higher education systems, we employ the age range 20–64 for the so-called 'working-age' population. Of course, this is not uniformly appropriate, but for a comparative pres-entation of the figures we felt it was worth the sacrifice.

3 This is a reference to different types of bees rather than flying machines. Funny how language can change so quickly and what we think of as a 'drone' changes!
4 Average residual life expectancy at that age will actually be more than fifteen years, especially in countries where deaths are more likely before that age. However, again, for comparison purposes this is not that important a point.
5 For detailed ageing indicators for all the world's countries, see reaging. org. Note that a counter-argument to the use of fifteen years might be that the length of time spent in worse health at the end of life has increased with life expectancy, so that a RLE of 20 (say) might be a more appropriate comparison.
6 Note that an economic contribution does not have to equate to paid work.
7 Whether this will on average be for longer or shorter periods of time than in the past is largely unknowable.

Chapter 7   Population and the Global Economy

1 Wikipedia is an example of a virtually weightless good, in dramatic contrast to the much smaller Encyclopaedia Britannica which weighs 65kg.
2 All figures from World Bank Global Development Indicators.
3 Personal communication from Dr Melanie Channon of the University of Oxford, drawing on evidence from the Nepali census.

Chapter 8   Population and Politics

1 There is no year 0. There was a census in 6CE. The author of the Gospel of Luke uses it as the narrative means by which Jesus was born in Bethlehem (Luke 2:1–5), and places the census within the reign of Herod the Great, who actually died ten years earlier in 4 BCE. No satisfactory explanation has been put forward which could resolve the contradictions, and most scholars think that Luke 'made a mistake', putting in doubt the other 'convenient' details.
2 Having three phalanges in the thumb (like in all other fingers) is a very rare congenital abnormality that usually results in it not being opposable. See https://en.wikipedia.org/wiki/Triphalangeal_thumb.
3 The full quotation starts, in the scientific language of the time: 'The almost infinite manifoldness of germ-plasmic recombinations can be relied on...'.
4 IQ is statistically contrived to fit a bell curve, as are many other statistics, e.g. the Programme for International Student Assessment (PISA) by the OECD of 15-year-old school pupils' scholastic performance on mathematics, science and reading.
5 In 2014–15, 29 per cent of all UK children (3.9 million) were already living in families in poverty, up from 27 per cent in 2012–13.

6 Many schools will inevitably try to manipulate these results, and want to lose pupils that perform poorly. Others appear to do well just because of their intake demography, but some of their children might have done better in a 'less good' school.
7 This can be seen in the increase in mental ill-health in children in the US and UK over the past thirty years, which is not reflected so strongly in the rest of Europe.
8 An obvious example is the reduced chances of going to university in China if you are born in an auspicious and hence higher birth-rate year.
9 Eusociality is the highest level of organization of animal sociality, and is defined by the following characteristics: cooperative care of offspring including those of other individuals, overlapping generations within a colony of adults, and a division of labour.

Chapter 9 Conclusion: Understanding Ourselves, Understanding Each Other

1 Unless you believe arguments that 'People Like Adam and Noah Really Lived to Over 900', and the reasons their proponents give to explain it! See https://answersingenesis.org/bible-timeline/genealogy/did-adam-and-noah-really-live-over-900-years.
2 The global volume of food wasted per year is estimated to be 1.3 Gtonnes, compared to the total agricultural production (for food and non-food uses) of about 6 Gtonnes. See http://www.greenfacts.org/en/food-wastage.

Bibliography

2020 Delivery. 2017. Deaths in the UK have risen by 50,000 per year since 2011. Why? 11 January, http://www.2020delivery.com/news/2017-mortality-analysis.

Adsera, A. 2005. Where are the babies? Labor market conditions and fertility in Europe. IZA Discussion Paper No. 1576, http://papers.ssrn.com/sol3/papers.cfm?abstract_id=530242.

Agence France-Presse. 2015. China promises rights to citizens born in violation of one-child policy. *Guardian*, 10 December, https://www.theguardian.com/world/2015/dec/10/china-promises-rights-citizens-born-violation-one-child-policy.

Akkoc, R. 2015. How Europe is slowly dying despite an increasing world population. *Telegraph*, 16 February, http://www.telegraph.co.uk/news/worldnews/11414064/How-Europe-is-slowly-dying-despite-an-increasing-world-population.html.

Al-Hadithi, T. S. et al. 2010. Demographic transition and potential for development: the case of Iraqi Kurdistan. *Eastern Mediterranean Health Journal*, 16(10): 1098–102.

Al-Monitor. 2015. Turkey offers cash rewards for marrying early. Al-Monitor Turkey Pulse, http://www.al-monitor.com/pulse/originals/2015/02/turkey-government-early-marriages.html#ixzz4AFuwyyno.

Arnold, J. 2003. Scotland seeks key to growth. BBC News Online, http://news.bbc.co.uk/1/hi/business/3216059.stm.

Arumainathan, P. 1973. *Report on the Census of Population 1970, Singapore.* Singapore: Government Printing Office.

Asia One News. 2008. Maid employer's nightmare. 23 December, http://news.asiaone.com/News/AsiaOne+News/Singapore/Story/A1Story20081223-110002.html.

Associated Press. 2010. Iran's leader introduces plan to encourage population growth by paying families. *New York Times*, 27 July, http://www.nytimes.com/2010/07/28/world/middleeast/28iran.html.

Baculinao, E. 2016. China braces for baby boom under new two-child rule. NBCnews.com, 4 January, http://www.nbcnews.com/news/china/china-braces-baby-boom-under-new-two-child-rule-n489641.

Baird, V. 2007. *The No-Nonsense Guide to Sexual Diversity*. London: New Internationalist Press.

Baird, V. 2011. *The No-Nonsense Guide to World Population*. London: New Internationalist Press.

Banister, J. 1984. An analysis of recent data on the population of China. *Population and Development Review*, 10(2): 241–71.

Basten, S. 2013a. Re-examining the fertility assumptions for Pacific Asia in the UN's 2010 World Population Prospects. *University of Oxford Barnett Papers in Social Research*, 13(1), https://www.spi.ox.ac.uk/fileadmin/documents/PDF/Barnett_Paper_13-01.pdf.

Basten, S. 2013b. Population Projections, POSTnote (Parliamentary Office of Science and Technology briefing note to UK Parliamentarians), March.

Basten, S. and Jiang, Q. 2014. China's family planning policies: recent reforms and future prospects. *Studies in Family Planning*, 45(4): 493–509.

Basten, S., Muttarak, R. and Pothisiri, W. 2014. 'The persistence of parent repayment' and the anticipation of filial obligations of care in two Thai provinces. *Asian Social Work and Policy Review*, 8(2): 109–22.

Basten, S., Sobotka, T. and Zeman, K. 2014. Future fertility in low fertility countries. In W. Lutz, W. P. Butz, and S. KC, eds., *World Population and Human Capital in the Twenty-first Century*. Oxford: Oxford University Press, pp. 39–146.

Basu, A. M. and Desai, S. B. 2012. Middle-class dreams: India's one-child families. Paper presented at IUSSP 2012 Conference, https://iussp.org/sites/default/files/event_call_for_papers/One%20child%20families_IUSSP.pdf.

BBC News, 2010. France hit by new wave of strikes over pension reforms. BBC News Online, http://www.bbc.co.uk/news/world-europe-11570828.

BBC News. 2016. Turkey's Erdogan warns Muslims against birth control. BBC News Online, http://www.bbc.com/news/world-europe-36413097.

Beck, U. 1992. *Risk Society: Towards a New Modernity*. London: Sage.

Becker, G. S. and Lewis, H. G. 1973. On the interaction between the quantity and quality of children. *Journal of Political Economy*, 81(2): 279–88.

Bengtsson, T. and Dribe, M. 2006. Deliberate control in a natural fertility population: Southern Sweden, 1766–1864. *Demography*, 43(4): 727–46.

Bijak, J. et al. 2007. Population and labour force projections for 27 European countries, 2002–2052: impact of international migration on population ageing. *European Journal of Population*, 23(1): 1–31.

Bijak, J., Kupiszewska, D. and Kupiszewski, M. 2008. Replacement migration revisited: simulations of the effects of selected population and labor market strategies for the aging Europe, 2002–2052. *Population Research and Policy Review*, 27(3): 321–42.

Billari, F. C. and Kohler, H.-P. 2004. Patterns of low and lowest-low fertility in Europe. *Population Studies*, 58(2): 161–76.

Bingham, J. 2015. Tory two-child limit on benefits 'fundamentally anti-family' – faith leaders. *Telegraph*, 10 November, http://www.telegraph.co.uk/news/politics/11986399/Tory-two-child-limit-on-benefits-fundamentally-anti-family-faith-leaders.html.

Bodewig, C. 2015. Is the refugee crisis an opportunity for an aging Europe? Brookings: Future Development, https://www.brookings.edu/blog/future-development/2015/09/21/is-the-refugee-crisis-an-opportunity-for-an-aging-europe.

Bongaarts, J. 2004. Population aging and the rising cost of public pensions. *Population and Development Review*, 30(1): 1–23.

Boserup, E. 1981. *Population and Technological Change: A Study of Long-Term Trends*. Chicago: University of Chicago Press.

Boyle, P. and Dorling, D. 2004. Editorial. The 2001 UK census: remarkable resource or bygone legacy of the 'pencil and paper era'? *Area*, 36(2): 101–10.

Brittain, V. 1933. *Testament of Youth*. London: Penguin.

Brockopp, J. E., ed. 2010. *Cambridge Companion to Muhammad*. Cambridge: Cambridge University Press.

Brookbanks, M. 2016. How the rise of childless women could change the face of Britain: Rampant infidelity. A struggling economy. Meltdown for the NHS. And shorter life expectancies. *Daily Mail*, 14 January, http://www.dailymail.co.uk/femail/article-3398484/How-rise-childless-women-change-face-Britain-Rampant-infidelity-struggling-economy-Meltdown-NHS-shorter-life-expectancies.html.

Byass, P. et al. 2013. Reflections on the global burden of disease 2010 estimates. *PLoS Medicine*, 10(7): p.e1001477.

Carlyle, T. 1842. *Chartism*. London: Chapman and Hall.

Carnes, B. and Olshansky, S. J. 2007. A realist view of aging, mortality, and future longevity. *Population and Development Review*, 33(2): 367–81.

Chan, R. K. H. 2009. Risk, individualization and family: managing the family in Hong Kong. *Journal of Asian Public Policy*, 2(3): 354–67.

Chang, C-K., et al. 2011. Life expectancy at birth for people with serious mental illness and other major disorders from a Secondary Mental Health Care Case Register in London. *PLoS One*, 6(5): e19590

Chapman, J. 2011. The collapse of family life: half of children see parents split by 16 as births outside marriage hit highest level for two centuries. *Daily Mail*, 18 April, http://www.dailymail.co.uk/news/article-1377940/Half-parents-split-16-births-outside-marriage-hit-highest-level.

Chappell, B. 2011. Along with humans, who else is in the 7 Billion Club? National Public Radio, 3 November, http://www.npr.org/sections/thetwo-way/2011/11/03/141946751/along-with-humans-who-else-is-in-the-7-billion-club.

Chappell, R., ed. 2005. *Focus on People and Migration 2005*. National Statistics publication. Basingstoke: Palgrave MacMillan.

Cheng, S.-J.A. 1996. Migrant women domestic workers in Hong Kong, Singapore and Taiwan: a comparative analysis. *Asian and Pacific Migration Journal*, 5(1): 139–52.

Chin, T. and Welsby, P. D. 2004. Malaria in the UK: past, present, and future. *Postgrad Medical Journal*, 80: 663–6.

Citi GPS and Oxford Martin School. 2016. *Technology at Work v2.0*, http://www.oxfordmartin.ox.ac.uk/downloads/reports/Citi_GPS_Technology_Work_2.pdf.

Clark, R. 2015. Muhammad really is the single most popular boys' name in England and Wales. *The Spectator*, 18 August, http://blogs.spectator.co.uk/2015/08/mohammed-really-is-the-single-most-popular-boys-name-in-england-and-wales.

Clarke, H. D., Goodwin, M. and Whitely, P. 2017. *Brexit: Why Britain Voted to Leave the European Union*. Cambridge: Cambridge University Press.

Cleland, J. and Wilson, C. 1987. Demand theories of the fertility transition: an iconoclastic view. *Population Studies*, 41(1): 5–30.

Coleman, D. A. 2002. Replacement migration, or why everyone is going to have to live in Korea: a fable for our times from the United Nations. *Philosophical Transactions of the Royal Society of London*. Series B, Biological sciences, 357(1420): 583–98.

Coleman, D. A., and Basten, S. 2015. The death of the West: an alternative view. *Population Studies*, 69(s1): 107–18.

Commission of the European Communities. 2005. Confronting demographic change: a new solidarity between the generations, Brussels, http://eur-lex.europa.eu/LexUriServ/site/en/com/2005/com2005_0094en01.pdf.

Connelly, M. 2010. *Fatal Misconception: The Struggle to Control World Population*. Cambridge: Harvard University Press.

Coonan, C. 2013. China law forces adult children to visit and care for their elderly parents. *Independent*, 1 July, http://www.independent.co.uk/news/world/asia/china-law-forces-adult-children-to-visit-and-care-for-their-elderly-parents-8681677.html.

Coulmas, F. 2007. *Population Decline and Ageing in Japan: The Social Consequences*. Abingdon: Routledge.

Crespo Cuaresma, J., Lutz, W. and Sanderson, W. 2014. Is the demographic dividend an education dividend? *Demography*, 51(1): 299–315.

Cumhuriyet. 2014. Erdoğan evlilik yaşına da karıştı, gençleri TÜRGEV'e davet etti. Cumhuriyet, http://www.cumhuriyet.com.tr/haber/turkiye/96093/Erdogan_evlilik_yasina_da_karisti_gencleri_TURGEV_e_davet_etti.html.

Daum, M. 2016. *Selfish, Shallow, and Self-Absorbed: Sixteen Writers on the Decision Not to Have Kids*. New York: Picador.

DaVanzo, J. and Dogo, H. 2011. China and India: the Asian giants are heading down different demographic paths. RAND Research Briefs, http://www.rand.org/pubs/research_briefs/RB9598.html.

Davey Smith, G. 2012. Epigenesis for epidemiologists: does evo-devo have implications for population health research and practice? *International Journal of Epidemiology*, 41(1): 236–7.

Dearden, L. 2015. Most popular baby names of last year revealed as official list published. *Independent*, 17 August, http://www.independent.co.uk/news/uk/home-news/most-popular-baby-names-2014-oliver-and-amelia-top-official-list-for-second-year-in-a-row-10458531.html.

Demeny, P. 2016. Europe's two demographic crises: the visible and the unrecognized. *Population and Development Review*, 42(1): 111–20.

Devlin, H. 2015. Genetic study reveals 30% of white British DNA has German ancestry. *Guardian*, 18 March, https://www.theguardian.com/science/2015/mar/18/genetic-study-30-percent-white-british-dna-german-ancestry.

DiDomizio, N. 2015. 11 Brutally honest reasons why Millennials don't want kids. Connections.Mic, https://mic.com/articles/123051/why-millennials-dont-want-kids#.imU5skTfX.

Die Welt. 2006. Europa wird islamisch, https://www.welt.de/print-welt/article211310/Europa-wird-islamisch.html.

Dominiczak, P. 2014. Pensioners to be given advice on how long they will live. *Telegraph*, 16 April, http://www.telegraph.co.uk/finance/personalfinance/pensions/10771507/Pensioners-to-be-given-advice-on-how-long-they-will-live.html.

Dorling, D. 2009. *Migration: A Long-run Perspective*. London: IPPR, http://www.dannydorling.org/wp-content/files/dannydorling_publication_id1834.pdf.

Dorling, D. 2013a. *Population 10 Billion*. London: Constable.

Dorling, D. 2013b. *Unequal Health*. Bristol: Policy Press.

Dorling, D. 2016a. Brexit: the decision of a divided country. *BMJ*, 354, doi: https://doi.org/10.1136/bmj.i3697.

Dorling, D. 2016b. Austerity, rapidly worsening public health across the UK, and Brexit. PSA Political Insight Blog, 11 July, https://www.psa.ac.uk/insight-plus/blog/austerity-rapidly-worsening-public-health-across-uk-and-brexit-0.

Dorling, D. 2017a. Policymakers should not act like scientists. *Nature Human Behaviour*, 1(9), 10 January.

Dorling, D. 2017b. Brexit, the NHS and the elderly middle class. *Soundings*, January: 50–3.

Dorling, D. 2017c. *Do We Need Economic Inequality?* Cambridge: Polity.

Dorling, D. and Lee, C. 2016. *Geography*. London: Profile

Dorling, D. and Rigby, J. E. 2007. Net cohort migration in England and Wales: how past birth trends may influence net migration. *Population Review*, 46(2): 51–62.

Dorling, D. and Tomlinson, S. 2016. The creation of inequality: myths of potential and ability. *Journal of Critical Education Policy*, 14(3): 56–79.

Dorling, D., Stuart, B. and Stubbs, J. 2016. Don't mention this around the Christmas table: Brexit, inequality and the demographic divide. LSE

European Politics and Policy Blog, 21 December, http://blogs.lse.ac.uk/ europpblog/2016/12/21/christmas-table-brexit-inequality-demographic-divide.

DWP. 2013. Autumn Statement announcement on a core principle under-pinning future State Pension age rises. DWP Background Note, https:// www.gov.uk/government/uploads/system/uploads/attachment_data/fi le/263660/spa-background-note-051213_tpf_final.pdf.

Easterlin, R. A. 1980. *Birth and Fortune: The Impact of Numbers on Personal Welfare.* New York: Basic Books.

Economist, The. 2007. Suddenly, the old world looks younger. 14 June, http://www.economist.com/node/9334869.

Economist, The. 2014. Age invaders. 26 April, http://www.economist. com/news/briefing/21601248-generation-old-people-about-change-glob al-economy-they-will-not-all-do-so.

Emmott, S. 2013. *Ten Billion.* Harmondsworth: Penguin.

European Commission. 2015. Monitoring the job market, http://ec.europa. eu/social/main.jsp?catId=955.

Eurostat. 2017. Unemployment statistics, http://ec.europa.eu/eurostat/stat istics-explained/index.php/Unemployment_statistics.

Fallon, T. 2015. The new Silk Road: Xi Jinping's grand strategy for Eurasia. *American Foreign Policy Interests,* 37(3): 140–7.

Foran, C. 2016. Donald Trump and the rise of anti-Muslim violence. *The Atlantic,* 22 September, https://www.theatlantic.com/politics/ archive/2016/09/trump-muslims-islamophobia-hate-crime/500840.

Frejka, T. and Gietel-Basten, S. 2016. Fertility and family policies in Central and Eastern Europe after 1990. *Comparative Population Studies,* 41(1): 1–55.

Frejka, T., Jones, G. W. and Sardon, J.-P. 2010. East Asian childbearing patterns and policy developments. *Population and Development Review,* 36(3): 579–606.

French, H. W. 2013. Demography is destiny, *Foreign Policy,* 2 October, http://foreignpolicy.com/2013/10/02/demography-is-destiny.

FT.com. 2015. Chinese hackers target Anthem for healthcare know-how, http://www.ft.com/cms/s/0/242c2f4e-7c2e-11e5-98fb-5a6d4728f74e. html#axzz3pxhLjaJ.

Fuchs, V. 1984. Though much is taken: reflections on aging, health, and medical care. *Milbank Memorial Fund Quarterly: Health and Society,* 62(2): 142–66.

Gietel-Basten, S. 2016a. Can't get a GP appointment? Blame George Osborne, not Romanians. *The Conversation,* 8 December, https://thecon versation.com/cant-get-a-gp-appointment-blame-george-osborne-not-romanians-69818.

Gietel-Basten, S. 2016b. Why Brexit? The toxic mix of immigration and austerity. *Population and Development Review,* 42(4): 673–80.

Gietel-Basten, S. 2016c. Why scrapping the one-child policy will do little to change China's population. *The Conversation,* 29 October, https://

theconversation.com/why-scrapping-the-one-child-policy-will-do-little-to-change-chinas-population-49982.

Gietel-Basten, S. 2016d. How China is rolling out the red carpet for couples who have more than one child. *The Conversation*, 7 April, https://theconv ersation.com/how-china-is-rolling-out-the-red-carpet-for-couples-who-have-more-than-one-child-57299.

Gietel-Basten, S. 2016e. Japan is not the only country worrying about population decline – get used to a two-speed world. *The Conversation*, 29 March, https://theconversation.com/japan-is-not-the-only-country-worry ing-about-population-decline-get-used-to-a-two-speed-world-56106.

Goldstein, J. R., Rößger, F., Jaschinski, I. and Prskawetz, A. 2011. Fertility forecasting in the German-speaking world: recent experience and opportu-nities for improvement. *Comparative Population Studies*, 36(2–3): 661–92.

Goldstein, J. R., Sobotka, T. and Jasilioniene, A. 2009. The end of 'lowest-low' fertility? *Population and Development Review*, 35(4): 663–99.

Goodkind, D. and West, L. 2002. China's floating population: definitions, data and recent findings. *Urban Studies*, 39(12): 2237–50.

Graebner, W. 1980. *A History of Retirement: The Meaning and Function of an American Institution, 1885–1978*. New Haven: Yale University Press.

Greenslade, R. 2016. Regional newspaper's EU poll shows massive support for Brexit. *Guardian*, 15 March, https://www.theguardian.com/media/greenslade/2016/mar/15/regional-newspapers-eu-poll-shows-massive-sup port-for-brexit.

Grigg, D. 1977a. Ernst Georg Ravenstein, 1834–1913. *Geographers: Bibliographical Studies*, 1: 79–88.

Grigg, D. 1977b. E. G. Ravenstein and the 'laws of migration'. *Journal of Historical Geography*, 3: 41–54.

Gu, B. and Cai, Y. 2011. Fertility prospects in China. United Nations Population Division, Expert Paper No. 2011/14, New York: UNDP.

Guilmoto, C. Z. 2009. The sex ratio transition in Asia. *Population and Development Review*, 35(3): 519–49.

Harding, S. 2004. Mortality of migrants from the Caribbean to England and Wales: effect of duration of residence. *International Journal of Epidemiology*, 33: 382–6.

Hatton, T. J. and Williamson, J. G. 2002. What fundamentals drive world migration? NBER Working Paper No. 9159.

Hatton, T. J., and Williamson, J. G. 2004. Refugees, asylum seekers and policy in Europe. NBER Working Paper No. 10680.

Heinrichs, R. 2015. Are childless millennials selfish A-holes? Flare.com, http://www.flare.com/culture/are-childless-millennials-selfish-a-holes.

Hiam, L., Harrison, D., Dorling, D. and McKee, M. 2017a. What caused the spike in mortality in England and Wales in January 2015? *Journal of the Royal Society of Medicine*, 1 January: 10.1177/0141076817693600.

Hiam, L., Harrison, D., Dorling, D. and McKee, M. 2017b. Why has mortality in England and Wales been increasing? An iterative demographic analysis. *Journal of the Royal Society of Medicine*, 1 January: 141076817693599.

Higgs, E. 2011. *Identifying the English: A History of Personal Identification 1500 to the Present*. London: Continuum.

Hinton, L. and Chen, H. 2016. Introduction to the special section: Eldercare in Asia: a call for policy development beyond traditional family care. *Ageing International*, 41(4): 331–4.

Hodal, K. 2012. Singapore's maids to get a day off. *Guardian*, 6 March, http://www.guardian.co.uk/world/2012/mar/06/singapore-maids-one-day-off-a-week.

Ikels, C. 2004. *Filial Piety: Practice and Discourse in Contemporary East Asia*. Palo Alto: Stanford University Press.

Iyengar, R. 2016. Shanghai citizens may soon have their credit scores lowered for not visiting their parents. *TIME Magazine*, 12 April, http://time.com/4290234/china-shanghai-parents-visit-credit-score-lower.

Jiang, Q. and Sanchez-Barricarte, J. J. 2011. The 4-2-1 family structure in China: a survival analysis based on life tables. *European Journal of Ageing*, 8(2): 119–27.

Jiang, Q., Li, Y. and Sánchez-Barricarte, J. J. 2013. The risk of mothers losing an only child in China. *Journal of Biosocial Science*, 22(2): 531–45.

Jones, C. 2015. Integration key to reaping benefits of migration, say economists. *Financial Times*, 27 December.

Jones, G. W., Straughan, P. and Chan, A. 2009. Fertility in Pacific Asia: looking to the future. In G. Jones, P. T. Straughan and A. Chan, eds., *Ultra-low Fertility in Pacific Asia: Trends, Causes and Policy Issues*. London: Routledge, pp. 204–14.

Kassam, A. 2015. Europe needs many more babies to avert a population disaster. *Guardian*, 23 August, https://www.theguardian.com/world/2015/aug/23/baby-crisis-europe-brink-depopulation-disaster.

Kaufman, J. 2006. The anatomy of a medical myth. Is Race 'Real'?: Web Forum of the Social Science Research Council, http://raceandgenomics.ssrc.org/Kaufman.

KC, S. and Lutz, W. 2017. The human core of the shared socioeconomic pathways: population scenarios by age, sex and level of education for all countries to 2100. *Global Environmental Change*, 42(1): 181–92.

Keating, J. 2014. Did Russia really boost its birthrate by promising new mothers prize money and refrigerators? Slate.com, 13 October, http://www.slate.com/blogs/the_world_/2014/10/13/russia_birth_rate_did_vladimir_putin_really_boost_the_country_s_fertility.html.

Ketels, G. 2015. Why Taiwan's single people are a national security threat. *Deutsche Welle*, 31 July, http://www.dw.com/en/why-taiwans-single-people-are-a-national-security-threat/a-18617944.

Khaleeli, H. 2014. Muhammad: the truth about Britain's most misunderstood name. *Guardian*, 1 December, http://www.theguardian.com/

uk-news/2014/dec/01/muhammad-truth-about-britains-most-misunders
tood-baby-name.

Kilpatrick, W. 2012. *Christianity, Islam, and Atheism: The Struggle for the Soul of the West.* San Francisco: Ignatius Press.

Ki-moon, B. 2015. UN Marks achievement in global malaria reduction. Roll Back Malaria Partnership, 19 November, http://www.rollbackmalaria.org/news-events/latest-news/2015/un-marks-achievement-in-global-malaria-reduction.

Kirby, P. 2016. *Leading People 2016.* London: The Sutton Trust, http://www.suttontrust.com/researcharchive/leading-people-2016.

Kirchgaessner, S. 2015. Pope Francis: not having children is selfish. *Guardian,* 11 February, https://www.theguardian.com/world/2015/feb/11/pope-francis-the-choice-to-not-have-children-is-selfish.

Kirk, D. 1996. Demographic transition theory. *Population Studies,* 50(3): 361–87.

Knoema.com. 2016. Demographics statistics of Vietnam, 2015. Knoema.com. Available at: https://knoema.com/xqdquqe/demographics-statistics-of-vietnam-2015?tsId=1008120.

Last, J. 2013. What to Expect When No One's Expecting: America's Coming Demographic Disaster. New York, NY: Encounter Books.

Lawson, S., Heacock, D. and Stupnytska, A. 2007. Beyond the BRICs: A Look at the 'Next 11.' New York and London: Goldman Sachs. Available at: http://www.goldmansachs.com/our-thinking/archive/archive-pdfs/brics-book/brics-chap-13.pdf.

Lee, R. and Mason, A. 2006. What is the demographic dividend? Finance and Development, 43(3): 5.

Lesthaeghe, R. 2014. The second demographic transition: a concise overview of its development. *Proceedings of the National Academy of Sciences of the United States of America,* 111(51): 18112–15.

Lipka, M. and C. Hackett. 2015. Why Muslims are the world's fastest-growing religious group. FactTank: Pew Research Center, http://www.pewresearch.org/fact-tank/2015/04/23/why-muslims-are-the-worlds-fastest-growing-religious-group.

Livemint. 2014. Falling total fertility rate in Kolkata sets alarm bells ringing, http://www.livemint.com/Politics/9jV7AFSSMgeCrJqyPgNwFI/Falling-total-fertility-rate-in-Kolkata-sets-alarm-bells-rin.html.

Lunsing, W. 2003. Review: 'parasite' and 'non-parasite' singles. Japanese journalists and scholars taking positions. *Social Science Japan Journal,* 6(2): 261–5.

Lutz, W. 2007. The future of human reproduction: will birth rates recover or continue to fall? *Ageing Horizons,* 7: 15–21.

Lutz, W., Butz, W. P. and KC, S., eds., 2014. *World Population and Human Capital in the Twenty-first Century.* Oxford: Oxford University Press.

Lutz, W., Scherbov, S., Cao, G. Y., Ren, Q. and Zheng, X. 2007. China's uncertain demographic present and future. *Vienna Yearbook of Population Research*: 37–59.

McRae, H. 2014. India will soon be the new China. It's the demography, stupid. *Independent*, 17 May, http://www.independent.co.uk/voices/comment/india-will-soon-be-the-new-china-its-the-demography-stupid-9391070.html.

Mahapatra, P. et al. 2007. Civil registration systems and vital statistics: successes and missed opportunities. *Lancet*, 370(7): 1653–63.

Mandelbrot, B. B. 1982. *The Fractal Geometry of Nature*. San Francisco: W. H. Freeman.

Marshall, A., Read, J. and Nazroo, J. 2014. An analysis of the demographic contributions to population ageing in England and Wales. *Radical Statistics*, http://www.radstats.org.uk/no110/Marshalletal.pdf.

Marshall, A., Nazroo, J., Tampubolan, G. and Vanhoutte, B. 2015. Cohort differences in the levels and trajectories of frailty among older people in England. *Journal of Epidemiology and Community Health*, 69(4), doi:10.1136/jech-2014-204655.

Masci, D. 2015. Europe projected to retain its Christian majority, but religious minorities will grow. Pew Research Centre, 15 April, http://www.pewresearch.org/fact-tank/2015/04/15/europe-projected-to-retain-its-christian-majority-but-religious-minorities-will-grow.

Matthews, F. E., Arthur. A., Barnes, L. E., Bond, J., Jagger, C., Robinson, L. and Brayne, C. et al. 2013. A two-decade comparison of prevalence of dementia in individuals aged 65 years and older from three geographical areas of England: results of the Cognitive Function and Ageing Study I and II. *Lancet*, 382(9902): 1405–12.

Michaels, A. 2009a. Muslim Europe: the demographic time bomb transforming our continent. *Telegraph*, 8 August, http://www.telegraph.co.uk/news/worldnews/europe/5994047/Muslim-Europe-the-demographic-time-bomb-transforming-our-continent.html.

Michaels, A. 2009b. A fifth of European Union will be Muslim by 2050. *Telegraph*, 8 August, http://www.telegraph.co.uk/news/worldnews/europe/5994045/A-fifth-of-European-Union-will-be-Muslim-by-2005.html.

Monbiot, G. 2015. We've almost stopped killing each other. Now let's spare the planet. *Guardian*, 15 December, https://www.theguardian.com/commentisfree/2015/dec/15/killing-planet-george-monbiot.

Morris, D. 2004. *Morris Review of the Actuarial Professional, Interim Assessment*. London: HMSO.

Mullan, P. 2002. *The Imaginary Time Bomb: Why an Ageing Population is Not a Social Problem*. 2nd edition. London: I. B. Taurus.

Myrskylä, M., Goldstein, J. R. and Cheng, Y. A. 2013. New cohort fertility forecasts for the developed world: rises, falls, and reversals. *Population and Development Review*, 39(1): 31–56.

National Archives. 2017. The changing census, 1801–1901. UK National Archives repository, http://www.nationalarchives.gov.uk/pathways/census/events/census3.htm.

O'Connor, J. 2012. Trend of couples not having children just plain selfish. *National Post*, 19 September, http://news.nationalpost.com/full-comment/joe-oconnor-selfishness-behind-growing-trend-for-couples-to-not-have-children.

Oeppen, J. and Vaupel, J. W. 2002. Broken limits to life expectancy. *Science*, 296(5570): 1029–31.

Ogawa, N., Kondo, M. and Matsukura, R. 2005. Japan's transition from the demographic bonus to the demographic onus. *Asian Population Studies*, 1(2): 207–26.

Olshansky, S. J. et al. 2005. A potential decline in life expectancy in the United States in the 21st century. *The New England Journal of Medicine*, 352: 1138–45.

O'Neill, B. et al. 2001. A guide to global population projections. *Demographic Research* 4(8): 203–88.

ONS. 2013. Why has the fertility rate risen over the last decade in England and Wales?, http://webarchive.nationalarchives.gov.uk/20160105160709/http://www.ons.gov.uk/ons/rel/vsob1/birth-summary-tables--england-and-wales/2011--final-/sty-fertility.html.

ONS. 2014. Population projections. ONS People, population and community, https://www.ons.gov.uk/peoplepopulationandcommunity/population andmigration/populationprojections.

ONS. 2015a. Statistical bulletin: baby names – England and Wales, 2014. Statistical Bulletin, http://www.ons.gov.uk/peoplepopulationandcomm unity/birthsdeathsandmarriages/livebirths/bulletins/babynamesengland andwales/2015-08-17.

ONS. 2015b. Birth summary tables, England and Wales, 2014. Statistical Bulletin, http://www.ons.gov.uk/peoplepopulationandcommunity/births deathsandmarriages/livebirths/bulletins/birthsummarytablesenglandand wales/2015-07-15.

ONS. 2015c. National population projections: 2014-based. Statistical Bulletin, https://www.ons.gov.uk/peoplepopulationandcommunity/pop ulationandmigration/populationprojections/bulletins/nationalpopulation projections/2015-10-29.

ONS. 2016a. Migration statistics quarterly report: May 2016. Statistical Bulletin, https://www.ons.gov.uk/peoplepopulationandcommunity/pop ulationandmigration/internationalmigration/bulletins/migrationstatistics quarterlyreport/may2016.

ONS. 2016b, Population estimates for UK, England and Wales, Scotland and Northern Ireland: mid-2015, https://www.ons.gov.uk/peoplepopul ationandcommunity/populationandmigration/populationestimates/bullet ins/annualmidyearpopulationestimates/latest.

ONS. 2016c. Parents' country of birth, England and Wales, 2014. Statistical Bulletin Available, http://www.ons.gov.uk/peoplepopulationandco mmunity/birthsdeathsandmarriages/livebirths/bulletins/parentscountryof birthenglandandwales/2015-08-27.

ONS. 2016d. Baby names statistics: boys, https://www.ons.gov.uk/peopl epopulationandcommunity/birthsdeathsandmarriages/livebirths/datasets/ babynamesenglandandwalesbabynamesstatisticsboys.

Palen, J. J. 1986. Fertility and eugenics: Singapore's population policies. *Population Research and Policy Review*, 5(1): 3–14.

PBS. 2014. Gold coins for babies? Iran looks for new ways to increase nation's birth rate. PBS Newshour, http://www.pbs.org/newshour/ rundown/gold-coins-for-babies-iran-looks-for-new-ways-to-increase-nat ions-birth-rate.

Pearl, R. 1927a. Differential fertility. *The Quarterly Review of Biology*, 2(1): 102–18

Pearl, R. 1927b. The biology of superiority. *The American Mercury*, 12(47): 257–66.

Perkowski, L. 2006. Muslim demographics in the European Union: widening the gap with US foreign policy. Research Report, Air Command and Staff College Air University.

Peterson, H. B., Darmstadt, G. L. and Bongaarts, J. 2013. Meeting the unmet need for family planning: now is the time. *Lancet*, 381(9879): 1696–9.

Phua, K. H. 2012. Health of migrants in Singapore. ASEF Presentation, https://www.asef.org/images/docs/Session%203_2_Kai%20Hong%20 Phua_Preliminary%20results%20of%20studies%20of%20Singapore%20 and%20Hon%20Kong%20SAR_1.pdf.

Pomeranz, K. 2001. *The Great Divergence: China, Europe, and the Making of the Modern World Economy*. Princeton: Princeton University Press.

Pope Benedict XVI. 2006. Address of His Holiness Benedict XVI to the members of the Roman Curia at the traditional exchange of Christmas greetings, Clementine Hall, 22 December, http://w2.vatican.va/content/ benedict-xvi/en/speeches/2006/december/documents/hf_ben_xvi_ spe_20061222_curia-romana.html.

Porritt, J. 2011. Who would have thought it? Population growth and famine would appear to be linked! Jonathan Porrit Blog, 11 July, http://www.jona thonporritt.com/blog/who-would-have-thought-it-population-growth- and-famine-would-appear-be-linked.

Pradhan, I. and Sekher, T. V. 2012. Is urban India moving towards single child families? An analysis of Kolkata City and West Bengal. *Demography India*, 41(1): 53–69.

Quarini, C. A. 2005. History of contraception. *Women's Health Medicine*, 2(5): 28–30.

RAND Corporation. 2005. Population implosion? Low fertility and policy responses in the European Union, Los Angeles, CA, http://www.rand.org/ pubs/research_briefs/RB9126.html.

Rauhut, D. 2004. Replacement migration to Sweden: an overview of possible sender countries. ITPS, Swedish Institute for Growth Policy Studies, Östersund, Sweden.

Renzetti, E. 2013. Why childless people are persecuted. *Globe and Mail*, 18 May, https://www.theglobeandmail.com/life/parenting/why-childless-people-are-persecuted/article12005541/?page=all.

Richardson, H. W. and Nam, C. W., eds., 2014. *Shrinking Cities: A Global Perspective*. Abingdon: Routledge.

Roberts, D. 2014. China's rapidly aging population drives $652 billion 'silver hair' market. Bloomberg Business Week, http://www.bloomberg.com/bw/articles/2014-09-25/chinas-rapidly-aging-population-drives-652-billion-silver-hair-market.

Ross, J. A. and Mauldin, W. P. 1996. Family planning programs: efforts and results, 1972–94. *Studies in Family Planning*, 27(3): 137–47.

Ross, T. 2016. Britain's green fields will have to be built over to provide new homes for migrants, warns Chris Grayling. *Telegraph*, 29 May, http://www.telegraph.co.uk/news/2016/05/29/britains-green-fields-will-have-to-be-built-over-to-provide-new.

Säävälä, M. 2010. Below replacement-level fertility in conditions of slow social and economic development: A review of the evidence from South India. *Finnish Yearbook of Population Research*, 45: 45–66.

Scammon, R. M. and Wattenberg, B. J. 1970. *The Real Majority*. New York: Coward-McCann.

Scherbov, S. et al. 2014. Re-measuring twenty-first century population ageing. In W. Lutz, W. P. Butz and S. KC, eds., *World Population and Human Capital in the Twenty-first Century*. Oxford: Oxford University Press, pp. 563–90.

Scherbov, S., Sanderson, W. C. and Gietel-Basten, S. 2016. Better way to measure ageing in East Asia that takes life expectancy into account. *Australasian Journal on Ageing*, 35(2): 139–42.

Scotsman, The. 2004. Why it's vital to lure the migrants north. Editorial, 25 February, http://www.scotsman.com/news/why-it-s-vital-to-lure-the-migrants-north-1-515169.

Seltzer, W. and Anderson, M. 2001. The dark side of numbers: the role of population data systems in human rights abuses. *Social Research*, 68(2): 481–513.

Sen, S. 2012. Where have Bengal's babies gone? *The Times of India*, 11 April, http://timesofindia.indiatimes.com/city/kolkata/Where-have-Bengals-babies-gone/articleshow/12617632.cms.

Shryock, H. S. and Siegel, J. S. 1993. *The Methods and Materials of Demography*. 8th edition. Washington, DC: US Government Printing Office.

Sian, G. L. 2015. Atmosphere of fear prevents pregnant maids from seeking help. *Straits Times*, 28 October, http://www.straitstimes.com/forum/letters-on-the-web/atmosphere-of-fear-prevents-pregnant-maids-from-seeking-help.

Siegel, H. 2013. Why the choice to be childless is bad for America. *Newsweek*, 19 February, http://europe.newsweek.com/why-choice-be-childless-bad-america-63335?rm=eu.

Singapore Government. 2013. *A Sustainable Population for a Dynamic Singapore: Population White Paper*. Singapore: National Population and Talent Division, https://www.nptd.gov.sg/PORTALS/0/HOMEPAGE/HIGHLIGHTS/population-white-paper.pdf.

Smith, C. H. 2010. Japan's economic stagnation is creating a nation of lost youths. Daily Finance, http://www.dailyfinance.com/2010/08/06/japans-economic-stagnation-is-creating-a-nation-of-lost-youths.

Sobotka, T. 2008. Does persistent low fertility threaten the future of European populations? In J. Surkyn, P. Deboosere and J. van Bavel, eds., *Demographic Challenges for the 21st Century: A State of the Art in Demography*. Brussels: VUBPRESS: Brussels, pp. 27–90.

Sobotka, T. and Beaujouan, E. 2014a. Two is best? The persistence of a two-child family ideal in Europe. *Population and Development Review*, 40(3): 391–419.

Sobotka, T. and Beaujouan, E. 2014b. Two is best? The persistence of a two-child family ideal in Europe. Vienna Institute of Demography Working Papers 3/2014, http://www.oeaw.ac.at/vid/download/WP2014_03.pdf.

Sobotka, T., Skirbekk, V. and Philipov, D. 2011. Economic recession and fertility in the developed world. *Population and Development Review*, 37(2): 267–306.

Squires, N. 2015. Italy is a dying country as babies no longer replace people who die, says health minister. *Telegraph*, 13 February, http://www.telegraph.co.uk/news/worldnews/europe/italy/11411907/Italy-is-a-dying-country-as-babies-no-longer-replace-people-who-die-says-health-minister.html.

Steger, I. 2013. Foreign baby formula, toy makers await China baby boom. *Wall Street Journal*, 18 November, http://blogs.wsj.com/moneybeat/2013/11/18/foreign-baby-formula-toy-makers-await-china-baby-boom.

Stone, J. 2016. Child poverty rises by 200,000 on previous year, official figures show. *Independent*, 28 June, http://www.independent.co.uk/news/uk/politics/child-poverty-increase-tories-200000-per-cent-2014-2015-official-figures-dwp-stephen-crabb-a7107306.html.

Stotesbury, N. and Dorling, D. 2015. Understanding income inequality and its implications: why better statistics are needed. Statistics Views, http://www.statisticsviews.com/details/feature/8493411/Understanding-Income-Inequality-and-its-Implications-Why-Better-Statistics-are-N.html.

Sullivan, J., Bicego, G. and Rutstein, S. 1990. Assessment of the quality of data used for the direct estimation of infant and child mortality in the Demographic and Health Surveys. In *An Assessment of DHS-I Data Quality*. Columbia: Columbia Maryland Institute for Resource Development, pp. 113–43.

Testa, M. R. 2007. Childbearing preferences and family issues in Europe: evidence from the Eurobarometer 2006 survey. *Vienna Yearbook of Population Research*: 357–79.

Testa, M. R. 2013. Lifetime fertility intentions in Europe: the role of women's education. Presentation at Workshop: Childbearing Intentions and Postponement in Times of Uncertainty, Lisbon, 30 May, https://duploadiamento.files.wordpress.com/2013/05/maria-rita-testa-lifetime-fertility-intentions-in-europe.pdf.

Testa, M. R. and Basten, S. 2012. Have lifetime fertility intentions declined during the 'Great Recession'? VID Working Paper No. 9. Vienna Institute of Demography, Austrian Academy of Science.

Testa, M. R. and Basten, S. 2014. Certainty of meeting fertility intentions declines in Europe during the Great Recession. *Demographic Research*, 31(23): 687–734.

Thévenon, O. 2011. Family policies in OECD countries: a comparative analysis. *Population and Development Review*, 37(1): 57–87.

Tiezzi, S. 2016. China's plan for 'orderly' hukou reform. The Diplomat, http://thediplomat.com/2016/02/chinas-plan-for-orderly-hukou-reform.

Tokudome, S., Hashimoto, S. and Igata, A. 2016. Life expectancy and healthy life expectancy of Japan: the fastest graying society in the world. *BMC Research Notes*, 9(482): 1–6.

UNESCO. 2017. 1703 Census of Iceland: documentary heritage submitted by Iceland and recommended for inclusion in the Memory of the World Register in 2013. Online UNESCO Repository, http://www.unesco.org/new/en/communication-and-information/memory-of-the-world/register/full-list-of-registered-heritage/registered-heritage-page-1/1703-census-of-iceland/.

UNPD. 2001. Replacement Migration: Is It a Solution to Declining and Ageing Populations? Population Division of the Department of Economic and Social Affairs of the United Nations Secretariat, New York, http://www.un.org/esa/population/publications/ReplMigED/ExecSumnew.pdf.

UNPD. 2011. World Population Prospects: The 2010 Revision. Population Division of the Department of Economic and Social Affairs of the United Nations Secretariat, New York, http://esa.un.org/wpp/Documentation/WPP2010_ASSUMPTIONS_AND_VARIANTS.pdf.

UNPD. 2015. World Population Prospects: The 2015 Revision. Population Division of the Department of Economic and Social Affairs of the United Nations Secretariat, New York, http://esa.un.org/unpd/wpp/DVD.

USCB. 2017. 1790 Overview, Census Day August 2nd 1790. United States Census Bureau online repository, https://www.census.gov/history/www/through_the_decades/overview/1790.html.

Van Bavel, J. 2010. Subreplacement fertility in the West before the baby boom: past and current perspectives. *Population Studies*, 64(1): 1–18.

Vanhuysse, P. 2014. Intergenerational justice and public policy in Europe. European Social Observatory (OSE) Paper Series, Opinion Paper No. 16.

Wang, F., Cai, Y. and Gu, B. 2011. Population, policy, and politics: how will history judge China's one-child policy? *Population and Development Review*, 38(s1): 115–29.

Wang, Y. and Fong, V. L. 2009. Little emperors and the 4:2:1 generation: China's singletons. *Journal of the American Academy of Child and Adolescent Psychiatry*, 48(12): 1137–9.

Waterfield, B. 2009. Mohammed is most popular boy's name in four biggest Dutch cities. *Telegraph*, 13 August, http://www.telegraph.co.uk/news/worldnews/europe/netherlands/6022588/Mohammed-is-most-popular-boys-name-in-four-biggest-Dutch-cities.html.

Wee, T. C. 2016. China in shock: why no baby boom? *Straits Times*, 21 January, http://www.straitstimes.com/asia/east-asia/china-in-shock-why-no-baby-boom.

Weeks, J. 2013. The origins of 'demography is destiny' revealed. Weeks Population Blog, http://weekspopulation.blogspot.co.uk/2013/11/the-origins-of-demography-is-destiny.html.

Wei, Y., Jiang, Q. and Basten, S. 2013. Analyzing the transformation of China's first marriage pattern using nuptiality tables. *Finnish Yearbook of Population Research*, 48: 65–75.

Wei, Y., Jiang, Q. and Gietel-Basten, S. 2015. The well-being of bereaved parents in an only-child society. *Death Studies*, 40(1): 1–9.

WHO. 2012. Civil registration and vital statistics, Geneva, http://www.who.int/pmnch/topics/knowledge_summaries/ks17.pdf.

WHO. 2017. Global health observatory data, http://www.who.int/gho/mortality_burden_disease/life_tables/situation_trends/en.

WIC. 2017. Wittgenstein Centre Data Explorer, http://witt.null2.net/shiny/wic.

Wiwa, K. 2005. Are you thinking what I'm thinking about immigration? *Globe and Mail*, 30 April, http://www.theglobeandmail.com/opinion/are-you-thinking-what-im-thinking-about-immigration/article736077.

Woodhouse, C. 2016. Britain risks migration timebomb as population set to swell by 500,000 a year. *The Sun*, 1 March, https://www.thesun.co.uk/archives/politics/274946/britain-risks-migration-timebomb-as-population-set-to-swell-by-500000-a-year-2.

World Bank. 2014. Learning about the unknown: the economic impacts of ageing in Europe and Central Asia. World Bank News, http://www.worldbank.org/en/news/feature/2014/04/25/economic-impacts-of-aging-in-europe-and-central-asia.

World Bank. 2016. *World Development Indicators*. New York: World Bank.

Wright, A. 2017, *Domesday Book: Beyond the Censors*. Kibworth Beauchamp: Matador.

Yap, M. T. 2003. Fertility and population policy: the Singapore experience. *Journal of Population and Social Security (Population)*, 1: 643–58.

Zakharov, S. 2016. Postponement and recuperation in Russia's cohort fertility: does the pronatalist policy contribute to the acceleration or deceleration of the postponement transition? Extended Abstract, http://epc2016.princeton.edu/uploads/160491.

Zhao, Z. and Chen, W. 2011. China's far below-replacement fertility and its long-term impact: comments on the preliminary results of the 2010 census. *Demographic Research*, 25: 819–36.

Zolfagharifard, E. 2015. The wasted generation: even millennials think they are self-absorbed and lazy, claims study. *Daily Mail*, 3 September, http://www.dailymail.co.uk/sciencetech/article-3221560/Millennials-self-absorbed-wasteful.html.

Index